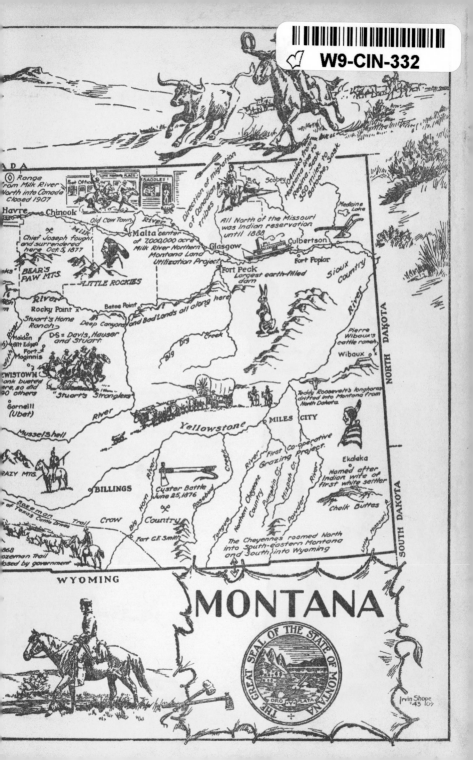

MONTANA

Montana

High, Wide, and Handsome

BY

Joseph Kinsey Howard

NEW HAVEN

YALE UNIVERSITY PRESS

LONDON · GEOFFREY CUMBERLEGE · OXFORD UNIVERSITY PRESS

For a valiant western woman,
my mother.

Colorado is high, having more peaks within its borders than any other state. Wyoming is wide, with the breadth of the plains between the Big Horns and the Grand Tetons. California is handsome, with a splendor of success. It takes all three adjectives to describe Montana.

DONALD CULROSS PEATTIE

CONTENTS

Endpaper map by Irvin Shope

FOREWORD

MONTANA IS REMOTE...

Home, home on the range,
Where the deer and the antelope play,
Where seldom is heard
A discouraging word . . .
And the skies are not cloudy all day!

IT is debatable whether that is an authentic cowboy ballad, but its frank, singsong melody is genuinely western, and its lyricist has managed to impregnate the naïve lines with some fragmentary feeling for the Great Plains —to sing, briefly and superficially, of the limitless arch of sky and the distant sharp-etched horizon and the spirit of those who people this land.

At any rate, America has accepted "Home on the Range" as the hymn of the prairies. A President of the United States has confessed a weakness for it. And what is more important, the people of the prairies love it and sing it and have adopted it as their own.

This is the story of that range, and the home on it, and what has happened to them. The song is chosen to open that story because in the few lines here quoted from it there live two concepts of range life which may have been true of the "romantic" period of the west, but are no longer true; and the lag in America's thought about the Great Plains, and in the thought of the plains people about themselves, as expressed in such misconceptions, has threatened frequently to destroy us—soil, grass, critter, grain, industry, people, and all.

No longer are the skies cloudless all day. There are clouds, but not of rain: they are clouds of earth—the rich, nitrogen-filled soil of the Rockies' east slope. And there are discouraging words, though fewer than justified, fewer even than are necessary. The west, traditionally cheerful and carefree, dodges self-analysis like a plague.

But this is not another book about dust storms. They figure but meagerly in it, partly because so little is known about them—though they are not as new as you may think: travelers in the northern "dust bowl" cursed them a hundred years ago. The wind rises somewhere to the west of us, in the vast canyons of the Rockies, stirs the grasses of the plains, gains in intensity, soars in a keening crescendo—and more of the precious soil is gone. It snows or rains and plainsmen smile; but the wind rises again, and in a few hours the snow cover is gone, the moisture is gone, soil is gone. Dust storms are not new, but they are worse.

Dust has its place in this story, along with drought (drouth in Montana), mineral bonanzas, the preciousness of running water, the food value of the prairie cactus, relief, death and taxes, mortgages, "busted" banks, absentee ownership, social disintegration, and the dream of a balanced society. Herein is the "discouraging word" that is seldom heard—born of the conviction that it is high time somebody in the west voiced such words more frequently and more emphatically. But here are some encouraging words, too.

This book is about Montana, largest segment of the northern Great Plains. Its problems to a large extent are typical of the region. Montana is a remote hinterland about as well known to the average eastern seaboard citizen as East or West Africa, and quite a bit like such ill-starred captive "empires" in other ways. A Boston shop clerk once asked the writer, who was arranging to have a purchase mailed to his home in a city of thirty thousand in Montana, if the state had regular mail service. Months after United States Army engineers began construction of Montana's $100,000,000 Fort Peck Dam, world's greatest earth-filled structure, a New York firm supplying some equipment on contract asked New York headquarters of the army how to address its shipment and was solemnly informed that there was no such place as Fort Peck, it had been abandoned in the '80's. The Montana press reported this incident with amusement shaded with a familiar sorrow: the state's isolation is an old, old story and responsible for much of its economic and social maladjustment.

Why Montana? Why not some better-known, culturally established, more romantically "colorful" state—Nevada (Comstock lode), or Utah (Mormons), or North Dakota (agrarian radicalism), or Arizona (gunplay)?

Well, Montana is singled out because it not only has had all these things, but because the conflicts brought about by the shift from frontier individualism to a machine-age economy almost within a generation have centered in this pitilessly exploited state which has fewer people (1940 census, 559, 456) than the cities of Buffalo, N. Y., or Milwaukee—still fewer now, because of World War II. . . . Montana, subject colony, has been the end of the cracked whip. Its story is that of the national social crisis, in miniature.

Montana never has had a stable economy; it never has had time to develop one. A little more than fifty years ago its first exploiters were slaughtering 150,000 buffalo a season on its plains, brawling in its frontier bars, robbing gold-laden stages, and swinging from Vigilante gallows. Many eastern communities—even many western ones—were thriving centers of civilization when, sixty-six years ago, Montana was finally won from the Indians by the defeat of Chief Joseph and his heroic band of Nez Percé in the last Indian battle in the United States.

This does not mean that Montana is "too new" to be chosen as an object lesson in American domestic imperialism. In the two-thirds of a century since Joseph surrendered to General Miles and those warriors who did not remain to be betrayed by our government drifted sadly across the Canadian border, Montana has lived the life of America, on a reduced scale and at breakneck speed. Its history has been bewilderingly condensed, a kaleidoscopic newsreel, unplotted and unplanned;

that of other states frequently has been directed, molded by tradition into a coherent and consistent drama.

But the history is all here. And even some tradition. . . . Tradition of recklessness, of violent living in a violent land, of putting little value on tradition because its span has been too brief. Montana is a country of great intensities, conditioned perhaps by its highly unreliable (but usually most enjoyable) climate—intense heat, intense cold. When it industrialized, it did so with a fierce impatience which drew from labor and agrarian elements opposition just as fierce, if less successful. Montana set out to grow wheat—and pyramided 258,000 acres of that grain to 3,417,000 acres *in ten years;* and the wheat boom collapsed just as suddenly. When its fledgling politicians and their masters decided to go in for corruption, they did so in a big way—$10,000 a vote; and when corporate industry decided to take control of the state's key functions, it did so without any serious attempt at subterfuge such as had been used in the east: it established an avowed dictatorship, and everybody in Montana recognized it.

Montana's battered elder generation has experienced most of the stages between the frontier and the machine-age economy—the era of self-contained handicraft industry, small farms, the "robber barons," speculative land booms, war—like any other section, but faster. The speed of Montana's transition, the apparently permanent instability of its economic life, have had important social consequences; more important, and a factor in this speed, is the combination of circumstance and destiny and mischance which made the territory a subject state of the east.

Before America's entrance into World War II social scientists had begun to fret about the breakdown of balances in American life, especially in industry and cash-crop agriculture, wherein the daily tasks could not be integrated, as one puts it, "either with the individual's whole life or with that of his community." Concentration of production, for efficiency, within fewer and fewer monopoly organizations during the war has done nothing to relieve this worry; and coupled with this socially disastrous factor is the decline in owner-operation of the means of production, especially the land. The conflicts arising from both of these processes have been immeasurably intensified in Montana, in peace or war. In Montana, machine-age tasks not only cannot be integrated with the individual's life or his community, they cannot even be integrated with his region: despite foredoomed "Buy Montana" campaigns the state can use only an infinitesimal part of its production and ships its resource wealth away. And Nature and man's greed have combined to rob Montanans of their birthright, the land. Less than 18 per cent of Montana's land is owned by individuals living on and operating that land; less than one half of Montana's farmers own all the land they farm.

Montana's is a cash-crop agriculture, hitherto exploited to the limit while the soil remained. There has been no continuity, no sense of debt to the land (with some noble exceptions), little realization of the social obligation implicit in land use.

Minerals, also, are a cash crop, to be yanked ruthlessly from the mountains, "high-graded" when profits are lean, and as little returned to the commonwealth or its people as possible. Here is "the richest hill on earth," at whose foot rests world-famous boisterous Butte—no longer the "richest hill" probably, for it has yielded up, in a few decades, $2,500,000,000 in mineral wealth. Here too is "Yankee bar"—richest of placer diggings for a little while; now over its scarred face crawl modern monsters, caterpillar-tread dredges, scraping hungrily for the crumbs the prospectors scorned.

Power is a cash crop—no cash, no crop: available sites seized by a monopoly holding company affiliate and permitted to stand undeveloped while rivers occasionally dry up and industry shuts down for lack of current, while public development is resisted by every agency of propaganda and political intrigue.

Men are a cash crop, in wartime; and so in World War I Montana contributed more of them, in proportion to its population, for military service than any other state, and lost more from enemy fire. Dead or alive, another mischance dictated that many of these men should not come back to Montana, because the opportunities which brought them to the state in the first place had vanished. And so there came about an odd unbalance of age groups, a shortage of earning-age citizens which has been aggravated by World War II's heavy draft levies and its drain of Montana workmen to west coast war industry—threatening, in future, a vast pension problem.

Montana has never had time to develop a Mark Twain or a Bret Harte to chronicle its wealth of frontier history and anecdote in order that it might become a cultural entity in the national consciousness, as have other states; and it has suffered greatly from that lack. Yet no other states have stories which are better than those you will find in this book—the one, for instance, of Thomas Francis Meagher, an Irish rebel sentenced to die at 25, Governor of Montana at 42, utterly vanished in a crude Missouri River town at 43; or that of pirate Fritz Heinze, at 30 triumphant (though briefly) over the great Standard Oil; or that of desperadoes "Rattlesnake Jake" and "Long-haired" Owens, and their heroic last stand against a whole town; or that of empire builder Jim Hill, who single-handed started a mass population movement culminating in the long, grim struggle of the dryland farmer; or that of the disastrous decade, and the federal financiers' curious excuse for having helped to bring it about.

Montana has crowded a lot of history into less than a century. Its gold rush was in the '60's, yet so strong is California cultural tradition that even some Montana pioneer days celebrations are called "Days of '49." But history is culture, and Montana has had little time for culture: it has been too busy, like the rest of America, making money. It has made a lot—for others; and more than a little bewildered, even occasionally discouraged, it faces a far-from-reassuring future. Those indices on its charts which should have gone up went down; those which should have gone down skyrocketed. America has not been doing so well, but Montana has been doing worse. In the 1930 census it was the only state to lose population, and though it came back in 1940, World War II started another decline. Its unbalance in population will affect all America; and that is the reason for singling out a state whose economy seems most precarious in the hope that discussion of its experience may encourage sympathetic understanding of steps already taken to aid it and help set in motion more such movements for all of the west.

This isn't solely Montana's problem, nor the west's. That must be emphasized. Balance of society, wrote Baker Brownell in *Architecture and Modern Life,* "depends in great measure on regional balance in population." And he continued:

> With many diversified soils, beautiful climate, with water power and mineral resources, the far west will become no doubt another region of large population. . . . Any policies that will tend to aid this kind of life and population will contribute to the balance of our society.
>
> The social problem in this respect is to prevent the urban east from exploiting other regions as a hinterland, draining wealth and youth from the south and west without corresponding return. Though economists may consider such a one-way drainage of wealth a fallacy, not a fact, there are some indications that it does take place.

There are, indeed. The reader will find them in this story of Montana.

Prairie...

I. THE GRASS

DONALD CULROSS PEATTIE once wrote: "Of all the things that live and grow upon this earth, grass is the most important."

This is the country of the "short grass"—the northern Great Plains. It is a land of little moisture, searing sun and wind, extreme cold—a land of brief spring greenness, yielding to long, hot summers during which the grasses cure on the ground, turning yellow, then brown.

What was the "short grass" before the white man came, and what is it now?

Now, save in especially favored seasons, it is sick: gray, scrawny, really "short"—a few inches tall at its best, growing sparsely in dun-colored clay fields or powdery sand, struggling to hold its ground against the Russian thistle (tumbleweed), introduced in the Dakotas in some unclean seed, and other less finicky but unpalatable plants. It is still nutritious, rich in protein, mineral salts, carbohydrates; this is because the short maturing season of the high-altitude plains develops protein and carbohydrates (sugar, starch, dextrin) more rapidly than it does crude fiber (roughage). Montana's altitude ranges from 1,800 to 12,850 feet, and its average is 3,400.

Seldom now—only in an exceptionally wet spring—does this grass grow tall enough to "roll in the wind like the sea," as the first white men saw it. It was blue grama, bluestem ("wheat grass") and "buffalo grass" and it stood a foot high— sometimes, especially the buffalo bunch grass, as high as three feet. So closely did it carpet the soil that one early visitor marveled: "You could graze all the cattle of the world upon this plain" and another added: "It [the grass] is the most nutritious that livestock ever fed on."

In the foothills, two-foot-high sagebrush formed little shelter belts for lush plots of grass.

Maturing rapidly and curing on the ground, the grass provided forage the year 'round; but Nature saw to it that these plains were not overgrazed. Thirty or forty million antelope ranged the Great Plains, and no one knows how many of them were in Montana. But they were dainty eaters, and restless; and there were no fences. In the foothills and on the higher plateaus where the antelope did not venture, thousands of elk maintained Nature's precarious balance of harvest; and deeper in the forest the deer took over the task.

The "thundering herds" of buffalo dramatically described in western fiction were here, too; but probably not, as too often indicated in novel or movie, all the time. How many? Now it is impossible to tell, but some estimates of their number also go as high as thirty million head. Lewis and Clark in 1805 reported seeing "vast herds" of buffalo in May and early in June on the plains of what is now Montana, at one time recording "a thousand." These explorers may have been watching the spring trek of the great beasts to the north; the first buffalo hunters established their "season" from December 1 to May, pursuing the bison southward through Montana into Wyoming and north again as the herds returned in the spring. The hunters reported large herds unusual before November or later than May, though smaller groups grazed Montana's plains the year around.

Montana's rich grasses were easily accessible to the bison because the almost unceasing wind swept the light snow of the plains from the cushioned sod, and many hundreds of thousands moved annually into this feeding ground from the snowed-under fields of the north and east.

There were scores of varieties of these native grasses. Some have disappeared, others, including the most valuable for forage purposes, have become virtually unobtainable in commercial seed form. Nearly all species, with the exception of those maintained in protected areas such as national forests, have changed drastically in physical character, in ground cover, and in nutritive quality.

The drumming hooves of the stampeding bison invariably provided dramatic opportunity for the pianist in the "silent movie" days, and more recently for the sound-effects technician. But these hooves served an important purpose, and no better instance can be given of Nature's meticulous planning than to cite the value of the bison's trampling.

Sturdy "blue bunch," the great perennial wheat grass of the Montana plains, wiry, drouth-resistant, nutritious, made up a large part of the ground cover of the bison's winter range. It grows only from seed; and the trampling of the bison's hooves (though not in stampede: he was king of the plains unless beset by Indian hunters) planted the seed. It was as simple as that: the grass flourished, matured, and dropped its seed; and as they foraged on the ripened crop, the bison planted it for next season. . . . But there were no sheep to crop to the roots the tender shoots of new grass when they came up in the spring, there were no cattle penned within fences, insatiably hungry—and above all, there were no desperate or greedy homesteaders to sink the murderous blades of their plows into this matted cushion!

This was Nature's controlled grazing: vast herds of ponderous, hungry bison ranging across millions of unfenced acres, eating their fill—but moving on. The springy sod which had been formed through centuries of growth and death of this grass cushioned pleasantly the great weight on their hooves; and the wind—for always there has been wind—blew the flowering heads of the bluestem against their bellies. The grass was thick, most of the time (not always, even then) because the soil was good; the grass was hardy, it needed and it got little moisture. But there were great subsoil reserves of water, and many little springs. These too attracted the bison herds to the eastern and central Montana plains.

"We found good fields of wild bluestem hay," wrote a buffalo hunter of his experiences in 1878. He and his partner, taking turns with a scythe, cut two hayrack loads in one day a mile or so from their camp, and then continued cutting for a week, "by the end of which time we had six or seven tons stacked in the corral." This was for use in emergencies only—bad weather, or, more likely, Indian attack—because "our horses did not go more than a mile from camp, which gave them more than 2,000 acres on which to graze." There was a spring at the camp site, and the horses came in every day for water "until the first good snowfall about December 1st; after that they did not take a drink all winter—they ate enough snow in grazing to give them all the moisture they needed."

Nothing so enrages the Great Plains stockman today as does a picture such as that given above of lush grasses waving in the breeze, the "mythical virgin forest of luscious grass" which he attributes to "theorists with vivid imaginations." (These impatient phrases are from *If and When It Rains,* a stockmen's publication). Some government reports he finds suspect and when they speak of such range conditions he seeks to discredit them on the ground that their authors have a bureaucratic ax to grind.

Nevertheless such a range did exist, though not all of the time. The stockman resents, justifiably, overdrawn descriptions of a paradise of forage, winter and summer, year in and year out; he resents the attendant implication that by overgrazing he brought about destruction of the natural ground cover and dust storms. He protests plaintively that stockmen have long urged and supported controlled grazing. That is not quite true; but neither is it true that he is solely responsible, or even responsible in major part, for the deterioration of the western range.

In recent years America has become dust conscious, especially since dust from the northern and central Great Plains has begun blowing clear to the eastern seaboard.

"The little black father," Jesuit Pierre DeSmet, visited Montana in 1841 and 1842. He wrote at that time: "Our beasts of burden were compelled to fast and pine, for scarcely a mouthful of grass could be found." Frontiersman Jim Bridger, about twenty years later, reported "forage unusually scarce, and the animals becoming much emaciated." Emigrants who came into Montana in the '70's reported dust and sand pounding against the weathered tarpaulins of their Conestoga wagons. Weather bureau records in Dodge City, Kansas, reveal that there were blinding dust storms there in 1890, 1892, 1893, and 1894.

There have always been drouth and dust on the Great Plains. Averages based upon weather records of thirty-five to fifty years indicate that in most of Montana there are one or two drouth years in every ten, and in the northern portion, two or three.

There were terrible fires which swept suddenly across thousands, perhaps millions, of acres of dry grass, destroying the ground cover for a season. Lightning started some; the Indians—especially after the white man's arrival had made their hunting more difficult—started others to drive game. Early settlers have left records of these fearful, uncontrollable disasters, sheets of roaring flame racing across the prairies thirty or forty miles an hour on a front many miles wide—stopped, sometimes, at the plowed fireguard around the settler's home.

So drouth dried and killed the grass and baked the soil; still the grass stood. And fire took it, leaving mile upon mile of powdery black ash—still its roots twisted and clung in the soil beneath. It would come up again next spring, greener than ever, not quite as rich, needing more rain because the cushioned mulch which held the moisture had burned. . . . But it would come up.

And then there came a man with a plow. Its sharp point crackled as it sliced through the new green grass of spring, the dry mulch of last season, the crisp topsoil. The point went a little harder as it cut deeper, severing the long roots, tough roots, of the native grass. And as the soil curled up beside the plow's gleaming blade the man was happy; for here was good, dark soil, cohesive; soil with moisture in it. . . . Perhaps the man loved the soil, had grown up on the soil—somewhere else. Perhaps he had been crowded there; and now as he gazed into this vast sky he felt free: here a man could stand up, here a man could do great things, grow incredible wheat crops, become rich. (But that sun *was* hot. There was nothing between him and the sun. Sure gets hot quick in this country!)

The man bent to his plow. (A man sort of gets a hankerin' to plow. Look at that grass! Wheat'll grow! They say they've got fifty, sixty bushels to the acre. . . . God damn, but it's hot!)

But on top of that limestone butte, glistening in the sun a mile away, a horseman is watching the farmer plow; and there is bitterness in his heart. The farmer's fence has cut across his range and his bewildered cattle and horses have blundered into it: the vicious twisted barbs have gashed their legs and he has been treating the wounds with axle grease or mutton fat.

But the horseman has greater ground for bitterness than this; for he genuinely loves the grass which the plow is destroying. He knows the farmer will fail. He has told Washington so, but Washington will not listen. It is to the interest of the east, just now, to push its discontented surplus population into the west; and it is to the interest of the railroads to carry the emigrants.

The watcher admits to himself that he, too, has abused this country, that spurred by competition he has overgrazed. But he has been here long enough to learn that cattle cannot be fattened on overgrazed range, that land abuse does not pay. And he has never broken the sod, so on his worst ranges the grass will come back in a year or two. After the farmer has failed, the grass may come back to his plowed fields—in twenty years. Or it may never come back. . . .

The horseman rides off to his herds. The farmer finishes his plowing, waits for rain that doesn't come. It is summer now; the wheat is heading out less than a foot above the ground. The stalk turns yellow, then brown; the heads droop. The farmer takes one in his hand, and it disintegrates into dust. It is not worth harvesting; and all about him the topsoil is cracked and crisped and curled up; gray, now, instead of the rich brown he saw when he plowed this field. He looks across his fence to the field of his distant neighbor, the cattleman. The grass is not so good, but it's better than this wheat. . . . And the stockman still has other ranges. (Well, it can't go on like this forever. A few good snows this winter and a wet spring—I'll be laughing at this first dry season. I can clean up!)

One day in the spring of 1883 as a Scandinavian farmer, John Christiansen, plowed his fields in Montana's neighbor state of North Dakota, he looked up to find that he was being watched—not by a stockman, as in the imaginary scene described here, but by an old and solemn Sioux Indian.

Silently the old Indian watched as the dark soil curled up and the prairie grass was turned under. Christiansen stopped, leaned against the plow handle, pushed his black Stetson back on his head, rolled a cigarette. He watched amusedly as the old Indian knelt, thrust his fingers into the plow furrow, measured its depth, fingered the sod and the buried grass.

Then the old Indian straightened up, looked at the farmer. "Wrong side up," he said, and went away.

For a number of years that was regarded as a very amusing story indeed, betraying the ignorance of the poor Indian. Now there's a marker on Highway No. 10 in North Dakota on the spot where the words were spoken—a little reminder to the white man that his red brother was not so dumb.

II. FIFTEEN SALADS

When you come to trade with the Indians of the northern plains, you will find that you have entered upon a tedious and exasperating undertaking: that often, before you are able to consummate the swap, you will have had to pick up your hides or other "trading stock" and make the motions of moving on to the next cabin, or the next village.

You will be shown moccasins when you seek gloves; and you will be shown nothing but moccasins until the tribesman finally is convinced that you will not have moccasins. Then miraculously there will appear a pair of gloves. Probably they will be too large or too small, but you will be assured that they are the only pair in the camp—until again you have gathered together your hides and made as if to move on. This maneuver will be more effective if you can accompany it with sound effects indicating extreme disgust with the whole deal, or resignation to a gloveless future. At long last, you will get the gloves you seek, at a fair price.

The Indian hates waste. He will show you no more than he must. For a generation he has watched you and your kind plundering the northern plains; he has learned that the more a white man sees, the more he seizes—and that what the white man takes he uses briefly and wantonly and casts aside. When the Indian feels the approach of death, he may, if you have been his good friend, leave you his ceremonial robes, his magnificent headdress, a valued medicine stone—for these, in some tribes, he cannot bequeath to his family. And in the beauty of the snowy, beaded buckskin garment, chewed to softness years ago by his squaw, in the savage splendor of the eagle-feathered bonnet or the mystic legend of his "medicine," you will find yourself more than repaid for any kindness you have done him.

But while he lives he will trade reluctantly, even with you, his friend. And this is not wholly due to greed—though the white man has taught him enough of that, too. No; it is because somewhere deep in his memories lie the images of rotting buffalo carcasses, of sod "wrong side up," of the game driven deeper and deeper into the mountains which he has always feared, mountains in which some plains tribes will not remain after dark. He remembers the luscious watermelon which he cultivated but which the white man has never been able to grow successfully in Montana. He remembers the vanished tobacco, the disappearing soap-yucca, the breadroot.

Today's "civilized" Montanan subsists upon a few staple domesticated plants and meats, as do his fellow citizens everywhere. Perhaps his diet is a little more restricted than that of some residents of other states because of his remoteness from markets and the costliness of fresh fruits; his beefsteaks, on the other hand, are the best in the world. His Indian predecessor selected his food from a great variety of native plants, mostly uncultivated, and he used many of these same plants in fashioning his implements, his ceremonial agents, his beverages, medicines, even poisons.

He wasted almost nothing. The fresh fruit of the serviceberry ("sarvis berry" to Montanans) was one of his finest table delicacies; but the same fruit was spiced and "put up," or made into wines, or mixed with others for jam, or pounded in with the fat of the buffalo to make pemmican, the staple condensed food of the plains for Indian and white alike. But he did not stop here; the woody stalks of the serviceberry plant he used for arrows and later for ramrods. Joints of the hostile prickly pear cactus were boiled until the soft, pulpy interior could be removed and this was then fried, making, the old settlers found, a very palatable food. Sometimes the reddish fruit of the prickly pear, spines carefully stripped off, was eaten raw, or was made into preserves. Old-timers learned from the Indians the exceedingly valuable properties of this plant in clearing muddy water and making it drinkable: the fleshy stems of the cactus were split and placed in the water and the extruding mucilage from the plant speedily absorbed all of the dirt.

The Indians chewed the dried roots of the chokecherry and the gum thus formed they placed upon wounds, to stop bleeding. They made the bark of this plant into a tea, as a remedy for dysentery. They used its wood for carved "medicine spoons." Its shoots they whittled into arrow shafts. Its fruit was eaten fresh, used in pemmican, or made into delicious wine or marmalade—a practice adopted with enthusiasm by housewives of the present day. The modern housewife does not, however, crush the fruit in a mortar, cut it into strips, dry it and store it for winter use, as did the tribesmen.

There are many other instances of the Indian's careful utilization of his natural foods, but these will serve to illustrate the point. More interesting, probably, is the amazing variety of foods and other products which Nature yielded up to his respectful harvest. Five plants served to make his arrows, two to make his bows. He made canoes from three Montana trees, fish nets from four plants, fish spears from another; one plant provided him with brooms, another with "digging sticks," forebears of our spades. One plant was treasured for pipestems, one made walking sticks, three made twirling sticks for ceremonials. And the thick, tough leaves of the lovely bear grass were woven into watertight bowls for his cooking.

That sufficed for his instruments, except for those he manufactured from stone. Another important field—that of ceremonial agents—used eight plants: two for writing incantations, five for incense, one for medicine spoons. For general utility purposes, he had the lodge pole pine for his tepee and nine trees, including this one, for lumber. He used five vines for ornamental landscaping, nine plants for cordage or fibers, eight for baskets, six for mats. Three served for clothing and bedding, two for soap and another for shampoo (the soap-yucca, which gave a luster to the hair no commercial shampoo of our times has matched). Essential oils were extracted from one plant, paints from six. Two were used in tanning, one for branding stock. One plant was reserved for weather prediction!

Now for his diet: He had thirty plants in the bulb, root or tuber classification, fifteen for salads, nine for greens, at least six edible tree or bush barks; he had fifty fruits. Twelve plants made his meal and flour, two made his sugar and syrup. And he topped this all off with ten plants for jellies, jams, or marmalades.

Five plants provided his beverages, and five he smoked. One of these latter was tobacco root, described by the first whites as a black and nauseating mess but enjoyed by the Indians. The native tobacco, however—it has now disappeared

—was found by the whites to be delicious when mixed with the kinnikinnick plant, and this smoking compound was adopted by many frontiersmen.

To arrest unwanted pregnancies, the Indians valued three plants, but the best of these was not native to Montana and was obtained by trade from tribes to the east. Two plants were snake-bite antidotes, two were valued as syphilis remedies, two provided antiseptics and three more astringents. There were five cathartics, three emetics, a hair restorer, seven lotions. . . . And all, save the one highly-regarded abortifacient, native to Montana!

There are scores of others. Twenty-six diseases were treated with plants, more or less successfully. One plant was a salivant, six made poultices, three provided styptics and there were six natural tonics. Not the least interesting were the thirst preventers. Two plants were used for this purpose, the most commonly employed being the familiar sagebrush. This plant, heavily impregnated with camphor, when chewed would give the illusion of coolness in the mouth. It was frequently used by Indians on long, hot rides or marches and was especially valuable to runners bearing messages from chief to chief.

The Indians had eight natural poisons including the water hemlock, that ancient bane, and the lovely translucent purple pasqueflower, which we call the crocus, first gay and delicate herald of spring on the upland plains, its deadly liquor distilled and saved by the redmen for special enemies. Besides these eight growing poisons, the medicine man had another, most revolting product of the Indian imagination: it was the distilled liquid of a putrefied toad.

Thirty-seven years have passed since J. W. Blankenship, Montana State College botanist, made the first serious study of the Indians' diet. (Most of the material in this chapter was derived from his *Native Economic Plants of Montana*.) During that period many more of these natural foods which enabled the tribesman to live well even in times of meat scarcity have disappeared. Many whites, however, have learned to appreciate his taste in fruits and berries and a few of his staples almost imperceptibly have been adopted into the Montana diet.

The Montana foothills and highway embankments still are

carpeted each summer with wild sunflowers; but no longer is this plant ground into meal and formed into cakes, boiled and mixed with grease, its oil extracted for use as a "cold cream," and the cakes packed away carefully for food for the war parties. According to the Indians, this "emergency ration" made from the sunflower sustained its consumer longer against exhaustion than any other food.

No; today the sunflower is a noxious weed, and mechanical scythes grimly eradicate it—for a season—from the roadside. A tourist may pause briefly to admire the yellow waxen perfection of the prickly pear blossom, a glistening opened rose; but the thorns will prick his fingers and he will curse the plant and agree with his wife that it must be an awful nuisance.

And so it is, to the modern agriculturist. Many of the native prairie plants, some of its grasses, are nuisances, noxious weeds.

But the Indian had no noxious weeds. If the weed was poisonous, he used it for poison. If it was an intoxicant, he got drunk on it, or at least pleasantly stimulated, for ceremonial purposes; for some reason drunkenness just for the fun of being drunk seems to have come with the white man's liquors. If he couldn't eat it, drink it, paint with it, squeeze out its juice (as with the milkweed) to brand his horse painlessly, he might try it out as an agent of abortion. If this didn't work (it seldom did) he'd keep on trying. And ultimately he would discover that it seemed to cure that last hangover headache, or fixed up his constipation, or healed a rash. . . . From then on, that plant had its place in his economy and his reverent partnership with Nature had advanced a little further.

He didn't expect any coddling. Nature did her part by offering her products to him freely; it was up to him to find the uses to which they might be put—without waste, and with respectful regard for her whims. There were cactus in the driest of years, years when the grass cracked and split and the dust rose in great clouds and his rain prayers lacked response; there was nearly always the bitterroot which he so loved: soaked in water it swelled enormously, becoming a bitter but exceedingly nourishing gelatin-like substance which the whites seldom could eat. There were always berries along the river banks and in the foothills. Even if the buffalo were starving and hard to find, as they were sometimes, there would be antelope, most delicious of meat animals and daintier eaters, not so hard hit by drouth. And there would be fish.

So even in times of relative scarcity and except when blizzards prevented travel or hostile tribes banished him to unfamiliar country, the Indian's diet was of greater variety than that of his white conqueror; and until he learned the white man's habits, it usually was better balanced—high in vegetable and fruit values.

Thus the people of this land lived in honorable alliance with their gods.

III. DRY BLEACHED PRAIRIE BONES

Among the relics of the old west in the glass cases which line the walls of the historic Mint saloon in Great Falls, Montana, there is a brief business letter. It originated, the old-fashioned letterhead tells us, in the "Office of B. M. Hicks, Dealer in Buffalo Bones," at Minneapolis, Minnesota. It bears the date of June 17, 1895, it is addressed to "Mr. John M. Lewis, Glasgow, Montana," and it says:

Dear sir:
  Replying to yours of the 14th offering 45,000 pounds of bones I beg to state that I can pay you for clean dry bleached prairie bones F.O.B. cars at your place $5.00 per ton. Railway rates at Minnesota transfer to be basis of settlement. Cars must contain 12 tons or over. If this is all you have perhaps you could load them all in one large furniture car such as the Great Northern runs.

The buffalo was a ponderous beast: a full-grown bull weighed 2,000 to 2,500 pounds. Three hundred and fifty pounds of that, however, was in his hide; and his fat flesh and bulky muscle and internal organs made up most of the balance. So it took a lot of buffalo to produce $5 worth of dry bleached prairie bones; and Mr. Lewis was only one of the shippers, Mr. Hicks only one of the dealers.
  The buffalo was a stupid beast, too, and easy to kill. So easy to kill that it took only about a dozen years—1870 through 1883—to annihilate most of the millions which roamed the western plains, and sell their hides for $3 or $4 each. After the hides were gone and the meat had rotted, there developed a market for their horns in the manufacture of ornamental hatracks for Victorian parlors; and the scavengers ranged the plains for skulls. Still later some demand appeared for bones, and the buffalo vanished from the plains forever, not even his bones remaining to fertilize the soil. . . . Today a buffalo skull is a prized relic of considerable value, even in Montana.
  Isaac P. Baker, a steamboat captain on the Missouri and Yellowstone Rivers who died in 1938, estimated his boats had

carried a quarter of a million buffalo hides from Montana to Bismarck, N. D., for reshipment overland, in just two years— 1881 and 1882; and this was only one transportation agency: hundreds of thousands of hides were transported overland from Montana annually in freight wagons.

Some Americans find such slaughter incredible, and because it is beyond their understanding, they are unmoved by accounts of it. Others, in recent years, have been profoundly shocked; they are sure that had they been here at the time, they should have done something about it. . . . Usually this latter attitude is expressed in contempt for the plainsman who permitted this bloody carnival and the buffalo hunter who was its principal performer.

Few of the hunters found it necessary to make excuses or to justify themselves before their fellows. Some who, unlike most of their fellow exploiters, settled in Montana after the great herds were gone, did analyze their motives and set forth their apology.

Almost unanimously they credited lust for adventure and for quick riches with drawing them into the business; and all agreed that they only hastened slightly a process which was inevitable. The buffalo had to go. The government encouraged the slaughter because until the herds were gone the Indians could not be controlled: starvation and not the United States Army won the west for the whites. Until the free-ranging beasts had been wiped out, cattle could not use the plains, and no settler's cabin was safe, if it lay in the path of a stampede.

Nevertheless, with this orgy of destruction the natural economy of the northern Great Plains perished, and none of the white man's devices has yet sufficed to restore the perfect balance of Nature, man, and food in this grim and unforgiving land.

The Indian, before the white man came, hunted the bison with bow and arrow. Consider the difficulty of bringing down a creature weighing a ton and whose hide is inches thick, racing at the top speed of a good horse—with a stick of chokecherry wood! The conditions of the Indian hunt made it impossible to avoid a stampede; and the stampede of a great herd of buffalo shook the earth for miles. A fall, a momentarily frightened horse, meant instant death. The buffalo hunter rated high in Indian society, as well he might; his was a skilled and perilous job.

A society which depended upon the prowess of its hunters, its ability to locate and trail the herds, lived an arduous life, a life which did not encourage overpopulation. Still, though the Indians knew hunger often in bad years, they husbanded their game resources cautiously even in times of plenty. They used the buffalo as sparingly, as thoroughly, as they used the plants. They had no way in which to keep meat fresh, so the meat they could not consume at once was preserved, usually in the form of pemmican. The hides made tepees, occasionally clothing. The bones were prized for their utility when fashioned into carving instruments and knives, especially useful in the treatment of buckskin for garments. The top of the skull and the horns often became a war bonnet, though the horns also had other uses.

Often buffalo were driven over cliffs, the "buffalo runs" or "pishkuns" under which Montanans still find rich harvests of arrowheads and other Indian implements. In such drives the Indians sought to cut out of the herd the fattest cows and spare those they could not use; naturally this was not always possible and unnecessary slaughter did occasionally result from this type of hunt.

When the white hunter invaded this paradise of game, he came armed with breech-loading Sharps rifles. If he could afford it he had two, one for reserve in case of mechanical trouble he could not repair, for he would be a long way from a gunsmith. They cost him $90 each, and each weighed 14 to 16 pounds. They were single-shot and of 45–120 caliber.

This white hunter may have been a ruffian, as many were; or he may have been an enterprising young man who would become an outstanding pioneer citizen, as some did. Certainly, despite his huge profits, his life was not easy; and his investment, for those days, was considerable.

The cowboy disliked him, complained that he was dirty; and so would the cowboy have been had he had to live under similar conditions. One of the most amusing passages in one of the best "true western" books of recent years—*We Pointed Them North* by Teddy Blue Abbott and Helena Huntington Smith—quotes Teddy Blue on the influx of prettier prosti-

tutes after the Texas cowboys came because the fastidious
Texans scorned the bedraggled bawds who had served the
buffalo men.

But unlike the trapper and the footloose cowpoke, the buffalo hunter was a businessman, the first of his class on the
frontier. Somewhere he had dug up the money to buy the
rifles, several Indian horses at $10 to $20 each, hundreds of
pounds of gunpowder and bar lead, tools and molds for making his ammunition, one or two "dead-ax" wagons—at least
$100 each—and a season's food.

Fred Whiteside was one of the enterprising young men who
were to remain in Montana to become outstanding citizens.
In an unpublished manuscript, "One Hundred Grand," he
has left an account of his experiences as a buffalo hunter.

In November, 1878, he set out for the buffalo range with a
partner, part Indian, who had hunted the same range before.
As they rode, Whiteside's partner told him of how the Indians
hunted:

Nearly every man, woman and child of the tribe came on the
hunt. Many generations had hunted here. Always it was a time of
labor for everyone, and preparation of food and living equipment
for all the next year. Each day the women and children made tons
of pemmican from the buffalo meat and the fruits they had
brought for this purpose. Also they dressed the skins for tepee
covers and for clothing and moccasins, and dressed and tanned
some robes. The implements used for fleshing and tanning the
hides were made from the bones of the buffalo; these knives were
prized and handed down from generation to generation as heir-
looms. The sinews of the buffalo were split into coarse and fine
threads. . . .

The rookie hunter and his experienced companion came
across a herd of antelope, and the older man shot one. The
herd stood stock-still and stared; it could have been wiped out
easily. But the buffalo hunters prized antelope as food and not
as an article of commerce: they could use only one so they did
not kill any more. Later they saw other, larger bands, many of
more than 1,000 head. The first buffalo they encountered
were in small herds of a dozen head; they did not disturb

them, and the older hunter said the frequency of their appearance so early in the season promised an early winter.

They established their camp in a coulee near a spring. Their first fuel was buffalo chips (dried buffalo dung); but later they came across a mound of vine cedar roots as large as a haystack, carefully cut into two or three-foot lengths, deposited under a ledge of rock in the coulee by rats whose feet had worn a trail six inches deep in the sandstone. The rats had been piling the roots there, it appeared, for centuries. At the bottom of the mound were the tunnels of the then-present generation of rodents, leading to the nests and food caches. The hunters used these roots for fuel for two winters, burning fifty wagonloads a season; each summer the rats restored the pile to its original size.

The hunters found a spring which a few years before had supplied a camp of fifty persons and two hundred horses. Their home was set up in a sandstone cave twelve by twenty feet, with a natural crevice, opened by an earthquake, to serve as a fireplace chimney. About a hundred yards away was a vein of coal, sandwiched between two strata of limestone; it too provided fuel.

They built a hayrack of quaking aspen taken from a grove along a creek, and cut several tons of wild hay—in mid-November. Buffalo hides are not "prime" until December, so Whiteside set off for a visit to Miles City, seventy-five miles away. With him he took two hind quarters of buffalo meat as gifts from his partner to Indian friends in the Nez Percé tribe. Their rebellion crushed the year before, they were prisoners in a military camp.

They were pleased to get the fine fat buffalo meat as a change from the stringy beef they were getting from the government. They were eager to hear all about our camp for they knew right where it was; they had been there many times. One of them wrote a letter to my partner and at the end he put down all of the names of the Nez Percé who thanked him for the meat. There is not much sentiment about an Indian, but as I pulled out with my load starting for camp, that little bunch of Nez Percé in a strange land followed me with wistfully longing, almost tearful eyes. . . .

Hunting started at dawn, after wind direction had been carefully noted: for the bison, poor of vision, was keen of scent. The killers approached when possible over broken country, to aid in concealment. They preferred small herds, to avoid the stampedes inevitable with the large ones. Best range was about two hundred yards. The first shot would scatter the herd, but it would pause for a moment, swing, and by some inscrutable instinct every animal would start in the same direction. The hunter then would shoot at the ground in front of them. This would turn the herd. He would continue this until the bewildered buffalo stopped running and stood helpless and terrified, to be shot down to the last animal. The number killed in one stand varied from a half dozen to eighty.

The meat was left to spoil; the hunters took hide, tongue, and a few tenderloin steaks from the youngest and fattest animals. And always they looked up at intervals for quick surveys of the horizon. Appearance of a rider on that horizon meant a quick break for camp or some vantage point for observation, lest the visitor be a member of a hostile Indian band. The sight and the stench of scores of wasted buffalo carcasses were apt to have unfortunate effects upon Indians, even professedly friendly ones.

Sometimes the hunt was so successful more help was needed for dressing out the hides, lest the hunters be forced to spend thus too much time which might more profitably be spent in killing. And a helper would be hired. Sometimes the hunters found their helper, left behind to work alone, propped against a rock, a bullet hole through his head, scalp removed cleanly down to his ears and eyebrows. . . .

So lived the buffalo hunter. His life was hard and dangerous, but it paid. As the herds dwindled or he began to lose his taste for slaughter—some did—he might work over the old ranges for horns, which he sold for 20¢ a pound. Dried buffalo horns do not weigh much.

He had learned the country, the climate, and hardship. Often he drifted into the cattle ranches, becoming cowboy, wagon boss, or even a rancher himself. The one whose story has been quoted partially here graduated into architecture, contracting, journalism, and politics, figuring spectacularly and honorably in Montana's greatest political scandal.

Today there are in the United States some 4,500 buffalo, all —with the exception of the few in zoos—confined on fenced reservations and fed hay when the grass is sparse, and through the winter. The largest of these reserves is that at Moiese, in Montana. There you may see, if you wish, the "thundering herds" whose wanton (but inevitable!) destruction appropriately inaugurated the era of exploitation of the west—the first and bloodiest incident in a history of wasteful pillage.

There remain 66,000 antelope in the United States. The last white-tailed deer disappeared in 1924 from Yellowstone Park. The toll among other and commoner game, pushed farther and farther into the mountains by the domestic herds, grows with each bad winter which curtails food supplies in the high country. The winters of 1930–31 and 1931–32 killed 35 per cent of all the deer in western Montana. In the winter immediately following these, 500 elk on the west fork of the Flathead River alone starved to death. The game of Montana is in a particularly precarious situation because in seasons of especially deep snow only 5 per cent of the national forest area is accessible to the animals for grazing. They drift back to the range; but the range has been depleted, and sometimes they raid haystacks. Indignant farmers kill them off. One Montana rancher (not representative of his class) advertised publicly for machine gunners to destroy wild game which blundered onto his foothills property. He was arrested and fined after he had killed a couple of elk.

In the same district heavy storms have occasionally driven thousands of elk to the plains and one year 1,070 head were slaughtered within a few weeks by men and women on foot, horseback, and in automobiles.

For a number of years prior to 1940, when the shamed game commission stopped the practice, hundreds of animals were slaughtered annually on the infamous "Park county firing line" near Yellowstone Park, an open plain where the elk had to run the gauntlet in direct line of fire from hunters, each of whom had to affix his state hunting license tag to his kill—his tag, or his wife's, or his child's, or all of them.

Late in the summer of 1882 a Texas cowboy, riding "drag" on one of the great trail herds pouring into Montana from the

Southwest, tenderly shepherded the weak and sick cattle in his charge and sang:

Whoopee, ti yi yo, git along, little dogies!
It's your misfortune and none of my own . . .
Whoopee, ti yi yo, git along little dogies,
For you know Montana will be your new home!

The sun was hot and the cowboy pulled his Stetson lower over his eyes, slumped in the saddle, almost dozed off. Suddenly his horse shied and stopped. The cowboy looked up, into the calm face of an old Indian brave, mounted and with a rifle held against his thigh. Behind him were two other Indians.

The Texan did not even reach for his gun. He did look around him fleetingly for his partner; but he knew the other rider was a mile away on the other side of the herd and probably had not seen the Indians approach and could not see them now.

He raised his hand in friendly salute.

"Buffalo," said the old brave slowly, as if reciting a piece he had learned, "gone. Cattle spoil much grass. Indian poor; no longer get enough meat. Want two steers."

"Okay," said the Texan, and added, to himself, "you thieving old bastard, I'll get you the sickest pair I got!" He was used to such trail incidents; but so was the old brave.

"We pick," the Indian said briefly, and his two companions rode quietly into the herd and chose steers which, allowing for the weakness that kept them among the drags, were in good shape. Deftly they cut them out of the herd, started them across the prairie. The old Indian watched their getaway, then dropped his rifle into its scabbard, wheeled his horse and rode off at a gallop, leaving the cowboy the target of his back.

But the cowboy left his gun in its holster. What the hell! This happened all the time. . . . He rode on, thinking.

As a matter of fact, that old brave had a lot more guts than most of 'em, who'd just ride up to the herd and beg a steer or two, and make nuisances of themselves until they got their meat. Getting good and hungry sure took the pride out of those babies!

Government had the right idea, starvin' them out. . . . But sorta too bad to break their independent spirit and take away their self respect.

Oh, what the hell! Cattle had to have range, didn't they? Shoulda plugged the old bastard; had the law on my side. . . .

Whoopee, ti yi yo, git along little dogies!
It's your misfortune and none of my own . . .

... and Prophet;

IV. 2,560 ACRES PER FAMILY

IN October, 1877, Chief Joseph of the Nez Percé, who like
many a great commander before him had won all his battles except the last one, surrendered to General Miles
near the Bear's Paw Mountains of Montana. All the way
from Oregon he had outmaneuvered, outsmarted, and out-
fought the United States Army; but now he was done. He was
outnumbered two to one; he had lost heavily in the Big Hole
massacre, when General Gibbons' troops had fired barba-
rously into his tepees in a surprise attack, killing not only warriors but women and children. He had rallied his braves after
this, turned on the whites and driven them back, but after this
three days' struggle in Montana against Miles' superior force
he had come to the end.

So Joseph relinquished the last claim of the red man to this
range. In half a dozen years the buffalo would be gone. The
white man's era had begun.

About the time of Joseph's surrender, there came to the
Great Plains and Montana a prophet. He came as a representative of the national government; and at that time the Terri-

tory of Montana paid little attention to the national government. He came, too, as a scientist—and Montana paid no attention whatever to scientists. For that matter, it later developed that the east and the nation's capital itself had little time for scientists, either.

This man was John Wesley Powell, director of the United States Geological Survey, first preacher of western water conservation. He left, in the Library of Congress, a brief report in a ponderous volume of congressional reports for the year 1878; and that report, considering its date, is one of the most remarkable studies of social and economic forces ever written in America. Not only did it forecast with what today seems to have been incredible prevision just what would happen to the Great Plains—it also set forth a draft constitution for a new society in the arid west, a coöperative, free society made up of individuals who recognized their responsibility to each other in a hard land, and acknowledged their debt to the soil itself.

The report proposed certain legislation to establish this society and to prevent inevitable ruin of the northern plains through the heedless greed of man. It attempted—this projected society—to preserve the best of Indian civilization, its reverent coöperation with natural forces which could not be tamed, and sought at the same time to eliminate most of the hardship of primitive life. It was the kind of state which might have been developed by the Indians through centuries of economic evolution had some phenomenal occurrence forced them to abandon their nomadic habit for one of agrarian stability.

Sixty years after Powell's legislation was drafted, a few of its suggestions became law—sponsored, probably, by men and organizations who never had heard of the geologist who had seen more clearly than anyone else the desolation, suffering, nationwide economic distress which would result from unrestricted exploitation of the west's soil resources.

Powell and his associates started with the soil. They took samples of the grasses and analyzed them chemically, studied and recorded growth habits of the native plants, dug in the earth to measure the thin but rich humus and depth of moisture penetration. They assembled reports laboriously compiled on crude charts by lonely weather observers in scattered plains stations, most of them volunteers. They compared this climatological data with their chemical studies to learn what made the western grasses so nutritious, so hardy in contest with the elements and yet so easily killed by man's herds and his plows.

Then Powell, synthesizing all this, gave to a deaf nation one of its earliest and finest examples of economic planning.

Thousands of men, women, and children have had their lives permanently blighted by poverty—hundreds have actually starved—thousands of head of livestock have perished, thousands of tons of food have been destroyed, and millions of acres of soil have been lost or damaged since Powell presented his plan for the plains—because Congress and the American people paid him no attention whatever. His warning was not heard, and the entire economies of communities, states, and a region were erected upon foundations of sand which collapsed in a hot, dry wind. That collapse, in Montana alone, has levied a tax in the last ten years of more than $1 on every man, woman, and child in the United States—and Montana is but one of the states Powell's plan might have saved. That collapse has disorganized the whole national economy and has compelled the federal government to adopt expensive and sometimes hasty, inadequately planned measures to restore the resources and the population balance of the west.

It would have been cheaper to listen to J. W. Powell. Sixty years late, some of his recommendations have been adopted; but—sixty years late—they cannot bring back all of the natural wealth so prodigally used. They cannot now recall the wasted man hours and put the lost human resources to fruitful use. Because even today selfishness and greed and jealousies obstruct and interfere, there are many things they cannot do.

In the summary of Powell's findings which follows, his predictions have been balanced against reports of Montana economists, principally Dr. R. R. Renne of the department of agricultural economics of the State College, and other current sources—the better to show the reader the amazing foresight of John Wesley Powell. Montana was not the only plains state he studied, and similar confirmation of his conclusions can be found in the Dakotas or Utah.

Reviewing his rainfall records, Powell declared flatly that

most of the western Great Plains never could be adapted to intensive crop cultivation because of inadequate annual precipitation and recurrent drouth. He warned specifically against exaggeration of the plains' value for crop farming based upon one or several years of better-than-average rainfall. The limit of successful agriculture, he said, is 20 inches annual moisture; and 20-inch moisture ceases about fifty miles east of Pembina, N. D. On the western and northern plains, he warned, "many droughts will occur; many seasons in a long series will be fruitless. It may be doubted whether, on the whole, agriculture will prove remunerative."

Nevertheless, in the decade 1909–19, which included a series of "wet" years, Montana's wheat acreage increased from 258,000 to 3,417,000! During most of this period, the state's annual average precipitation was 18 inches—still considerably under the total Powell had held necessary for successful farming—but that of the northern and central region where most of the new wheat development occurred was even less; and calamitous drouth followed, carrying the average in some sections to as low as 5 inches.

Irrigation of the dryland sections, said Powell, would be important for support of a limited agriculture (for gardens and hay lands), but he warned against "crude and careless" methods which would result in gullying, sheet erosion, and especially alkalization of the soil. This caution, too, was ignored or forgotten; and thousands of acres fell victim to wasteful runoff or alkali condensation.

The luxuriant grasses of Montana Powell described as "quasi hay," but with this acknowledgment of their richness he coupled his most important admonition: these lush prairies must not be overgrazed nor the natural sod cover be destroyed. The grasses would be particularly vulnerable to domestic feeding within fences; this led to the conclusion that the herdsman must have a large area for support of his stock. With this as his initial postulate, Powell set out to plan his model land use system.

"A quarter-section of land alone will be of no value," he said. "The pasturage it will afford will not suffice to maintain a herd that even the poorest man will need for his support." Four square miles would be the minimum; but he fixed upon 2,560 acres as the best standard land unit per family.

Sixteen years before Powell spoke, Congress had passed the Free Homestead Act. It had not yet affected the northern plains very much, for farmers had found more fertile, less hostile country; there were few foolhardy enough to attempt to wrest a living from 160 acres of dry soil entirely surrounded by Indians. But perhaps Powell despairingly foresaw the Enlarged Homestead Act of 1909, the so-called "dryland farm act," which gave the government's blessing to the plundering of the plains. At any rate, he warned anxiously against any attempt to apply the Homestead Act to Montana. The 160-acre allotment, he reiterated, would be worthless. (Certainly he could not have regarded the 1909 allotment of 320 acres as any better; and he would have grieved—he died in 1902— over another provision of the 1909 act—the requirement that at least one eighth of the farm area had to be *continuously* cultivated for agricultural crops *other than native grasses* beginning with the third year of entry!)

Writing in 1936, Dr. Renne said of the expansion of Montana crop agriculture and the resultant overdevelopment of social services:

It was based upon a production pattern which is impossible in most areas of the state. The land was homesteaded. . . .

Correction of present maladjustments depends largely upon the grouping of these small, uneconomic farm parcels into units of proper size.

Powell's fundamental principle, therefore, was this: Large acreage is essential to support of human life on the plains. How sound that principle was and how amazingly accurate the deductions he derived from it, America did not learn for half a century. Upon this principle he built his suggestions for social organization, and these in turn stemmed from three sub-principles: First, surveys should conform to the topography; second, farm residences should be grouped; third, pasturage should not be fenced.

If the lands were surveyed regularly, as in the township surveys of the fertile east, all the water sufficient for a number of pasturage farms might fall entirely within one owner's property. On the other hand, irregular surveys conforming to topography and permitting each settler to get a portion of the

essential stream might prevent, Powell said, monopolization
of water rights by a few individuals and consequent imposition of "an intolerable burden" upon the people. Nevertheless the lands were surveyed in townships, water rights were
monopolized (and water power rights, too), and the "intolerable burden" was imposed, just as he had predicted. Surveys in the traditional eastern manner, he warned, would
result in only those divisions which had water being taken up;
"and the farmer obtaining title to such a division could practically occupy all the adjacent country because he would own
all the water necessary to its use."

(It is interesting to note that one of the causes of the 1885
Northwest Rebellion in semi-arid Saskatchewan across the
border from Montana was the Canadian Government's insistence upon township surveys, resisted by the métis [mixed-
bloods] who knew the value of water on the plains and who
insisted on the French system, giving each his portion of the
vital stream).

Powell pointed out that a brook carrying water sufficient to
irrigate 200 acres could be made to serve 20 acres on each of
10 farms, supplying stock water and irrigating gardens and
hay meadows. This could be brought about if the surveys
were so drawn as to give the greatest possible number of
"water fronts." They were not so drawn. The current projects
of the Federal Land Utilization Division, Bureau of Agricultural Economics, according to a press release are "based on
evidence that land which has been proved unsuited to crop
production should be turned back to range, *with the exception of small tracts for family living and feed.*" Sixty years
late.

It followed naturally, if individual tracts were to be large
and yet residences were to be placed, so far as possible, on
water fronts, that these homes could be grouped for social
services. The large acreage required for support of a family
would result in sparse population and vast untenanted spaces;
attempts to establish county governments on the eastern pattern, Powell reasoned, would prove to be prohibitively costly.
Therefore he proposed what he called a "colony" system by
which citizens might obtain benefits of the usual social organizations—schools, churches, etc.—and coöperate in construct-
ing roads, bridges, and other improvements, without estab-

lishment of formal incorporated communities and counties and their expensive political accessories.

Today Montana is full of bankrupt or near-bankrupt counties and ghost towns. The national land planning unit of the national resources committee has said of the Great Plains:

The cost of political and social institutions is still too high, sometimes exceeding total county tax receipts. One must conclude that in part this is due to county units being far too small; in part, however, it is due to an institutional program not adjusted to basic land productivity. . . . Consolidation of county units and zoning of rural residence to achieve lower road and school cost might achieve some economy.

Zoning of rural residence was proposed by Powell sixty years before that report was issued.

Powell's third sub-principle—that cattle must graze unfenced lands—grew naturally out of his determination of soil and forage qualities:

The great areas over which stock must roam to obtain subsistence usually will prevent the practicability of fencing the lands. It will not pay; hence in many cases the lands must be occupied by herds roaming in common. For poor men co-operative pasture is necessary, or communal regulations for the occupancy of the ground and for the division of the increase of the herds.

Such coöperative grazing districts, Powell said, should have "home rule" and should be closely integrated with the "colony" social organization which he had projected. Fifty years after this recommendation had been submitted to Congress and forgotten, America's first such coöperative grazing district was established, and it was in Montana. In 1928, by act of Congress, there was created an organization which was regarded (but would not have been by Powell) as having revolutionary implications. It bore the homely western name of Mizpah-Pumpkin Creek Grazing Association, and six years after its establishment, as a result of its success, there came the Taylor Grazing Act. This act—though without, as yet, complete efficiency—provided for controlled coöperative grazing throughout the west.

Federal legislation was required to set up that first grazing association because public domain was included in the lands it was to administer, and passage of the bill was obtained on the plea that it would be a valuable "experiment" in land use on the Great Plains—an "experiment" fifty years late! Now economists agree that there should be voluntary grouping of ranchers to form coöperative grazing districts and the bureau of agricultural economics reports as a fundamental policy the encouragement of "local grazing associations" in order to provide "additional range to a point where enough cattle can be raised to earn their owners a livelihood without necessitating overgrazing."

The processes of democracy are slow; unhappily, those of the "rugged individualism" to which our American way gave free rein in the west, are swift. The sixty-year lag in social and economic thinking since the report of a government scientist was put aside and forgotten has taken an incalculable toll of the nation's real wealth. The lesson to be read in the brittle yellowed pages of the volume of 1878 Congressional Reports should earn for modern postwar planners a more sympathetic hearing than the one which was accorded to singularly clairvoyant J. W. Powell.

Today the traveler can drive for hundreds of miles on hard-surfaced highway which has replaced the Bozeman Trail and for scores of those miles, in Wyoming and Montana, he will never see a fence. There will be long, hot stretches in which he will not see a house; though he may see, and puzzle over, an occasional derelict privy: neighbors helped themselves to the drylander's abandoned house, but the privy was not worth salvaging. After a few more years the last of the privies will have disintegrated in the wind; all of the post holes where the fences used to be will have filled up. Some of the grass will have come back, helped along with chemicals and seeding. More and more grazing associations are established, more and more herds wander freely over unfenced plains.

And the heart of J. W. Powell would bound if he could ride that trail today and see beside it the signs which have been placed by highway authorities:

"OPEN RANGE
WATCH OUT FOR
LIVESTOCK"

Prospector,

V. MR. ROGERS SECEDES

MONTANA'S first sizable city was named in honor of the wife of Jefferson Davis, president of the Confederacy.

This was in the roistering '6o's, when the Territory was full of gold, Indians, whisky, and fugitive Rebels. For half a century before this, there had been only the Indians and the tough and lonely mountain men, the trappers, many of them métis. It was one of these, François Finlay, known as "Benetsee," who discovered gold. His find was made, apparently about 1856, at Gold Creek, midway between the present cities of Helena and Missoula.

The first really profitable gold discovery was made by John White in 1862 on Grasshopper Creek and there arose the camp of Bannack, Montana's first capital and site of the first territorial legislative session in 1864. By the time it had attained this honor, however, Bannack's thin gold placers were already worked out, and it was destined to become a ghost town in another couple of years. The little group of Union-minded prospectors who had sponsored Montana's territorial pretensions drifted fifty miles east to Alder Gulch, scene of a richer discovery in 1863.

The founders of the Alder Gulch camp chose to call it Varina, but a federal judge of Idaho Territory, of which Montana in 1863 was still a part, refused to accept this tribute to Mrs. Jeff Davis in his court records; he changed the name, by judicial fiat, to Virginia City. So the Alder Gulch miners' gesture was futile. It was, nevertheless, significant.

The first newspaper, save for a couple of single-sheet bulletins which lasted only a few weeks, was the *Montana Post* of Virginia City. (Bannack, though briefly the capital, never managed to support one.) So auspicious were the *Post's* beginnings that its founders, who had arrived in the gold camp with nothing but a case of battered type and an old hand press, were able to retire from the hazardous field of journalism and take up mining after just three weeks. They sold the *Post* for $3,000.

The second issue of that newspaper, dated September 3, 1864, bore a headline noteworthy for its implications: "News from America." Montana had become a Territory in its own right in May, 1864, and previously, at one time or another, had been a part of six—Missouri, Nebraska, Dakota, Oregon, Washington, and Idaho—but it nevertheless chose still to regard itself as back of beyond, as a remote, independent, and untouchable empire. It resented and continually obstructed, ungratefully, the federal controls which accompanied the blessings of territorial recognition; and an active and noisy section of its citizenry held that it should continue to be the last refuge of the Confederacy's unreconstructed belligerents. Montana has a legend to the effect that "the left wing of the army of Confederate General Price in Missouri never surrendered; it retreated to Montana."

It was some time before Montana got around to calling the rest of the country "the States." In October the *Post* was still referring to an alien land—"the Yellowstone expedition will weigh anchor on the 18th inst. and sail for America"—and the reference was repeated in later months. This particular attitude was not, of course, solely Montana's: it was to be found somewhat generally in the Territories and may have originated in California. On that golden coast, however, it had been speedily modified by the influx of northerners who

followed the southern pioneers to the new diggings, whereas
Montana got not only the Californians but hundreds who had
abandoned stricken homes in the south, or had fled northern
vengeance for Civil War outlawry.

So strong was this concept of the Territory as a detached
and autonomous state that its first delegate to the Congress of
the United States solemnly warned his amused colleagues in
1865 to have a care lest certain legislation they were contem-
plating should offend the fractious frontiersmen who had sent
him to Washington from the high country. It had been hard
enough, Samuel MacLean told them, to win Montana's somewhat suspect loyalty to the Union; and he would not put it
past his constituents, if annoyed, to quit the United States
forthwith and team up with similarly gold-minded British
Columbia. (It is worth noting that this westernmost Canadian
province, culturally akin to pioneer Montana, later caused
the Dominion similar headaches by its regard for its "independence" and the high price it set for confederation.)

The fact that the United States might object to any such
summary transfer of one hundred forty-seven thousand square
miles of its Louisiana Purchase as was hinted by MacLean
was not acknowledged in his speech nor in the early debates
of the Territory's Rebel-sabotaged legislature, many of whose
delegates apparently regarded the Union as merely a political
fancy to which they owed no more than nominal recognition.

It came as no surprise, therefore, save to a few federal officials and the *Montana Post* (it was better informed on the
duties of citizenship than were its readers) when the first
territorial legislature, meeting in Bannack, attempted to seat
a speaker who flatly refused to take the prescribed oath of
allegiance to the United States.

The *Post's* special correspondent in the legislative halls—a
log cabin—was properly shocked by this "most impudent attempt of a Rebel to get into the Assembly." He was a Mr.
Rogers, and in his little gesture the Confederacy fought a last
battle for the western Territories, and lost . . . not, however, through lack of friends: the Montana assembly was so
sympathetic that when he declined to swear to the "ironclad,"
incorporating the pledge not to take up arms against the
United States, the assembly obligingly changed the oath to
suit him. At its indulgent suggestion, Rogers agreed to "sup-

port the constitution of the United States and the organic act
of this Territory, and to demean myself faithfully while in
office." Thereupon he was seated, to the horror of the *Post*
and of Governor Sidney Edgerton.

Governor Edgerton promptly notified the assembly that
until Rogers took the regulation oath as prescribed by the
Government of the United States—or until he were unseated
—there would be no communication between executive and
legislative branches of the government, and—more to the
point—the legislative branch would go unpaid. The delegates
raged and there was fierce talk of secession, but Rogers tired of
the futile comedy and resigned. The assembly settled down to
a debate over another "impudent" development, an attempt
by two booted and spurred racketeers to get a franchise for a
toll road to Salt Lake City on a route they had merely ridden
over and "claimed." Despite the *Post's* protests, dozens of such
"franchises" were granted to political favorites who thus were
enabled to exact tribute from the Territory's citizens. The
session then subsided into the apathy since characteristic of
Montana legislatures, and the *Post's* special correspondent
complained: "This dull town makes one long for the fleshpots
of Madison County [Virginia City]."

For years this rebellious spirit, like the wild winds of Montana, tore at the Territory's rickety new political structure.
Over its thousands of citizens—many, perhaps a majority of
whom, were secessionist Democrats and all of whom were un-
ruly—had been set a group of federally appointed officials
who were members of the opposing Union party. Besides,
these officials were mostly easterners, pilgrims and tenderfeet;
the "hill rats" and "hardrockers" didn't take to them, and the
feeling was mutual.

Thousands of the prospectors who streamed into the Alder
Gulch-Virginia diggings were either actively hostile to feder-
alism or indifferent, and they had had nothing to say about it.

They had nothing to say, either, about the editorial policy
of the Territory's only newspaper—like a good many newspaper readers before and since. The *Post,* heroically indifferent to the overwhelming Democratic sympathies of its nine
thousand paid subscribers, was Union—and somewhat given
to breast-beating about it, too. Thus, admitting humiliating

defeat in the first congressional election, October, 1864 (its candidate obtained a bare majority in but three of the twelve precincts whose returns it reported), the *Post* said:

On Monday, came off the long-expected election. The day was fine, and upon the whole, the behaviour of the large crowd assembled was as orderly as could be expected and much more so than really was anticipated. The Democratic ticket has obtained a majority in this vicinity . . . The friends of liberty and of the government of their fathers are in no ways dismayed, but wait the event, with the calmness of men who have done their duty to their God and their own consciences.

The angry political winds soon blew Edgerton out of the Territory—Edgerton, who had been justice of Idaho Territory, who had gone to Congress with nuggets in his pockets and had persuaded it to give Montana its own government. He left for Ohio, ostensibly to see to his daughters' education, and from there sent in his resignation. A subsequent legislature erased his name from the map by changing Edgerton County to Lewis and Clark; the Helena *Herald* applauded the vindictive act and not even the Unionist *Post* dared protest.

Upon Edgerton's departure, Montana Territory acquired a new secretary who served for a year as "acting governor" and who was one of the most colorful characters the west has ever known. He was Gen. Thomas Francis Meagher, Civil War hero, almost legendary Irish political saint, world-renowned explorer, writer, and orator. The Territory's already badly confused political situation was hopelessly muddled by his intervention. The Union party, which dominated executive and judicial departments, was Protestant and Masonic; Meagher was a staunch Roman Catholic. The Democratic party, which controlled the legislature, was—to put it mildly —only lukewarm in its loyalty to the United States; Meagher was a Democrat but unswerving in his devotion to the Union.

The Territory, when Meagher arrived, was without government; there was not even paper and ink for transaction of territorial business in Virginia City, to which he moved the capital from Bannack immediately upon his arrival in 1865. Meagher, after first ruling that he had no authority to summon either a special territorial legislative session or a constitutional convention as a step toward statehood, suddenly decided he did have such power and called both—defying the procrustean legalism of the judges. (But the judges were later upheld and the laws passed at his special session, which by then had served their purpose, were stricken from the books. As for the convention, the constitution it drafted was mysteriously lost en route to St. Louis and was never heard of again.)

Meagher's message to the special session was uncompromising: "We are going to have nationality without sectionalism, we are going to have an enlightened civilization, religion without puritanism [the hostility to his own Catholicism rankled, naturally] and loyalty without humiliation."

The legislators didn't like the lecture, and a good many of them hadn't wanted to come, anyway. Word reached them, however, that Meagher, who had brought a military escort with him from the States and still retained it, was prepared to enforce martial law in Virginia City; it was rumored, probably falsely, that he intended to keep all food, and—what was worse—all whisky from his puppet legislature until it had done his bidding. The orders, he announced grimly in a public statement, were to pass laws so framed that "no judge, whatever his powers or consequence, should dispute or disobey them," such laws to be enforced "with the whole power of the county of Madison and if need be, with the whole Territory"—which meant Meagher's storm troopers, his personal military escort.

Montana was restive under the iron command of Meagher, its first dictator; but his name, unlike Edgerton's, is still borne by a Montana county, and a statue of him stands before the state's capital. He was one of the greatest soldiers of fortune who ever lived. A strikingly handsome and effective Irish patriot at twenty-four, in the space of twenty years his adventures carried him around the world and ended with his mysterious death in the rough river town of Fort Benton, Montana Territory, where as late as 1882 visitors were warned, "Walk in the middle of the street and mind your own business; this is a tough town!"

He was little more than a boy when he drove the moderates out of the Irish independence movement and whipped the peasants to the point of revolt with a famous address hailing the effectiveness against tyranny of "The Sword." After the uprising of 1848 he was sentenced to be hanged, drawn, and quartered, but the sentence was commuted by Queen Victoria to life imprisonment in Van Diemen's Land, now Tasmania. He escaped, spent a week on a nearby island living on shell-fish, finally reached New York. There he lectured and published an Irish newspaper, then explored Central America, wrote travel articles for magazines, and on the outbreak of the Civil War formed the 69th New York Regiment, which came to be known as the "Bloody Irish." After the war he was appointed secretary of Montana Territory, of which he may never have heard up to then. He demanded a military escort and waited in Omaha until he got it.

Meagher's Montana career lasted but two years. In June, 1867, he rode with a party to Fort Benton to board a steamer which would carry him downriver to pick up arms sent by the government for use in suppressing new Indian outbreaks. He went aboard a ship owned by an old Irish riverboat skipper on the night of July 1—and was never seen again. Meagher was ill at the time of the common "summer complaint" of horsemen, and it was officially decided that he had fallen off the boat and drowned; but no trace of the body was found in the shallow river despite offer of $10,000 reward. He was forty-three years old.

There were ugly rumors that he had been murdered by the Vigilantes. A month earlier he had pardoned a gambling table brawler, James Daniels, who had killed a man in a fight and had been sentenced to prison. This culprit, said one Montana historian, was "indicted for a crime he did not commit [indicted for murder, but convicted of manslaughter]; tried by a court without jurisdiction, reprieved by a governor by mistake, and lynched by a mob." That was the way things happened in Montana; life was a little confused. . . . After Meagher freed Daniels, the man was hanged by Vigilantes in Helena, to which he had returned mouthing threats against those who had "sent him up." Pinned to his coat when he was cut down was a message to the "acting governor": "Do this again and you'll meet the same fate."

In 1913 an old man suffering from delirium tremens "confessed" in a small Montana jail that he had killed Meagher at Fort Benton and had been paid $8,000 for the job. He was rushed to a city hospital, recovered speedily, and repudiated his story. Then, a decade or so later, David M. Billingsley, ninety-seven and self-asserted former Vigilante, claimed in a newspaper interview that he had been present the night the Vigilantes had condemned Meagher to death. The story was instantly denied by other former Vigilantes and descendants of Vigilantes, most of them among Montana's "first families."

No more bums with alcoholic jitters, no more aged and eccentric pioneers, have risen to confound Montana historians; the "accident" verdict stands. Montana has virtually forgotten Dictator Meagher; but in Ireland they still sing of a gallant fighter from a fighting race who died on his way to get more guns to do more fighting.

A Methodist church was established in Virginia City late in 1864, partially through the efforts of one George Forbes, who had arrived in the first gold rush possessed of a few hundred dollars and had left three years later with $75,000. Pastor of this church was the Reverend A. M. Hough, and in later years this dominie confessed his bewilderment about Montanans: "One of the things I could never understand was that in communities where the population was ready to rise en masse and hang men guilty of great crimes, or sustain an organized vigilance committee in doing it, a legal conviction and execution will not be sustained." Perhaps that was due to Montanans' resentment of federal interference. Certainly the incessant political warfare between Unionist judges and Democratic citizens was a factor. During the two or three years between the major Montana gold discoveries and the separation of Montana Territory from Idaho, there was virtually no law. Into the camps streamed the diggers from California and Idaho and the fierce men who had fought their way through the brush wilderness to British Columbia's Fraser River fields. Hard on their heels came the outlaws of the plains, Civil War deserters, bushwackers from Kansas and Nebraska and Missouri—especially Missouri. Holdups and claim jumping were common and murder occurred almost daily.

When these conditions became intolerable, a citizens' agency was born to stamp out outlawry—Montana's famous Vigilantes. Their story has been told so frequently that it

merits only the briefest review here. A half dozen men—all or
most of them members of the Masonic order—formed the
Vigilance Committee of Virginia City in a series of secret
meetings late in 1863. Quietly recruiting reinforcements from
among Virginia's 10,000 population, they gathered evidence
against the ruthless "road agents" who had been terrorizing
the stage routes for months, and struck swiftly, wiping out the
outlaw element in a few weeks. Two dozen men were summarily hanged and scores more fled or were banished.

Chief of the outlaws was Henry Plummer, who had so ingratiated himself that he had been elected sheriff at Bannack
and had made his highwaymen lieutenants his deputies. By
virtue of their official position, they knew in advance the
movements of all prosperous citizens and were informed of
transfer by stage of gold dust. This gang was accused of 102
known murders, confirmed by discovery of the victims' bodies
or by confessions of the killers, and suspected of scores of
others. Their total loot has never even been estimated, but it
ran to many thousand dollars. Plummer, after "persuading"
the Virginia City sheriff to yield his office to him, virtually
ruled both gold camps.

The road agent chief was a "gentleman," cultured and
shrewd. He married a teacher who knew nothing of his
crimes, but ten weeks after the wedding she left him, and
after his death she remarried in another state. Only a few
weeks before he was hanged he entertained several territorial
notables, including the governor and some of the Vigilantes,
at an elaborate dinner in his home, for which he had obtained by stage from Salt Lake City a forty-pound turkey. It
cost him three ounces of gold dust, probably $50 to $60. Vigilantes among his guests, who already had decided to hang
him, apparently saw nothing untoward about thus enjoying
his hospitality; and turkey, after all, was a rare treat.

Men were rough and their tempers short, and women were
scarce. The Vigilantes relinquished the task of preservation
of the peace to federal judges; Virginia City's first grand jury
brought in its report on New Year's Eve, 1864, and hurried
to a saloon. The greatest number of indictments returned for
any one sin against the Territory's brand-new criminal code
was not, as one might have supposed, concerned with mascu-

line combat: five astonished Montanans found themselves solemnly charged with—adultery. There had been, the jury decided, one "attempt to commit murder," two "assaults with deadly weapons," two major thefts, one instance of fraud, one each of bigamy, incest, and mayhem, and two (how times had changed!) of "exhibiting deadly weapons."

The law had come to Montana, or said it had; but it was to have its hands full. Nothing much came of those indictments, especially the ones for "exhibiting deadly weapons"—thirty years later Montanans were still exhibiting them. It was, indeed, hardly to be expected that any such abstract principle as that of social sanctions could be impressed immediately upon the frontier. One could put up with road agents just so long—it was a free country; but finally one hanged them. One could not do anything about the weather, which was frequently damnable: therefore the *Post* could report, under the facetious heading "Pleasant Traveling," that trip through Portneuf canyon when the coach had to traverse a suddenly formed lake four miles across and breast-deep, mules swimming and coach floating. Sure, that was weather, and one accepted it . . .

But when the fault was mechanical or human, that was something else again. A man made himself into a highwayman, and the only way to unmake a highwayman, if he wouldn't go away and annoy somebody else, was to string him up. Men made coaches, and men drove them, often inexpertly. One day in the winter of 1864 the *Post* commented curtly as follows on an incident of travel: "The passengers on one of Oliver & Co.'s coaches which left this town on the 17th instant had a break down, got mad, and burnt up the coach on Snake River."

The writer knows a Montana mountain man of current vintage who beats his balky Ford truck with a stick of firewood.

VI. THE SCALES WERE CROOKED

The trail which led to the independent, devil-may-care life of the frontier was, however, a two-way road: outgoing traffic balanced, and occasionally exceeded, that which was coming in. The gains—a certain implicit freedom from restraint, a gay and unbuttoned spirit—could never quite compensate for the losses, for the transitory character imposed upon the community, the initial acceptance of the disastrous colonial concept.

Here in Montana was a no-man's-land, to be looted by the strongest and, as soon as possible, abandoned. One owed it no allegiance.

So little more than a year after the gold discovery at Virginia City, the *Post* was saying bon voyage to leading citizens: "Sam Schwab, one of the proprietors of the Montana Billiard Hall, has made his pile, sold out, and gone to his 'faderland.' A happy and speedy voyage to you, Sam." . . . Not, however, without faint misgivings; even in that early *Post* there must have been some realization that all could not go well in such a self-seeking society: "Daily we see teams loaded with men [*sic*] that have made their pile, leaving the country, some to return in the spring, some never to see this fair Territory any more."

It was an inauspicious beginning for a Treasure State, for thus was established a social and economic pattern of spoliation which subsequently was impressed upon the laws, customs, and even minds of Montanans and their eastern exploiters. The pattern originated in hardy individual enterprise on the log-cabin frontier and to some extent could be justified and even defended: while it hurt the frontier, it strengthened the men. But it has survived to maintain itself by corporate cunning born in today's air-conditioned Wall Street offices.

Life in Montana was not only strengthening—if you could take it—but it was also fun. Hurdy-gurdy houses, the dance halls of their day, were most prosperous properties, despite the *Post's* fruitless copybook moralizing. Reporting that citizens of the near-by town of Summit were about to "abate the nuisance before pauperism becomes the rule," the newspaper said of these institutions: "With the hardest part of the mountain winter before them, our citizens would do well to lay up a store of something more tangible than pirouettes, more nutritious than varsouviennes and more profitable than smiles and tickets per agreement."

But how could one "lay up a store" of those other, estimably practical commodities on the frontier? There was always too much going on!

Con Orem, Virginia City saloonkeeper who "made it his doctrine to touch, taste or handle not either spirituous or malt liquors, or use tobacco in any form," was matched for a fight with Hugh O'Neil, miner, who touched, tasted, and handled 'em all, with delight. About the only respects in which they were evenly matched were nationality and spirit—both were Irish and both dearly loved to fight. Con Orem was only 5 feet 6½ inches tall and weighed but 138 pounds; his opponent was 2 inches taller and 52 pounds heavier.

The battle between the forces of good and evil lasted for 185 one-minute rounds, from two in the afternoon until sunset. It ended in a draw, all bets off, after scores of knockdowns and lots of blood. The spectators, apparently more exhausted than the principals, helped persuade the two men's backers to call the fight off. The *Post's* sportswriter, who was also its editor, reporter, and printer, and was the village schoolmaster to boot, recorded the contest in a style somewhat reminiscent of that of George Gordon, sixth Lord Byron, and concluded admiringly that the participants were perfectly willing to continue their epic contest all night. The moral issue at stake was never satisfactorily resolved, but the saloons, especially Con's, were very busy after the fight. Each fighter got $1,000 and they shared the "ring money"—sacks of gold dust tossed to them by enthusiastic fans.

That fight, Montana's first professional sport event, was staged outdoors in midwinter.

Not all entertainment was so violent. It was on the whole a time of simple pleasures, and the *Post* summed up its readers' social characteristics one day in this manner:

The great features of our people are enterprise, restless activity,
and contempt for danger or privation. Hospitality is general and
unaffected. There is a sort of rough, though genuine courtesy
much in vogue among the mountaineers which makes them excellent companions in danger or hardship. Majors, colonels,
judges and doctors include about one-third of the adult males, but
the reverence usually accorded to those high-sounding cognomens
is left at home; and in the gulch Major Blank wheels, while Colonel Carat fills.

Virginia City had a "reading room" for members only
where books and magazines were provided at a fee which appears to have been $5 a month, and it was a very popular re-
sort. The mining camp, a year after gold's discovery, was
staging amateur theatrical performances and had organized
a lyceum committee to engage touring musicians and lec-
turers. The legitimate theater flourished.

But none of these innocent pursuits threatened the favored
position of gambling as a pastime or the dominant popularity
of saloons. Operators of the games and bars brought hetero-
geneous cultures to the camps: the professional gamblers were
frequently traveled and polished "gentlemen" with a background of Mississippi riverboat experience, and at least one
of the scores of saloonkeepers who set up shop in Virginia at
one time or another was "of royal blood." He was Count
Henri Murat, nephew of Joachim Murat, whom Napoleon
made King of Naples.

Count Henri, who seems to have been a rather engaging
rogue, came to America with his German wife in 1848 and
joined the California gold rush. His Virginia City sojourn
lasted only a month or two in 1864 and the exact nature of
his specialized talents was not discovered until after he had
sold out and left for Colorado, where he first became a barber
(his wife took in washing) and later a "speculator." After his
departure from Montana the *Post* made an upsetting discovery:

Count (H. Murat), we kindly remember thee for sundry and
divers drinks taken in your Arcade, for which we paid you on your
scales—with extra heavy weights. Your successor, having found
these weights, placed them in the hands of some officers, who
showed them to us. You have got $8,000 gulch dust, have you?

The *Denver News* ran across the *Post's* item and was shocked. Denver had been making quite a fuss over the count, and the *News* commented, "We hope it isn't true." "Sorry," retorted the *Post,* "it is." The Virginia City paper might well have added that this was not the first time, and would not be the last, that Montanans had been short-weighted.

Because they were short-weighted, because bread occasionally cost $2.50 for seven pounds and flour at one time $150 a hundred pounds (in 1864, when the populace staged a pigmy communist uprising and "nationalized" Virginia City's supply), Montanans were nearly always broke. Of course their reckless habits had more than a little to do with it, too: an Omaha man wrote a friend in 1866 that his brother "whom I left in the mountains has lost eighteen thousand dollars in gambling within a short time; for that reason I start tomorrow for Montana."

Because they were broke, development of the gold properties Montanans discovered had to be financed by others, as the discoveries themselves had been "grubstaked." Mining camp economy was highly unstable. A good discussion of this in Harrison A. Trexler's *Flour and Wheat in Montana Gold Camps,* points out:

Many a miner with no credit but his apparent honesty was "grubstaked" by the merchants who in turn borrowed of such parties as had money. The whole economic fabric thus rested on a none-too-secure foundation. If the miner "struck it rich" he could settle with the merchants and the latter could afford to pay the high interest rate. If the miner was unlucky—all parties suffered.

It was a fertile field in which to plant money and watch it grow. At the Trout Creek diggings in 1865 the interest rate was 1 per cent a day. To build a sawmill in Helena A. M. Holter paid interest of 10 per cent a month, and despite this appalling burden he prospered because of the great demand for lumber for mine sluices and timbers. Even churchmen participated in the interest racket: one Bishop Tuttle, Episcopal missionary, obtained $3,500 from the east for a new church but decided to postpone erection of his House of God for a time, meanwhile lending the money to a Helena merchant at the comparatively Christian rate of 25 per cent a year.

In 1865 Samuel T. Hauser, miner and budding banker, went east to interest moneyed men in Montana Territory's gold. As a result of his efforts, large investment began in these frontier ventures, among the first companies being the Missouri & Montana Mining Company of St. Louis. Hauser's success was the more remarkable because of the very unflattering opinion of Montana which had taken root in the east. The great Daniel Webster had been dead only a dozen years, and he had paid his respects to the western frontier in no uncertain words:

What do we want with this vast worthless area, this region of savages and wild beasts, of shifting sands and whirlwinds of dust, of cactus and prairie dogs? To what use could we ever put those great deserts or endless mountain ranges, impenetrable and covered to their base with eternal snow?

The magic word "Gold!" however changed all this. And Hauser had some canny advice. Hezekiah L. Hosmer, a Montana friend, wrote him to get in touch with a Dr. B. H. Throop of Scranton, N. J., who would buy some mining claims himself and interest others. Hosmer also suggested that it might be advisable "in order to get the Territory into notice, to present some [mining] claims to the Herald [New York]. Advise with Dr. Throop about this."

Not all the letters Hauser received from home during his eastern junket were of that sort. Nathaniel P. Langford, a Vigilante leader and Masonic grand master, suddenly remembered some tall tales he had told his family, whom he had asked Hauser to visit, and sent off a frantic letter. After explaining in panting phrases that he had had to hurry to get his message aboard a Missouri boat, Langford cautioned his friend:

Hauser, you remember I told you of my "blowing" to my nephews and nieces in Utica about *our* Yellowstone trip. [Hauser had made a famous and hazardous journey into the Indian-infested Yellowstone country from which he barely escaped with his life; Langford had not been with him]. Now don't you for the world say a word about it, as if I wasn't there, for I would not have them know that I was *gassing*, for anything. It was a piece of foolishness that

I'll never repeat, but not a word from you. So be careful:—and don't let this letter be seen. Burn it up.

Hauser perhaps fancied this letter as a club to hold over his friend in the future. At any rate, he didn't burn it.

Out of this trip of Hauser's grew Montana's first bank, established in Helena in 1866. It was not long before this institution was figuring in a struggle of titans to obtain the major share of Montana's mineral wealth; no longer would its backers have to hunt about for capital, for it was to be thrust upon them.

A. J. Davis started a bank in Butte twelve years later and wrote Hauser of his attempts to interest a young Irishman who was to become famous in Montana—Marcus Daly—in the Territory's mines. Daly was then a representative of George Hearst and J. B. Haggin of the Comstock lode. Davis' letter also introduced another budding copper king, William Andrews Clark, who he reported was outbidding one Warren for "a corner lot." Thornton and Rosecrans, he wrote, had bought a mine which was gradually declining in silver but improving in copper. They had mortgaged everything they owned to pay for this property on borrowed money at 2 per cent a month. "Thornton, as usual," commented Davis drily, "goes his bottom dollar on a single card."

But Thornton was a Montanan and hence a gambler. Besides, it was a time to gamble: the copper industry and its notorious capital, Butte, were being born.

As the placers, worked by gold pan and crude "rocker" or homemade sluice, were cleaned up, the quartz miner, the hard-rock man, moved in. His operations required a mill for extraction of gold from the ore and consequently were costlier; the local "grubstake" was inadequate and the subtle change to the western debtor-eastern creditor relation began, in journeys such as Hauser's.

Nevertheless these first eastern promotions differed from the Montana "grubstake" only in scale. The financiers merely loaned their money to the operators and control for the most part remained with the latter. There is considerable evidence, in fact, that the easterners were wont to complain over the cavalier manner in which they were treated. They importuned their Montana partners constantly for more comprehensive reports of their operations; as the years passed, Hauser's St. Louis agent, a relative, grew increasingly petulant because the westerner couldn't be bothered to write letters.

The returns from these gold ventures were quick and comparatively sure, and as long as the investors or lenders got their money Montanans could let them whistle for their reports.

All that was to change.

The mining, smelting, and refining of copper is a long and very expensive process. It takes big money, and money that can wait. Development of a "limited portion" of one lode in Butte's copper discovery mine, the Anaconda, cost $250,000.

Some of this big money was overseas, mostly in England. In the '60's and '70's, the United States was not a capital-exporting nation, and the panic of 1873 had seriously curtailed even the domestic flow of money for investment. What American capital was available was timid or greedy: Montana found easterners reluctant to finance a copper operation but willing to buy it, if they could get it cheaply. The usual interest rate for American money was 2 per cent a month; the English, with more money to spare and longer investment experience, were content with much less. In the '70's and '80's Englishmen invested thousands of pounds in Montana mines and ranches.

Then suddenly in 1887 Congress passed a law prohibiting aliens from owning any real estate in the Territories, and the foreign capital market instantly dried up. This prohibition did not apply to the States, and it hastened Montana's application for statehood. When the 1889 constitution looking to this end was submitted to the people, its drafters made a particular point of the fact that statehood "will relieve us of that unjust inhibition by which we are prohibited from selling our mines in foreign markets, and will invite capital and emigration [sic]."

The bill had been slipped through Congress when Montana wasn't looking, and Montana was mad, with good reason. Its first Senator after statehood, seeking to relieve remaining Territories of the crippling handicap, commented bitterly in debate on the selfish motives of the measure's proponents—

"it seemed entirely agreeable to prohibit the investment of foreign capital everywhere except in the districts of the voting members." It was a dog-in-the-manger law, he concluded.

Even had ample domestic capital been available, Montana probably would have preferred the foreign money because there were fewer strings tied to it. The trust was being born, and the new state feared that it would lose, through economic pressure, that independence for which it had fought so vigorously in the political field.

There was a gloomy prescience about this: Montana has pretty nearly always known in advance the things that were going to happen to it, but has been unable to do anything about them. Thus the first elected governor of the state, Joseph K. Toole, said as the cornerstone of the capitol was laid in 1899:

There are some wise men bold enough to insist that these stupendous combinations of capital are the offspring of humane impulses exclusively, and that they are designed solely to ameliorate the sufferings of mankind by cheapening the costs of production. . . . Many of the so-called benefactors of mankind who lived in other days appear to have been made of the same clay as those of the present time, and like the latter did not always hang a lantern over the pit they dug. . . .
In the light of history, then, we may be pardoned if in our ignorance or incredulity some of us should take issue with the incorporated humanitarians and seek to prevent that which, in our judgment, will destroy competition, limit production, restrain trade, and raise prices, for the sole purpose of adding to the wealth of the few and the poverty of the many.

Even as the governor spoke, the "incorporated humanitarians" were dickering for an opportunity to extend their benevolence to unsuspecting Montana. Henry H. Rogers, Standard Oil millionaire, was plotting with Marcus Daly the organization of the Amalgamated Copper combine.

Daly, an Irish immigrant who had been a New York newsboy, came to Montana in 1876 as representative of a Utah mining syndicate and bought a silver mine. A couple of years later he returned and bought another, this time with the backing of Hearst. This second mine was the Anaconda, destined to found the world's most famous mining dynasty and to establish the legend that somewhere out west in little-known Montana stood "the richest hill on earth."

The Anaconda, a silver mine, was sold to Daly for $30,000. It was pretty well worked-out, and historians do not agree as to whether Daly, who shrewdly kept his own counsel, had already discovered that it was a promising copper property. Certainly it was to surpass anything he could have expected of it at this time. He soon closed the mine and word got around, perhaps with his help, that he had been bilked; at any rate he quietly bought up other claims surrounding the Anaconda as they were thrown on the market, and quietly moved in machinery.

In 1881 Daly founded the Anaconda Silver Mining Company. Within a few months he found in his mine a copper seam fifty feet wide, and realized that the Anaconda was the richest copper mine the world had ever known. Wealth beyond the dreams of a one-time poor Irish newsboy was within his reach, and grasping for it, Daly sold Montana's greatest industrial resource to Standard Oil.

According to Thomas W. Lawson, who later exposed the machinations of Amalgamated, Daly went to Rogers to make a deal with the Standard Oil crowd to buy out the Anaconda, in which Haggin and Lloyd Tevis, associates of the late George Hearst, were his partners; Daly was to remain secretly a partner in the new, Standard-controlled, company. For the Anaconda, which had cost Daly and his backers $30,000 about twenty years before, Rogers gave $24,000,000; for three other mines and some additional land, timber, and mercantile establishments, he added $15,000,000. The purchaser was the Amalgamated Copper Company. Within a few days after its expenditure of $39,000,000 for the Montana properties, it was capitalized at $75,000,000 and its stock offered for sale to the public.

This "watering" was the first of the "crimes of Amalgamated" which were exposed in 1905 in a sensational series of articles in *Everybody's Magazine* by Lawson, a participant in the "crimes," and later incorporated into his book, *Frenzied Finance*. Amalgamated, he said, "plundered the public to the extent of over one hundred millions of dollars." Its maneuvers in Wall Street, their exposure by Lawson, its

battle for life in Montana against an equally cunning and unscrupulous adversary, and the vengeance it subsequently
wreaked upon him in New York were largely responsible for
the financial panic of 1907.

The Amalgamated, wrote Lawson in 1905, "has from its
birth to the present . . . been responsible for more hell than
any other trust or financial thing since the world began. Because of it the people have sustained incalculable losses and
have suffered untold miseries." But Lawson was not concerned with Montana. The foundation of the whole hollow
pyramid was Butte Hill, and this he barely mentions. We
are not here concerned with what happened to eastern investors; we must look now into the personalities of the amazing triumvirate who became known as the "copper kings" and
who waged war over their prostituted state, debauching her
courts, her politics, and her people, sending gunmen among
her miners to play out, half a mile underground, one of the
most fantastic dramas of American frontier history. These
men were Marcus Daly, William Andrews Clark, and Frederick Augustus Heinze.

First of them was Clark. . . .

VII. THEY HAD TO GROW UP

Once there were three Irishmen.

One was Scotch-Irish, one German-Irish, and one just Irish. Two things, and two only, they had in common—ambition, and cupidity.

The Scotch-Irishman was William Andrews Clark. He was a tight white starched little man, proud and pinchfisted, and when he went on a vacation trip to celebrate a business coup, he peddled pork en route to pay expenses. Never a dollar got away from him except to come back stuck to another, or to buy some splendid flourish for his vanity. He was a Presbyterian and a patriot: in later years he loved to be asked to sing the national anthem in public places, and he sang it in a tight thin voice and blessed America, which had permitted him to harvest scores of millions.

He had no humor and no vices. He was intelligent, efficient, ruthless. And uncouth, easy-going Montana was somewhat in awe of him.

Originally a Pennsylvanian, Clark came to Montana from Missouri, where he had saved enough from his meager pay as a schoolmaster to join the gold rush. He was twenty-four and penniless when he reached the Territory in 1863. Nine years later, when he went to Butte, he was a prosperous merchant and banker, one of the Territory's leading men. In the interim he had mined a little, sold merchandise and cattle, been a moneylender (2 per cent a month), become partner in a Deer Lodge bank, and scrimped until he could buy his partner out. Starting with borrowed money, he never had lost a penny on any venture.

Clark bought the Original, Butte's silver discovery mine, and several other silver properties, and promptly departed for the Columbia School of Mines, where he spent a year learning how to manage his new business. Excessive transportation costs for his Butte ore to the smelters of Colorado irked him, and he loaned money to another Butte miner who was building a silver stamp mill. Before long he had possession of this mill and of the mine which his guileless debtor had pledged as security. It had been agreed that Clark was to work the mine until the loan was repaid; the ore, of course, suddenly became low grade and inadequate to meet the debt, so Clark foreclosed.

For a few years this mill brought him rich profits, for he charged all the traffic would bear; then competitors sprang up, and Clark built a smelter, permitting the recovery of copper as well as silver from Butte's ore.

In the meantime another of Butte's three Irishmen had appeared.

Marcus Daly had landed in New York with the peat smoke still in his rough clothes. He was fifteen and had no money. He worked as a newsboy and messenger in New York long enough to accumulate a stake sufficient for steerage passage to San Francisco, and thence drifted to the rich Comstock, where he earned a reputation as a skilled and hard-working miner.

"Mark" was short, stocky, dark, and ruddy. He was a fighter, rough where Clark was pretentiously cultured, convivial and friendly where Clark was usually cold and withdrawn. Though there is a legend that the men were once friends, it is more likely that they hated each other on sight and maintained for a time a surface semblance of cordiality only for social and family reasons: Mrs. Daly and the wife of Clark's brother were sisters.

Hundreds of theories have been advanced by friends of the two men, and by historians, for the cause of their epic feud. One of the best-informed commentators of that era, Christopher P. Connolly, lawyer, writer, and stenographer for the constitutional convention over which Clark presided, attributed it to a Clark sneer directed at Daly's "uncouthness as measured by Clark's standard, and referring to his discovery of the Anaconda mine as an accident."

Certainly the first public shot in their war was fired by Daly, and it was all but murderous. Given an adversary with less cold determination and a thinner skin, the feud would have ended then, and Daly would have ruled Montana unchallenged, until the arrival of the third Irishman. Despite all the theories, Daly's blow may have originated simply in the fact that a man of his temperament couldn't stand Clark.

In 1888, while Montana was still a Territory, Clark de-

cided that his meteoric rise to wealth and influence merited
wider recognition, and he became a candidate for congressional delegate. The support of Daly, who was a Democrat
too and whose interests as a miner were presumed to parallel
those of Clark, was taken for granted. Clark spent money
lavishly on his campaign and prepared happily for his debut
in Washington.

When the votes were counted, it was discovered—to the
amazement of almost everyone except Marcus Daly—that
Clark had been humiliatingly beaten by an upstart young
Republican lawyer and former book agent, Thomas H. Carter, who had swept every district in which Daly had any influence. He won even Clark's own ward.

Montana, traditionally fond of fights, was pleased to learn
that the two titans of this last frontier of unregulated capitalism had locked in mortal combat. Clark supporters instantly
accused Daly of jealousy, of harboring political ambitions
himself. He retorted bluntly: he respected men who had
made public affairs a field of study, but as for himself he believed in staying in "my proper sphere." The intended insult
to Clark, whose sphere also was mining, was manifest; Daly
had paid him for that sneer, if it was ever spoken.

But a truce was declared.

Montana was clamoring for statehood. The Territory
needed that foreign capital, and it was tired of what it contemptuously called "carpet-bagger government." In most instances the territorial governors appointed by Washington
had been eastern politicians or generals with no understanding of the west and no desire to learn about it. Statehood
had been sought in 1884, but the move failed. Now (1889)
another memorial went to congress; it complained that "the
policy which has so long prevailed, of sending strangers to
rule over us, has become distasteful to us, and is wholly unsuited to our present condition and growing importance of
the diversified interests of our country."

The constitutional convention, in which Democrats were
in the majority, seated Clark as chairman, then spent the next
couple of days wrangling—incredibly—over whether a permanent record of its proceedings should be kept. Appointment of a stenographer and authorization of the record finally carried by a narrow margin after opponents had em-

ployed every conceivable argument against these steps, including the claim that such service was too expensive and
posterity wouldn't be interested anyway. Actually it was only
too evident that a good many of them dreaded having their
names and positions on certain controversial issues placed in
a permanent record; and even after the vote had been taken
a few of the delegates prefaced their remarks with the hopeful suggestion that the stenographer suddenly become deaf.

The reason for the Clark-Daly truce became apparent when
the convention got to the crucial point in its deliberations—
mine taxation.

The mine owners had come around reluctantly to the realization that they were going to have to pay some taxes.
(Throughout the territorial period, save for seven unhappy
years, they had been required to pay none whatever). The
point was to pay as little as possible.

The congressional committee on Territories had reported
in 1888: "The property returned for taxation [in Montana]
does not embrace the mining interests, which are exempt
from taxation under the law, nor does it include the 1,626
miles of railroad now in successful operation. The mines of
the Territory last year yielded over $25,000,000."

The Montana legislature, memorializing Congress in 1889
and pleading for some special favors for the mining industry,
acknowledged that its income had then risen to $40,000,000
annually, but insisted "we consider it practically in its in-
fancy."

Congress snorted and the mining millionaires and million-
aires-to-be sadly decided that they would have to take off
their short pants and grow up; they could no longer get into
the show free. Nevertheless, if they could fix a *constitutional*
pattern for their future contribution to society, they could
make it difficult for future legislatures (there was always the
chance that one would get out of hand) to increase the levy
upon them, for a majority vote of the state's citizens would
be required.

Hence the selection of Clark to rule the convention and
hence, probably, the reluctance of some of the delegates to
be put on record; for the project was not to be easy. The old
war of stockman against miner flared up instantly and kept
the assembly embroiled until its final session; but the stock-

men, as usual, were outnumbered. And some of the delegates who, geographically, belonged with the stockmen, were found when the votes were counted to have moved profitably to Butte.

The mine tax provision was submitted to the convention in virtually the same form as it had appeared in the proposed 1884 constitution, also drawn by the mining interests. It read:

All mines and mining claims, both placer and rock in place, containing or bearing gold, silver, copper, lead, coal, or other valuable mineral deposits, after purchase thereof from the United States, shall be taxed *at the price paid the United States therefor,* unless the surface ground, or some part thereof, of such mine or claim, is used for other than mining purposes, in which case such surface ground . . . shall be taxed at its value for such other purposes, as provided by law; and all machinery . . . and all property and surface improvements upon or appurtenant to mines and mining claims . . . and the annual *net proceeds* of all mines and mining claims shall be taxed as provided by law. [Italics this writer's].

"The price paid the United States therefor" was $5 per claim; in some of these claims, whose surface area was only 1,500 by 600 feet, copper ore already in sight underground was worth millions. And while provision was made for taxing machinery and surface property, the constitutional limitation automatically prevented legislative adjustment of the levy to the property's increase in value on development—as for instance a farmer's soil increases in value with cultivation, which costs the farmer more in taxes.

The stockmen bellowed, but the miners had them; there was no formula by which they could assess the probable value of a mine, admittedly a hazardous operation. So the fight centered on the "net proceeds" provision, the range men and farmers attempting unsuccessfully to strike out the word "net" or the whole section and leave determination of how the proceeds should be taxed to future legislators.

Leader of their fight was W. A. Burleigh, a Republican lawyer from Miles City, cow country capital. Most of the argument occurred in committee of the whole, thus giving opportunity to Clark to take the floor and unburden his pious soul:

I stand here today as a representative of the mining interests, and I will venture to say that there is no class of men engaged in any industry in this Rocky Mountain country that has a higher regard for integrity or is more disposed to make a fair and equitable return of their property . . . but they do contend that the only way to reach a fair and equitable assessment of their values is to base it upon the net proceeds of their mines. . . . It is the only method whereby the state can secure from this species of property a reasonable and just revenue, and at the same time protect those men, those brave pioneers who have come out here and made the wilderness blossom as the rose, and opened up these great mountains and brought their hidden wealth to light; yea, I say, it is the duty of the members of this convention to throw such safeguards around this great industry as are proper and just; this great industry that is the foundation of almost all the prosperity of this country, and has made all the valleys and mountains of Montana productive.

Burleigh had yet to see a blossom growing out of a mine shaft, and he was not impressed. He offered an amendment to the "net proceeds" provision: "And the legislature shall provide some stringent means to ascertain the actual income. No salaries paid officers of the mining corporations shall be accounted as an expense or deducted from the gross earnings. The levy shall not be less than two per cent of the net earnings."

The amendment was lost. Burleigh got his wind back after a while, however, and moved to strike the entire "net proceeds" section. He lost, though he finally succeeded in obtaining a record vote—in which only nine stood with him and fifty stood against him. Finally he showed signs of losing his temper and read his colleagues a lecture:

I think this is a matter that should by every principle known to constitutional law and to other law, be left in the hands of the people to be exercised by their representatives. . . . I know of no reason which would justify us in legislating upon mines here, prescribing the rules by which they are to be governed or taxed, any more than upon stock, cattle or breeding mares, or other species

of property. . . . Is it possible that there is an industry in this
country that is of so precarious a nature that the owners and promoters . . . are afraid to submit [its taxation] to the people to be
determined by them? If so, I would advise all such men to abandon such a vocation and pursue some calling which is not of so
precarious a nature. . . . I know these mines should be fostered,
and I believe the people will foster them so far as they are entitled
to be fostered!

It was a gallant but hopeless fight. It took Montana more
than thirty years to undo the work of Clark and his lackeys
in this constitutional convention, to force even moderate additional taxation upon the "brave pioneers who made the
wilderness blossom as the rose." A dozen years after the constitutional convention, as Montana's capitol was being dedi-
cated, a fearless and farseeing pioneer named Col. W. F.
Sanders took occasion to remind the citizens of how they had
been short-weighted by Clark and his allies:

With the courage which was a conspicuous trait in their character,
to assist a hazardous, hopeful industry, they [the founders of the
commonwealth] took upon themselves a portion of its burdens by
absolving it from its share of taxation. When thus delivered the
interest and amount involved was small, but it has now grown to
colossal proportions . . . but the advantage thus given has not
been relinquished and what was in its nature and purpose designed to be temporary, by the forethought and adroitness of
greed has been taken from the domain of legislation and become
interwoven in constitutional enactment as a permanent policy of
the state. It does not require a wide knowledge of human nature
to discern that when the ownership of private property does not
carry with it the equal burden which that ownership implies, a
disregard of the sanctities of titles is begotten which may wreak
abounding mischief. Absolute equality of taxation . . . is primal
essential justice unless it is desired to cultivate a superior class to
own the property and a proletariat or peasantry to become their
serfs.

After the constitutional convention, Clark returned to
Butte and the war with Daly, flushed with acclaim; he had
been, as was to be expected, an excellent presiding officer.
The first round of the great feud had been Daly's. The
second, also a setback for Clark in that he again failed to

reach Washington, was so confounded by other political factors that the Clark-Daly issue was not clear-cut. It came about when the first state legislature split and elected two sets of United States Senators. All four set off for Washington and laid the decision in Congress' lap. The Senate seated the Republicans, who included Colonel Sanders, and sent home the Democrats, one of whom was Clark.

It began to be apparent that it was going to take more than his personality (which was none too good) and prestige to send Clark to Washington, so in 1893 when election of a Senator again was before the legislature, bribery for the first time assumed major proportions as a political expedient in Montana. But Clark still had not sufficiently loosed the tight purse strings; and as fast as he bought a vote Daly bought it back for his candidate.

Clark was confident of victory. He sat in the legislative chamber, an honored guest, while the ballots were tabulated. He was smiling a little, fingering the speech of acceptance in his pocket.

He lost by three votes.

It was time for the tight white starched little man to win a round.

VIII. TRIAL·AT·ARMS

The constitutional convention had provided that the people of Montana should select, by vote, their state capital city. Helena wrested the seat of government from Virginia City in 1875 after nearly a year of legal controversy over the election results; two earlier attempts by Helena, when it had been more humbly known as Last Chance Gulch, had failed. The Virginia City *Madisonian* reported churlishly that "a mongrel outfit of poor mules and lank cayuses" freighted the state's property north to "the county town of Lewis and Clark county." It was a hard trip—four days in the mud.

Helena had no challenger until, in 1892, Daly for the first time sought the capital for his town, Anaconda, owned body and soul by his copper company. Boulder, Bozeman, Butte, Deer Lodge, and Great Falls were also in the running, but it was a Helena-Anaconda fight, and Helena won, 14,010 to 10,183.

Daly tried again in 1894, and Clark determinedly backed Helena. This time it was "for keeps," because the constitution had provided that the winner of a runoff between the two highest-vote cities should retain the capital unless two thirds of the state's voters approved its removal.

Both copper titans spent fortunes. C. P. Connolly reported in *The Devil Learns to Vote:*

Taking into consideration the vast sums of money Daly afterwards gave away in the form of mining leases to his supporters, he must have spent, in round figures, over $2,500,000 in the contest. Clark and his friends must have spent over $400,000. The vote of the state did not exceed 50,000 in the capital election. [It did, however; but only by about 2,000]. The cost of each vote was, therefore, approximately $38 [sic].

Actually, it probably was not the bought votes which decided the election. The balance of power was held by the thousands of respectable, uncorrupted citizens who cared not a whit for either principal or for the copper industry; they could not stomach establishment of their capital in a copper-owned town, so Helena won, 27,024 to 25,118. It is likely that, no matter what his expenditure, Daly could not have won for Anaconda; it is equally probable that Helena would have won without Clark's costly help.

On election night the jubilant citizens of Helena took the horses out of the shafts of Clark's carriage and dragged it through the streets, cheering its occupants: Clark and John M. Quinn, editorial writer of Clark's *Butte Miner.* The drinks in every Helena bar were on Clark, the pious Presbyterian, and old-timers today declare it was the drunkenest night Montana ever had, which was going some. . . . Bartenders finally ceased pouring drinks and tossed bottles, including champagne, to those of the suppliant thirsty still erect and able to catch them. The revel lasted all night, and amazed visitors from out of town went home asserting they had seen every man and woman of Helena and some of the children drunk before exhaustion ended the party.

Clark was now encouraged to renew his campaign for political prestige, and although he failed to elect his candidates to the state legislature (which at that time chose the United States Senator) he bribed that body so successfully that he was elected on January 28, 1899. Several days before the final roll call, Fred Whiteside, whom Clark had sought to use as an agent in bribery of other legislators, pitilessly exposed the conspiracy on the floor of the house and turned $30,000 of bribe money over to the state treasury. Clark's servile delegates took advantage of a technical question regarding Whiteside's seat to oust him from the assembly, and the bribery continued. Clark's son, his political manager, was reported to have said, "We'll send the old man either to the Senate or the poorhouse"; 47 votes were bought in eighteen days for a total of $431,000, the individual price ranging from $5,000 to $25,000. Thirteen senators refused bribes which totaled $200,000. Clark, a Democrat, was able to buy all but 4 of the 15 Republican votes in the Senate.

Jeers and catcalls echoed in the galleries as the vote was taken and onlookers shouted, as legislators' names were called, the price Clark was known to have paid for their support. Political morality had ceased to exist in Montana. Another all-night drunk (cost to Clark, $30,000) celebrated his triumph, and the ambitious little peddler might have taken his place in the United States Senate with little more than some public grumbling had he not, in his hypocritical eagerness to clean his skirts, overplayed his hand. His newspaper made the charge that the $30,000 which Whiteside had offered as evidence of Clark's bribery actually was money provided by Daly in an attempt to "frame" the would-be Senator. Enraged, Daly had his agents assemble documentary proof of the bribery, and through Montana's Senator Carter, a Daly supporter, challenged Clark's election on the floor of the Senate.

Several months of senatorial investigation exposed Montana's shame to the world. And on the eve of the report which was to recommend that he be refused his seat Clark resigned, asserting that he was "conscious of the rectitude of my conduct."

By his resignation the scheming little man assured a vacancy in the office of Senator. Governor Robert B. Smith, an implacable enemy, was now lured out of the state ostensibly (and in good faith, so far as the Governor was concerned) to act as expert counsel in some California mining litigation. The Lieutenant Governor, a Clark man, rushed back into the state from neighboring South Dakota where he had been attending a convention; and as acting Governor he promptly appointed Clark to the "vacant" Senate seat. Governor Smith hurried home, denouncing "this contemptible proceeding," and notified Clark, who was still in Washington, that the appointment was revoked.

Clark, with a wary eye on the hostile Senate elections committee, did not attempt to serve the term to which he had been first elected illegally and then appointed by fraud. Instead he came home, calling himself "Senator," and set about to obtain "vindication." This he finally accomplished through an alliance with F. Augustus Heinze which enabled him to elect a legislature in 1900 pledged to send him to the Senate. He served one six-year term without distinguishing himself as a statesman.

Immediately after his election, his great enemy, Marcus Daly, died.

This alliance with Clark was the first large-scale political venture of Frederick Augustus Heinze—"Fritz." Before he was thirty, Heinze had established himself as the most adept pirate in the history of American capitalist privateering up to his time; and probably no one has equaled his achievement to this day. Certainly he was one of the few men who ever has been able to make the mighty Standard Oil Company sweat blood.

This gay, handsome, industrial desperado and demagogue convinced thousands of Montanans that he was Robin Hood reincarnated. He was the son of a German Lutheran father and a mother of the Irish Lacey family, which had been reinforced with Connecticut Yankee blood. He had intelligence, even genius; with this he had Irish flair and Yankee cunning—and he had also great determination and acquisitiveness.

Heinze came to Montana in 1889, at the age of twenty, and went to work as a mining engineer for the Boston & Montana Consolidated Company, later to become a part of the great Standard Oil combination, Amalgamated. His salary was about $100 a month; one chronicler of the incredible "copper wars" suggests that the Boston & Montana would have done well had it paid him $100,000 a month to stay away.

Young Fritz had been in Butte only a few months when he discovered the mousehole which was to admit him to the copper trust's treasure house; but he needed capital to press his audacious campaign. An inheritance, two years after he came to Butte, of $50,000 from his grandmother's estate helped, but it was not enough. He went to Germany for a few months, studying mining and smelting methods (he already was a graduate mining engineer), and returned to an assistant editorship of the *Engineering and Mining Journal* in New York—an ideal position from which to interest capital in his Montana ventures.

Establishment of a Butte smelting company was his next step, perhaps as a screen for his contemplated raid upon the "richest hill on earth," for soon he was moving in cautiously on the completely unsuspecting Boston & Montana, his old boss, by purchase of the Rarus mine.

Before going ahead with his major offensive, however, Heinze, now twenty-six, tried a diversion: he went to Trail,

British Columbia, established a small smelter, and suddenly launched a promotion for a railroad to the Pacific coast. Panic-stricken mining interests which faced heavy penalties because they could not supply Heinze's smelter with the ore they had contracted to deliver besought the Canadian Pacific Railway in which they also held stock to buy him out; and after Heinze had gone so far as to obtain a land grant from the provincial parliament for his projected line, the C.P.R. surrendered. Fritz came back to Butte richer and more confident than ever; he was ready now to exploit the knowledge he had obtained as a hundred-dollar-a-month engineer for the Boston copper interests.

The Rarus mine adjoined a rich B. & M. property, the Michael Davitt. Shortly after Heinze's return to Butte, word reached Col. A. S. Bigelow in Boston, president of the company, that Heinze, operating through his Rarus, was encroaching upon B. & M. ore bodies. The issue was joined: the B. & M. sought an injunction, and Heinze sat back and waited, serene in the knowledge of his trump card.

That trump was the complexity of the "apex" theory of mine ownership. The federal mining law of 1872 provided that a claim constituted a surface area 1,500 feet long and 600 feet wide in which a vein came to its apex—in other words, an area of the prescribed size which contained the surface outcropping of a presumably continuous ore body. The locator could follow this vein any distance underground as long as he remained within the 1,500-foot *length* of his claim; there was no restriction on the *lateral* variation of the vein underground. Heinze realized that the increasing depth of Butte's mines had resulted in greater complexity of the ore pattern: the veins were faulted, and frequently neighboring veins intersected. Given a battery of "experts" and a friendly court, it was anybody's guess whose vein apexed where.

He had made sure of the friendly court by his political alliance with Clark. Now, as the Amalgamated combination took over the Boston properties before the first suit came to trial, Heinze rolled up his sleeves and pitched in: Amalgamated lawyers, studying Bigelow's injunction, suddenly found themselves buried under scores of retaliatory restraining orders issued by Heinze's judges and charging that Amalgamated ore bodies apexed within Heinze claims. His most spectacular attack involved a claim he had ironically named the "Copper Trust." It was a triangular sliver of land seventy-five feet long and ten feet across at its base, and Heinze asserted that within it the veins of three major Amalgamated properties—the Anaconda, St. Lawrence, and Neversweat—apexed.

Judge William Clancy (a saloon hanger-on and shyster before his sudden ascent to the bench) granted every injunction Heinze asked, but the one based on the "Copper Trust" claim and closing these three mines lasted only a few hours. Three thousand angry miners, thrown out of work, descended from the hill and announced that they were going to lynch the judge. Clancy promptly dissolved the restraining order.

But Amalgamated did not realize the implications of the miners' spontaneous march which had terrified Heinze's bought judge. Whereas Heinze continually used the people and ingratiated himself with them, New York's arrogant Standard Oil ignored them, almost to the end; and when Standard did go to the people it did not go, as Heinze went, with an appeal—it went with a club. Heinze and Clark shrewdly granted the 8-hour day (the cost to them was relatively small as compared to that to the huge Amalgamated) while Amalgamated rejected it. Heinze, years ahead of his time in his mastery of propaganda, kept his own personality vividly before the people in his Butte newspaper the *Reveille,* and in any others which would print the releases of his skillful publicist, P. A. O'Farrell, a former New York newspaperman; and he pounded everlastingly at the "soullessness" of Standard and its bosses. Neutral Montanans (there were some) might laugh at Heinze's flamboyant manner and deplore his methods or his morals; but they despised H. H. Rogers, fighting coldly from his Wall Street office. Heinze had made him a symbol of wolfish monopoly capitalism, to which this individualistic west was traditionally hostile.

So, despite a tactical victory in the "Copper Trust" incident, Amalgamated was soon desperate. It was burdened by more than a hundred suits and Judges Clancy and Edward Harney signed every decision written for them by Heinze's lawyers. While Amalgamated was enjoined from operating its own properties, poacher Fritz drilled into them from his adjoining claims and lifted hundreds of thousands of dollars'

worth of his enemy's high-grade ore to the surface through
his shafts and sent it off to his smelter. All the decisions were
appealed, but while Amalgamated waited for the ponderous
functioning of the Supreme Court, Heinze delved deeper and
fed his illicit profits into his war machine.

For Heinze, too, had a lion by the tail and could not let go.
With each victory he had to attack on a new front; it is
always thus with aggressors. Absolute ruin faced the con-
tender who quit, and given two such contenders, a stalemate
was feasible. The cost to Heinze of a contest of this magnitude, which unquestionably had grown far beyond what he
had originally contemplated, had long since exceeded the
legitimate proceeds of his own small properties. To keep
going he had to plunder, plunder.

Inevitably, the climactic phases of the drama moved out
of the law courts and into the streets of Butte—and the hot,
dark treacherous avenues half a mile under the streets. For
this had ceased to be, if it ever had been, a contest-at-law:
it had become a trial-at-arms for the major conflict of the
dawning American industrial century.

Here on Butte hill was the testing ground: here one man,
alone, confronted a giant "monopoly," a newborn business
behemoth which was none too sure of itself just yet, but could
fight tooth and claw, nevertheless, to establish itself in the new
exploitative economy. The monster had no suave philosoph-
ical apologists, no columnists nor commentators; this was the
era of "the public be damned." But it had the economic
power, the money, for the long pull.

No knight who would dare enter the lists against such a
formidable foe could help but become a glamorous figure;
and Heinze's glamour did not evolve solely from this circumstance. He was handsome, young, rich, reckless—and hu-
manly wayward, fond of liquor and love. He was inevitably
a leader, albeit an outlaw—so was Jesse James. Loyalty was
not bound by the merits of his cause; Montana was with him
then and is with him still. And it is significant, and important,
that while he was fighting on his own ground, not all the
wealth or power of the world's greatest trust could win from
this thirty-year-old desperado anything better than a draw!

IX. STANDARD OIL COFFINS

The Michael Davitt mine adjoining Heinze's Rarus had been closed since the beginning of the Heinze campaign by a federal court injunction which forbade both litigants to work its veins. But Heinze had to have that ore. He transferred his interest in the mine's disputed riches to a new puppet company which, according to the letter of the law, was not bound by the injunction; and he began a systematic looting of the Michael Davitt, working from his own Rarus by means of secret crosscuts.

Amalgamated, whose Pennsylvania mine adjoined the Michael Davitt on the other side, soon became aware of the raid. After some espionage by its engineers and a good deal of wrangling by its lawyers, it obtained a federal court order forcing Heinze to admit Amalgamated engineers through his secret tunnels to investigate.

Meanwhile, however, Heinze's miners in the Michael Davitt and Rarus and Amalgamated's men drilling through from the Pennsylvania had had several clashes. In an effort to drive each other out of the ground legally forbidden to both, they had fought with rocks, smoke, powdered lime, steam, and blasting powder; at least two had been killed and a dozen or so injured. The trust's lawyers told the court, "If we cannot stop this [looting] the government might better abandon its courts and leave litigants to determine their rights by the shotgun." Montana had gone native again and the only way to stop a claim jumper was to shoot him.

Amalgamated's engineers found that Heinze had looted the Michael Davitt of $1,000,000 worth of ore. He was fined $20,000, but Amalgamated could not recover damages in a civil action against the phantom "Johnstown Mining Company" because it had no tangible assets. And no sooner had this case been decided than the war flared up on a new front —in the Amalgamated's big Leonard mine, adjoining Heinze's Minnie Healy.

The trust was grimly resolved now, and as fast as Heinze's crosscuts bore into the Leonard, blasts destroyed them; Amal-

gamated even went so far as to destroy some of its own drifts
to keep the interloper out. Finally the Leonard's pressure
water system was secretly directed into the Minnie Healy,
Heinze's miners were told to get out, and the valve was
opened. In a few seconds Heinze's entrances to the Leonard,
much of his timbering, some of his machinery, and considerable of Amalgamated's own property had been destroyed or
damaged.

No lives were lost in this last major encounter; and this
ended the underground war. An excited mob gathered at the
Leonard after a rumor spread that the Minnie Healy's men
had been drowned like rats; an Amalgamated superintendent,
at rifle-point, forced Heinze's officials to explain that ample
warning had been given and all had escaped. The next day
engineers and superintendents of the belligerent companies
agreed to call off the fight and leave it up to the courts.

There is no authentic record of the human casualties in
the whole "copper war." At times both parties to the conflict
leased sections of disputed veins to individual miners, thus
avoiding direct responsibility for fights and "accidents." In
most instances the opposing foremen notified each other of
offensive plans so the men could escape; there were a few
slip-ups. Deaths were few—only two or three were recorded;
but scores were hurt in mass combat or private fights in the
mines and on the streets. There were humorous incidents,
too. One day an Amalgamated spy fell twenty feet down a
Heinze crosscut almost into the lap of an enemy foreman.
"Hello," said the foreman; "where did you come from?"
The spy got up and brushed the muck from his clothes.
"County Galway," he said, and walked off.

After his failure in the Leonard, Heinze was near the end
of his rope, but he had a few tricks left.

He directed his agents to buy stock in two of Amalgamated's
subsidiary companies and to bring suit in Butte demanding
a receivership on the ground that Amalgamated, under Montana law, was an illegal trust. Judge Clancy announced that
he would hand down a decision in this action and in the suit
over ownership of the Minnie Healy on the same day.

A packed courtroom heard the tobacco-chewing judge who
already had handed millions of dollars' worth of stolen property over to Heinze solemnly declare the great Amalgamated

combine illegal and permanently enjoin its subordinate corporations from paying dividends to it. At the same time he affirmed that Heinze was the owner of the Minnie Healy. (This Minnie Healy decision, based on a verbal agreement by the mine's owner to sell it for $54,000—an agreement never put in writing and repudiated by the maker under Amalgamated pressure—was one of the very few Clancy rulings ever to be upheld by the state supreme court.)

It appeared to be Heinze's greatest triumph. For the time being, at least, he had humbled his giant foe to a greater extent than he had ever dreamed was possible: Amalgamated, great metal trust, was legally dead.

But law or no law, Amalgamated was the economic master of the state of Montana, and its patience was exhausted. It had no intention of yielding the "richest hill" to a piratical pipsqueak and a virtually illiterate district judge. . . .

President William Scallon of Amalgamated and his board of strategy may have suddenly remembered the "Copper Trust" incident, when three thousand miners had frightened Clancy into canceling his injunction; or they may have heard from New York—though this latter they always denied. At any rate, the day Clancy's ruling was made telegrams sped about Montana from Amalgamated's Butte offices; and in a few hours every Amalgamated operation in the state—Butte's mines, Anaconda's smelter, Great Falls' copper refineries, Missoula's lumber mills, coal mines, gold mines deep in forgotten canyons, company stores—shut down. Montana's only major industry died overnight.

Twenty thousand men were out of work next morning. In the next day or so thousands more—retail employes, service workers, railroaders, craftsmen, the masses dependent upon the business of the men who drew their pay from Amalgamated—were laid off. It was October; a hundred thousand people, workers and their families, faced a penniless winter.

The day the Clancy decisions were handed down a final report of distribution of the estate of Marcus Daly, who had died three years before, was filed in Montana courts. He left $3,000,000 in cash, millions more in investments; few bothered to read the details. "Butte on Verge of Desperation," a headline said; there were angry crowds in the streets of the stricken cities.

Heinze issued a statement: Amalgamated was trying to force its own stock down on the market so that its controlling manipulators could buy more of its shares from lambs it had not yet fleeced; besides there was an oversupply of copper and the trust could well afford to curtail production. He would double his own mining force, and he pledged himself "to the limit of my means to see that no head of a family shall want for necessities."

Three days passed, days of idleness and worry and more threatening crowds on street corners. Amalgamated said nothing; there was nothing it need say. And slowly, inevitably, the tide turned against Heinze. Hitherto independent (or nearly so) newspapers in other towns decided that it was all very well to bait the trusts, but a whole state could not permit itself to be destroyed in a private fight, much as it liked fights; this one was no longer funny. Railroader Jim Hill, Governor Joseph K. Toole, Senator Clark were called upon to mediate; they tried and failed. Then a compromise was proposed: the miners' union, with money borrowed from Clark and Daly banks, would buy Heinze's interest in the companies involved and dismiss the suits—whereupon the Heinze agents who had brought the suits disappeared. The union appealed to Heinze. He promised to give his answer the next afternoon from the steps of Butte's courthouse, perched on a steep slope of the "richest hill."

Fifteen thousand men, women, and children confronted Fritz Heinze when he appeared promptly on the courthouse steps at four that afternoon, October 26, 1903.

Some of them were his own loyal miners, but most of them were frightened or angry or both; and he wasted no time on banter.

My friends, I could have met the committee of the miners' union in my private office, but as a free American citizen, relying on the justice of his cause and not afraid to place it before the people of Silver Bow county, I preferred to meet that committee here in public.

He denied that he was harassing the Amalgamated. On the contrary, the trust had ordered him, years ago, to quit the state or be driven out. "I fought my own battles, explaining them to the public when I had the opportunity." He did not, he intimated, make the helpless wives and children of miners do his fighting. . . .

President Long of the miners' union, who with several other union officers was with Heinze on the courthouse balcony, interrupted impatiently. What about the miners' proposition to buy those shares in the Amalgamated companies?

For an instant genial Fritz forgot himself. He had the floor, he told Long curtly; he would make his speech in his own way. Long, angry, gathered his aides about him and stalked off into the crowd. Then Heinze, the tilt adding sharpness to his voice, struck out:

My friends, the Amalgamated Copper Company, in its influence and functions and the control it has over the commercial and economic affairs of this state, is the greatest menace that any community could possibly have within its boundaries. That stock [the stock involved in the suits outlawing the Amalgamated] is a bulwark to protect you from the aggressions of the most unscrupulous of corporations, the Standard Oil Company. Rockefeller and Rogers have filched the oil wells of America, and in doing so they have trampled on every law, human and divine. They ruthlessly crushed every obstacle in their path. They wrecked railroad trains and put the torch to oil refineries owned by their competitors; they entered into a conspiracy with railroads, by which competitors were ruined. . . .
The same Rockefeller and the same Rogers are seeking to control the executive, the judiciary and the legislature of Montana!

Heinze knew this argument could not fail to move his audience. Montanans had always hated and feared the trusts. Only a year before Colonel Sanders had warned the state solemnly against monopolist greed and political aggression.

Perhaps Heinze, in this supreme scene of his melodramatic career, really believed himself to be what he proclaimed—champion of the little man, beset on all sides by overwhelming, inhuman forces. Certainly he would not have been the first to persuade himself that the public was best served—even heroically served—by the course which coincided with his own material interest. Whatever the cause—conviction of

the validity of his "mission," or fear lest he go down with the
whole collapsing structure—there was genuine emotion in
Heinze's voice as he went on. He drilled his points home.
Were they not experiencing, right now, a sample of the malignant power of which he warned them?

These people are my enemies—fierce, bitter, implacable. But they
are your enemies, too. If they crush me today, they will crush you
tomorrow.
    They will cut your wages.
    They will raise the tariff in their company stores on every bite
you eat and every rag you wear. . . .

Heinze paused, glanced shrewdly over the crowd; it was
quiet, intent; some of the fifteen thousand heads were
nodding, urging him on.

. . . They will force you to dwell in Standard Oil houses while
you live—and they will bury you in Standard Oil coffins when
you die!

Again he waited, waited for the little grumble to grow to
the full-throated roar, helped along by his own miners. The
roar came quickly from the brawny men of Butte; he silenced
it, and said quietly:

You and I are partners and allies. We stand—or fall—together.

The miners were cheering now. Lost jobs, fear of hunger—
they were forgotten for the moment; here was a man!
"Tamp 'er down, Fritz!"
    It was a scene, as Connolly pointed out in *The Devil
Learns to Vote,* worthy to stand beside Marc Antony's achievement; indeed the cultured Heinze may well have patterned
his hour-long speech on the Shakespeare model. There was
the same documented denunciation of his foes, the same
digression into history, and in conclusion the same appeal to
his hearers' cupidity and gratitude: as Antony had recounted
Caesar's bequests "to every several man, seventy-five drachmas
. . . all his walks, his private arbours, and new-planted orchards . . ." so did Heinze offer his proposition:

He would sell the shares of the Amalgamated companies at cost to the miners' union. He would submit the whole copper war to arbitration; he would choose two of the arbitrators, Amalgamated would choose two, and the four would elect their own neutral chairman. In return Amalgamated had only to sell to him, at the price it had paid, its small share in a mine of which he owned the major interest. As for him, that was enough: who could say Fritz was greedy? But Amalgamated also would have to take care of his friends, the miners. . . .

It would be required to contract with the union to keep its mines running (on the pre-shutdown basis) for at least a year, and to maintain the existing high wage scale for three years.

The cheers thundered up and down Butte's precipitous Granite Street. Miners waved their caps, grabbed the handbills thrust at them by Heinze's men, handbills setting out in fearless black and white the proposition Heinze had just made verbally. These they took home, and talked it all over that evening with their neighbors. What could be fairer than Fritz's offer?

It had been one of Butte's great afternoons, and Heinze had won the people back; but actually he gained only a few hours. The trust was awake now to the power of public opinion, and it rushed into print with its angry answer.

Heinze knew very well that there was no provision in Montana statute for arbitration such as he suggested. If the arbitration award went against him, there was nothing to prevent him from refusing to recognize it—and that, said Amalgamated's Scallon, was just what wily Fritz would do. There were several objections to his demand that Amalgamated sell him its minor interest in his mine, one of them the fact that the price he proposed was only a fraction of its present value, as Heinze himself had once acknowledged in court testimony. And as for his insistence upon a guarantee to the miners' union—that was an insult! "As if the miners' union needed any whip or driving by Mr. Heinze to protect their rights! . . . Neither Mr. Rogers nor myself [Scallon] would stand for any cut in wages!"

But the guarantee against a mine shutdown was not mentioned by Scallon. The retort on the whole was clumsy, com-

pared to Heinze's deft performance; but it was no longer
"the public be damned." Amalgamated was learning. And
there was still the club.

Nothing happened. Miners' wives unused to having their
men about the house chased them impatiently into the streets.
Businessmen's committees brought their worries from other
towns. Scallon received them politely; but he was sorry, there
was no more to say. Shutdown: no mine whistles, no clank
and rattle from the hoists, no shuttling clangor from the ore
cars, no hiss of steam or tap of drill or boom of blast, no
jokes or horseplay. Shutdown, the grisly specter in every
mining town, bigger and grimmer in mighty Butte. Shutdown
of a whole state! Butte's worried mayor closed the saloons and
the redlight district. He could not keep the grumbling men
off the streets of their own city.

There was a week or so of this conditioning of Montana.
Then one day a rumor appeared in the press: Scallon had let
it slip to a miners' committee that if the governor could be
prevailed upon to call a special session of the legislature to
pass the "fair trial" bill, Amalgamated might reopen its mines.

The "fair trial" bill provided that any litigant, merely by
charging a judge with prejudice—not proving it—could force
that judge to disqualify himself and call in another. The law
is still on Montana statute books. Amalgamated would never
chance another Clancy or Harney!

Petitions poured in upon Governor Toole, and November
10 he called the special session. Mine whistles in Butte (but
not on Heinze mines) blew for a full hour. Impromptu parad-
ers first marched, then staggered, and finally rolled down the
streets of Butte, Great Falls, and other company cities: the
bars had opened again. Miners' and smeltermen's bands gave
unrehearsed and reckless concerts on the corners, pausing
after each number for refreshment and inspiration. Next day
the mines reopened and thousands of men, a lot of them with
hangovers, hurried to the "rustling lines."

Heinze looked on sadly from the windows of his luxurious
apartment on Broadway in Butte, the apartment which had
been the scene of elaborate banquets for Butte's self-conscious
society, and then—after his guests had left for their proper
beds—had been flung open to the ragtag and bobtail girls of
saloon and street. Socialite or slut, you got champagne at

Fritz's table . . . But watching them now, Fritz knew he had lost the people. The war was just about over, and two years later, almost to the day, Heinze was to start negotiations to sell out to Amalgamated.

The "fair trial" bill passed as a matter of course. Heinze wisely did not fight it, for, ironically, at the next election Amalgamated ousted his judges and elected its own; thereafter the legislation it had paralyzed a state to obtain proved a lifesaver for its enemy, who could escape the judicial steamrolling that he had originated.

But in April, 1905, the supreme court affirmed Heinze's ownership of the Minnie Healy, a mine considered to have a potential value of $10,000,000. Fritz, who had been hanging on the ropes, was in the ring again; Amalgamated cursed and made its bitter decision: buy him off. Heinze celebrated his triumph characteristically, staging a big dinner in his apartment and then taking eight cronies (all men) to New York in his chartered private car, "The Rival."

The day Fritz's admiring friends, several of them veterans of the mines, boarded his "palace coach" with its staterooms, library, bar, observation and dining rooms, and kitchen—that day William A. Clark, "Senator" by grace of his purse, who had learned a little something about public relations too, entertained 9,000 children at Columbia Gardens, the park he had given to Butte. He bought them ice cream, soda pop, food, and rides on the carrousel; there wasn't a vote in the whole 9,000, but they were Montanans and not too young to get used to free drinks and rides on a merry-go-round!

On February 14, 1906, sale of the Heinze properties to Thomas F. Cole of Duluth, heading a new Amalgamated subsidiary, was announced in New York City. The price, not announced, was reported to be $10,500,000, plus some stock interest. The litigation had cost Amalgamated $1,000,000 a year for at least six years, and Heinze had robbed its mines of uncounted sums—$1,000,000 from the Michael Davitt alone. Most of his legal expense had come from his adversary's mines.

Seventeen years before, he had gone to work for the Boston & Montana for $100 a month.

In March, 1906, one hundred and ten suits pending in Butte district court and involving claims totaling more than

$70,000,000 were dismissed. Court attachés and judges felt lost: for the first time in nearly a decade they were free to deal with ordinary litigation and routine business.

Before he left for New York for bigger and better conquests, Fritz gave his last big dinner in the Broadway apartment. To the friends assembled to bid him good-by he told some of his plans: his new United Copper syndicate would rival Amalgamated, his banks would rule the financial world. One guest shook his head. "When they get you on their own ground, Fritz," he said, "they'll chase you up a tree."

Heinze laughed; but within a year he had written this friend: "They not only treed me; after I was up, they shook me down!" For in that year Standard and its allies had stripped him of nearly all the money he had wrested from the copper trust, they had smashed his United Copper, bankrupted his stock exchange firm, and had all but wrecked his banks, in which he was allied with Charles W. Morse, ice trust king and notorious market manipulator. And in the process of their vindictive campaign the Standard forces had loosed upon an unprepared financial community the elements which precipitated the nationwide panic of 1907; other firms than Heinze's went under as selling swept the market, and other banks succumbed to runs. One was Knickerbocker Trust, whose president killed himself. President Theodore Roosevelt threw $25,000,000 of federal money into the whirlpool in an attempt to slow the pace of disaster, and at last Standard decided it had eliminated upstart Heinze and his allies, and it helped to prevent further losses.

Morse and Heinze were indicted for fraudulent banking practices. Morse was convicted and went briefly to prison (he was pardoned by President Taft); Heinze was triumphantly acquitted and cheered by a courtroom crowd.

Fritz came back to Montana, an engineer again, and vowing bloody vengeance. But he had virtually no interests left in Butte: Amalgamated had drawn his teeth most carefully. Only forty, he was tired, too; the fighting spirit was gone, even if his public statements were as belligerent as ever. And his health was poor. Fritz had lived hard, happily, and unwisely. He still owned a mine in Utah and one in Idaho, and could live in his accustomed luxury on their proceeds. He even married, finally—a New York actress, Bernice Henderson—

but divorce ended that in two years and she died soon thereafter.

Fritz died suddenly in 1914 of cirrhosis of the liver, while at Saratoga, N. Y. He was forty-five years old.

F. Augustus Heinze, Robin Hood of copper, did Montana incalculable harm. Strangely enough, he actually enriched his detested enemy, the Amalgamated Copper Company.

Hero of the common people, Heinze nevertheless forced the trust, in self-defense, to thrust its finger into every man's pie and to make brutally manifest its absolute economic domination of the state, its power of life and death over the common man. This extension of trust control might have occurred anyway—it had in other sections—though it was under muckrakers' fire; in Montana Heinze speeded up the process and made it inescapable.

His cynical manipulation of the courts struck at the basis of the social community, respect for law, and forced his opponent, finally, to humble the public state as no other had ever been degraded: a corporation forced the Governor to summon the legislature, at state expense, for the sole purpose of doing that corporation's bidding on a single bill. Governor Toole held out briefly against this unprecedented humiliation of the people; but the abstract ideal of an independent democracy could not, in this test, stand against the threat of a wageless winter, and the people themselves forced him to yield.

After the Heinze war was over and the subsequent purchase of the Clark interests, the Amalgamated (it became the Anaconda as a result of Roosevelt trust-busting efforts, but remained unbusted) owned the city of Butte—its mines, public services, some of its stores, its press, usually its government. It controlled, though less obviously, half a dozen other major cities of Montana, and still does. It owns most of the state's daily newspapers, including Butte's two and the two in Helena, state capital, and because of its dominant business position it usually is able to dictate to the few it does not own. Company agents do its bidding within some of the unions, in the chambers of commerce, in hundreds of political offices, on school boards, in taxpayers' associations, on bank directorates, in real estate companies. Through some of these agencies it is able to discourage the entry of new industry into resource-rich Montana: it wants no more Heinzes, nor competition in the labor market.

"The Company" has controlled virtually every Montana legislature since it drove Heinze from Montana. Its legislative organization of lobbyists, entertainers, writers, and bill clerks is so far superior to the state's own machinery that newspapermen tell (but not in print) of incidents when state employes appealed to the Anaconda's Helena offices for help on some confused point.

And "the Company" has waxed fat on ore discovered for it by Fritz, whom aging buccaneer H. H. Rogers angrily called an "impossible" man. . . . The strangest part of the whole strange story is the fact that Heinze, skilled but unorthodox in his engineering and pressed by an ever-urgent need for ore, found copper in Amalgamated's mines where Amalgamated had no idea it existed.

Fritz taught Amalgamated a lot about mining engineering, and more about public relations, politics, and general public skulduggery. By rights, the copper trust owes him a statue; and the Butte courthouse, scene of his great speech, would be a good place for it. The statue of Marcus Daly, which used to stand before the post office, has been moved to the School of Mines.

The base of the Heinze statue could be inscribed: "They will force you to dwell in Standard Oil houses while you live, and they will bury you in Standard Oil coffins when you die."

Because a lot of Montanans figure Fritz was dead right.

X. BOISTEROUS BUTTE

You round a corner on a highway clinging to the Continental Divide and there, suddenly, is Butte. It is sprawling and slovenly, a bully of a city, stridently male, profane and blustering and boastful: "The biggest mining camp in the world!" "A mile high and a mile deep!" "The richest hill on earth!"

Butte is no longer any of these; certainly it is no longer what its police chief once called it, "an island of easy money entirely surrounded by whisky"—though it still behaves like that. There was a time when the mine pay rolls of Butte averaged $50 monthly for every man, woman, and child, when miners made $10 to $20 a day on contract. Now money is not so easily come by, but it is still easily spent: the habit persists.

This city remains what Joseph Pennell called it in his *Wonders of Work*—"the most pictorial place in America." It could be one of those selected centers of sin which columnist Heywood Broun once facetiously suggested America might establish as places in which the ordinarily virtuous citizen might occasionally blow off steam, for Butte is notorious the nation over as a "good time" town. Indeed, its chamber of commerce has hinted delicately but nonetheless frankly in its literature: "Here they [visitors] may relax in the tradition handed down from the days of wayfaring prospectors, mining and cattle men, laugh and play in the red-blooded manner that is peculiarly Butte's. . . . Doors are wide open, nothing is hidden."

Butte is the black heart of Montana, feared and distrusted. From the sixth floor of one of its office buildings go forth the corporate commands to politicians, preachers, and press, all the pensioners and servile penny-a-liners of corporate capitalism. Butte is a sooty memorial to personal heroism, to courage and vigor even in rascality; and it is a monument to a wasted land.

It is a mile high, even a little more; but it is not a mile deep —the deepest mine is still a thousand feet short of that. If it is no longer "the richest hill on earth," probably it was: above the city, denuded of grass or tree, gray-tan and dirty, squats the mountain of copper which has yielded up metal worth $2,500,000,000 in half a century. Black triangles crowned with circles, like children's classroom compasses slightly askew, thrust up through the crust of this hill to stamp fantastic abstractions on the limitless Montana sky. Under the city twist 2,700 miles of tunnels, and in their dim hot depths thousands of men have worked and fought and died; thousands of feet in the earth, at the bidding of their masters, they have thrown up barricades, fashioned crude grenades of mine powder, and prepared to blow each other up—while their masters, securely above-ground, fought in corrupted courts for possession of a disputed vein.

Bullets have raked the tired streets hung awkwardly on this mountainside as these men have fought one another or have been fought by their bosses; and the battles have helped build vast fortunes—for other men. The miners have risen in wrath and smitten the Lords of the Hill, and struck, and fought again; and they have been betrayed and defeated and driven back into their holes. But sometimes they have won and wrested away a little more of their Hill's riches for themselves. Then the surface has rocked with Rabelaisian mirth, the drinks have been on the house, the girls on "the line" have bought new dresses, the effigies of the scab have been cut down from telephone poles, and everyone has gone cheerily back to work.

Butte was born in violence, bred in it, and lives it. Back in the boom days the mines killed or injured a man a day; there were sales on crutches in drug stores. Even today there are many cripples, frequent deaths, despite vast improvement in methods and efforts by employer and union to elevate safety standards. Rock dust fills the miners' lungs and sulphuric acid dripping from the walls of a drift (the copper is in a sulphur formation) burns their clothing and their flesh. The city's file of death certificates provides the tragic coda for the dramatic song of Butte: "Occupation, miner; cause of death, silicosis; was deceased's occupation responsible? Yes." About twenty years ago federal Bureau of Mines experts asked Butte workers to appear for silicosis tests; of the 1,018 who came voluntarily for examination 42 per cent had silicosis—

"miner's con." The intervening years have brought the "wet drill" and vastly improved ventilation; employers claim—for public consumption—that silicosis is now virtually non-existent. Yet men continue to die of this and other pulmonary disorders. Butte's county, with one tenth of the state's population, contributes about one fourth of Montana's tuberculosis deaths.

Butte's dead are speedily carted to one of its six cemeteries and added to their 40,000-odd census; for this city, only seventy-five years old, has about as many dead as alive; its present population, including all the "metropolitan area," is about 50,000, a drop of 11 per cent in one decade, 16 per cent in two.

In the carriage days there were races back from the cemeteries to the saloons, and there the miners downed "boilermakers"—whisky with beer or ale chaser—in memory of the departed comrade; frequently this funereal treat was paid for out of the deceased's estate, by his command. Some still observe the traditional ceremony.

Butte has fascinated countless thousands of visitors, won their affection and finally their citizenship. It has repelled and shocked others, who have spoken and written savagely about it. Even this writer, fond of Butte, finds the temptation to exaggerate its distinctive character almost irresistible. But the temptation must be resisted; travelers like Glenn Chesney Quiett, author of *Pay Dirt,* should stop over for a day or so. Butte is not as ugly as he would have it in his rather terrifying impressionist portrait, nor does his impatient dismissal of it do justice to its notable history:

So today the mining of Montana . . . has come to be symbolized by the city of Butte on its grim and naked hills surrounded by gaunt mountains gnawed out by an iron tooth. Over the vast honeycombed hill is spread a nightmare network of trestles, railroad tracks, scaffolds, wooden buttresses, crazy stairs, bunkers, fences, houses, rusty iron pipes, electric transmission lines, hoists, buildings black and red—a cosmic junk heap created by some ingenious and saturnine Joe Cook of the gods. In this appalling Dantesque waste land, where no flower blossoms, no seed grows, there are acres of burnt slag, mountains of black boulders, mazes of chemical-incrusted iron. It is burnt-out, ravaged, raped and

discarded, and as the train slowly creeps through it on a hot summer day, the traveler can only wearily pull down the curtain and
say, "Take me away from Butte."

For half a century American writers have been discovering
delightedly that Butte's lusty history, its social and economic
habits, provide as rich a lode for their prospecting as the
famous hill provided for the mining entrepreneurs, but none
has captured the impious and indomitable spirit of the brawling big town.

Nor has any skilled historian tried to do justice to the city's
violent past—the story, for instance, of a now-vacant lot, once
occupied by a hardware store. At 10 o'clock one night in 1895
that store caught fire, and Butte's fire department responded
to the call. Ladders were against the building, firemen on
the ladders, the chief and one other on the roof. Blasting
powder illegally stored inside exploded, annihilated the Butte
fire department save for one or two men busy with hose some
distance away. Paralyzed for an instant with horror as frag-
ments of the firemen's bodies hurtled about them, the watching miners then surged heroically into the blaze in the hope
of saving a few of the victims. There was another blast, and
a third. . . . Fifty-seven men were blown to pieces that
night. Butte men today tell how with hundreds of other boys
they stood around the morgues, watched gunny sacks filled
with human particles—heads, hands, bones, or just seared
flesh—brought in for the task of assembly and identification.
The task was finally admitted to be hopeless.

Down another street was the miners' union hall. (Now the
miners own the once-luxurious Silver Bow Club, where the
Lords of the Hill entertained at least one President of the
United States, scores of famous actors and actresses, and other
notables, where thousands of dollars changed hands in epic
poker games.) The union hall was blown up by dynamite
June 13, 1914, in the midst of a bitter internal dispute which
the miners still believe was inspired by the bosses. Butte was
Local No. 1 of the Western Federation of Miners, toughest
union in America in the '90's, the union of Big Bill Haywood.
(It is still Local No. 1 of the WFM's successor, International
Union of Mine, Mill & Smelter Workers, CIO.) In 1914 the

IWW sought control of the WFM, and in the process it destroyed the Butte union's hall. Martial law followed (there was a strike in progress, too, and big war profits were endangered) and Butte's Socialist antiwar mayor, elected by the miners, was driven from office. The strike was broken and the miners' union did not come back until the days of NRA.

On top of the "richest hill," almost in the center, is the Granite Mountain mine. On the night of June 8, 1917, the flames of a miner's carbide lamp ignited the uncovered and frayed insulation of a temporary power cable near the 2,400-foot level. The timbers caught, the roaring draft down the shaft pushed smoke and gas throughout the workings. Within an hour 163 men had perished, all but 2 of them from suffocation. The unhappy miner whose cap-lamp had started the fire survived it; he had a German name and so far had the pendulum swung in once antiwar Butte that there was lynch talk, but investigators proved him to be guiltless.

As you drive out of Butte onto the highway leading to the smelter city of Anaconda, you come to a concrete underpass which replaces an old wooden trestle. The night of August 17, 1917, a gang of masked men seized Frank W. Little, an IWW organizer, as he lay in bed in a Butte rooming house, dragged him into the street without permitting him to dress, took him to the trestle and there hanged him. The victim, said the company press, "made no outcry." Such courage must have been difficult unless Little had fainted—at the time of the lynching he had a broken leg. None of his attackers was ever publicly named or tried, but there are those in Butte who will name them, and who will tell of the amazing retributive fate which has caught up with most of the murderers—violent or horrible death in one form or another. As for Frank Little, he gained the measure of immortality available for men of his hazardous calling—a commemorative ode in the IWW song book.

A narrow little street winding up the hill is Anaconda Road, traversing Dublin Gulch. One day in 1924 a close-packed mass of striking miners started up that road to picket a mine at the top. They were met by murderous fire from the guns of deputies and company guards. Several men were killed; oddly enough they were leaders who had been cold-bloodedly warned before the march that they would be killed if they did not get out of Butte. A reporter squatted behind a post and wrote an eyewitness account of the "battle."

Butte's exciting past is important only because few American communities are so enslaved by their own tradition—a tradition, in this case, which has helped to make Butte the outstanding example of exploitation by the American imperialist capitalism which has stripped the resources of the nation's own frontiers in half a century. Butte is not "the biggest mining camp on earth." It is not a mining camp at all; it is a northwestern metropolis, center of state and regional industry, metropolitan in aspect and influence. Nevertheless Butte thinks like a mining camp, acts like one, and was built like one. This must continue, inevitably, as long as every man, woman, and child in this city is dependent in greater or less degree upon its only industry of importance, the absentee-owned mines.

Pierce Williams, writing in *Survey Graphic* on permanently depressed areas, called Butte "the outstanding example of community vulnerability to economic forces in the mining industry." It is that and more: it affords unequaled opportunity for scrutiny of the major economic trend of our era, the reversal of the frontier and monopolist concentration of the means of production. The men came west, but more and more of the products of their toil and the resources of their earth have gone east; and due to recurring market crises, war, technological advancement, and curtailment in real wages, less and less has come back.

The ideals of laissez-faire capitalism have been committing suicide in Butte. Individualism has made a last stand, and the compulsions of an industry caught in the disorganization of capitalist markets have been destroying in Butte that individual initiative which capitalism has always said it lived to defend.

Copper miners have always been individualists; as such they have contributed innumerable heroic or comic episodes to the saga of Butte. They may be, and usually are, loyal and militant unionists; but they would rather work "on their own" by contracting with the company on a piecework basis than work for the union minimum scale. These men are no slaves of the assembly line. Despite the great advance of metal mines technology since World War I, their job is still personal and integrated: the contract miner still "breaks" (blasts), shovels the ore into cars, and timbers the drift; it is a unified task and complete. His is still a man's work, a man's contest with Nature jealous of her riches, a fight against dust and heat and fire and gas.

But the contract system is the bane of the miners' union. Some 80 per cent of the men, according to union leaders, work under that system: they agree to a certain price per cubic foot of ore produced. This is an individual contract between miner and employer and the union has no control over the price except that, on contract or not, the miner must receive at least the union minimum. The contract price can be, and has been, cut at will by the Company; and as the men strive to maintain their wage standards, the union charges, a speed-up results which is similar in effect to the speeded assembly lines of a motor plant.

The union strives constantly to increase the daily minimum wage in the hope that it may thus destroy this contract system. In time, the leaders argue, the contract miner may decide that the profits of his "free enterprise" bargain with his boss are not sufficiently greater than the minimum to be worth the extra effort. Then he would become a good deal more interested in union standards than he has been hitherto. Individual initiative, so dear to the heart of the industrialist, would be dead; but so would the speed-up be dead. The Company, on the other hand, insists that the contract system rewards the best worker, and it usually does. The miner, however, cannot choose his own drift and may be assigned to an unproductive working; this, says the union, encourages favoritism by foremen and impairs the independence of the men.

Technological unemployment is an old story by now, and Butte cannot claim that its distress as a result of it is unique. Nevertheless it is a grave problem for Butte. Copper production in this war will exceed that of World War I, but far fewer men will be needed to get it out. Production in 1938, in fact, was equal to that of the best years of the first World War, but peak employment was 7,800 and that was 5,000 less than in the war period. Such was Montana's man-power crisis in World War II, however, that even this reduced number could not be found to man adequately the mines of Butte; and although many were released from the army to dig copper there, most of them found they preferred military life to Butte's hot workings, and went back to it.

Net production in pounds per man year when Butte started as a copper camp (1882) was 10,000; in 1930 it was 45,000. When Butte began producing, imported copper was only 8 per cent of American exported copper; in 1930 imports were 108 per cent of exports. Increasing imports in peacetime are bound up with technological change because it is cheap labor abroad which forces installation of machinery to supplant costlier labor in Butte. Because mining is still a man's job and no machine has been devised which can handle the three essential operations listed above, the changes have been few. But they have been remarkably effective in reducing employment. Principal mechanical aids have been the high-speed hoist and the machine loader, or "mechanical mucker." This latter device, somewhat resembling a baby scoop shovel mounted on a truck, lifts the ore after blasting into a mine tram car. Two sizes of these machines have been introduced in Butte; the union estimates that the smaller one will displace two men and the larger, three.

The specter of the machine which does the work of the man first rose over Butte Hill in 1927, when the Anaconda Copper Mining Company installed high-speed hoists in the Belmont, Badger State, and Mountain Con mines. By means of these hoists it was possible to bring the ore from several mines to the surface through a single shaft in less time than it had taken before to lift the output of one. Many of Butte's mines are connected; thus the Badger and Belmont each work parts of several other mines. The effect of this consolidation of operations was immediate, particularly upon surface employment, and miners believe the hoists, rather than the mechanical loaders, are primarily responsible for the decrease in jobs.

Montana mines employment decreased 10 per cent between 1919 and 1929; in the same period there was an increase of 40 per cent in the rated horsepower of electrical or other power equipment.

Of all the cities which claim the unique and unhappy distinction of being the first to feel the effects of industrial recession and the last to recover, Butte's claim is better than most. The metal mines industry usually follows, seldom leads others into large-scale production, and Butte is forever down or up, never level.

Thus in the winter and spring of 1937–38 Butte mine employment plunged from 7,800 to 800. Virtually all the city's 50,000 people depended upon those 7,000 jobless miners, directly or indirectly. WPA and direct relief certifications skyrocketed and business collapsed; retail trade dropped 50 per cent. This crash came on the heels of a brief upturn which had followed an earlier long period of shutdowns, and the miners, if they could ever accumulate reserves, had not had time to do so. Few could, anyway, for Butte living costs are high, its spending temptations almost innumerable. And life is hard in the mines; when a miner can afford it, he likes to lay off. That is one reason, the miners claim, that the Company permits Butte's notorious "openness." The miner who is always broke cannot lay off and he cannot—when he tires of his dangerous and unhealthy job—quit and "drift" as he did in other, plushier times. The Company likes to have big "rustling lines" before the mines' employment offices; federal relief, keeping large numbers of workers rooted in a community many of them otherwise would have left, has helped.

Butte businessmen accept as a matter of course their dependence on mines in which virtually half of the city's wage earners are employed. The more cynical among them will say that "the Company's loudest critics are usually on the Company's pay roll"; they have had considerable experience in Butte with *agents provocateurs*. This, however, does not lead to business confidence and businessmen do not make any save the most essential commitments. Loans and discounts of Butte banks plunged from $18,000,000 in 1929 to less than $3,000,000 in 1939 while the banks' cash reserves more than doubled.

Business has been tolerant, too, of the big gambling establishments which, though closed in intermittent reform waves, have given the city a nationwide reputation. They re-

sent bitterly much of the sensational publicity, insisting
"other towns are just the same, but not so honest about it."
There is a measure of truth in this, but Butte's gambling
has certainly been on a scale one would be unlikely to find
in other cities of 50,000. An indication of its magnitude as
an industry might be seen in the fact that the Arcade, one of
the largest establishments prior to a statewide shutdown in
1940, was located on Butte's busiest, highest-rent corner. Curley Darragh, its operator, was hostile when questioned: "Get
wise to yourself; if we weren't wanted in Butte we wouldn't
be here!"

Operators of the games and bars in Butte and in its good-
time suburb of Meaderville have always insisted that a very
large share of their business comes from visitors, and a police
officer once bitterly confirmed this. "We have to police not
only Butte but the five adjoining counties too," he complained. "There's many a man who will live like a respectable
gopher all week in Deer Lodge so he can get drunk and raise
hell in Butte come Saturday night!"

Only about a third of the city's people are American born
of American parentage. This has much to do with Butte
politics, industrial practice, and social life. It is responsible
for much of its color and some of its bad reputation. It has
restrained any tendency to become "stuffed shirt": a dance
hall proprietor boasts, "All our patrons have to dress; see,
they all have coats on." Though this proportion of foreign
born and foreign or mixed parentage is much higher than in
the average American city, it does not indicate a lower literacy
standard. Butte, in fact, has less than half the national urban
percentage of illiteracy—1.2 against 3.2.

Another Butte statistic perhaps sheds some light on the
city's famous restricted district. It's still a man's town: it
has more men in proportion to women than any other American city its size and far more than the average. In 1930, 54.3
per cent of its population was male; the national average was
49.5. Mining is more attractive as a career to unmarried than
to family men, and Butte's dependence on that single industry
also limits the field of employment for single women.

That is one reason "they treat sporting people very well
in Butte," which is the way one of the "sporting people"—a
girl in Butte's "Venus Alley"—put it. "After we go out of

the alley we're just like anybody else. We work for our money; in good times the take'll run to $100 a week for some of the younger and prettier ones. . . . Butte figures we give value for the money and we're just as good as anybody so we can live in nice places and it doesn't matter where we eat, even if they know we're sporting people. They don't kick us out of restaurants or make it tough for us, like some places I've been. . . ."

The restricted district is in a narrow alley-courtyard just two and a half blocks from Butte's new modern high school and on the same street. When the school was built there was some reckless talk of closing the line, but it had been there for many years, it was accepted, and Butte decided it was necessary. So a compromise was reached: the three entrances were closed off with fences built somewhat like a maze, painted green and bearing the words "Men under 21 Keep Out." Youths mature rapidly in Butte and may be skilled miners before they are twenty-one, so the phrase is not as foolish as it looks. Further to protect Butte's knowing youth, the girls were ordered to abandon their "day shift" and not to appear in the alley before five o'clock.

The girls are protected from racketeers and cranks and disturbances are rare. However, the "line" is a cold-blooded business proposition. Its "cribs" are dingy, crude offices for a revolting "business," which even in tolerant Butte is a little furtive, a little afraid.

Under the leadership of an enlightened and progressive mayor who, unfortunately for Butte, died in office, the city began a few years ago with federal help to tackle its unique problem—to break with paralyzing tradition and the powerful forces which maintain that tradition: in the words of that mayor, Charles A. Hauswirth, "to refrain absolutely from boosting Butte as a mining camp, but advertise it in every conceivable way as an up-and-coming city."

Butte has behind it three quarters of a century of haphazard mining-camp development, decades of municipal mismanagement, and a community psychology born of miners' tradition—generous but heedless. Here are people oddly different from their nearest neighbors, even in other Montana cities. A spontaneous gesture of good-fellowship, perhaps a

benefit dance to provide a "seeing eye" dog for a blind musi-
cian, can find wholehearted, immediate support; but Butte's
patience is short and its vision dim, so a long-term program
of community planning is more apt to run up against the
phrase, "Oh, the hell with it!"

The handicaps under which such planning will have to
proceed are worth special consideration. This "most pictorial
city" of Joseph Pennell earned the artist's attention, he wrote,
because

Its mountain is crowned not with trees but with chimneys. Low
black villages of miners' houses straggle toward the foot of the
mountain. The barren plain is covered with gray, slimy masses of
refuse which crawl down to it—glaciers of work—from the hills.
The plain is seared and scorched and cracked with tiny canyons,
all their lines leading to the mountain. . . .

That, accompanying Pennell's sketch of Butte, was published in 1916. His incisive, if superficial, judgment could
have stood until the last decade; but the Butte which he saw
is gone. It was an overgrown mining camp sprawling over
some five square miles, completely without benefit of planning, cursed with offset streets and blind streets, even streets
higher on one side than on the other. Some of its sewers—
since replaced—were fifty years old and ran diagonally across
the city; one had been laid by a mining magnate to connect
two points for which he wanted sewer service, with complete
disregard to the needs or convenience of the intervening
sections. Much of the city had no sewer service until "new
deal" public works projects were inaugurated, and relied on
cesspools; the soil formation of Butte is unsuitable for these
so scores of families were kept continually digging up their
back yards in an exhausting struggle to dispose of their own
waste.

But Butte's most incredible feature—it has struck casual
visitors as very funny indeed, though it isn't—is its boundary.
The city limits defy every rule of logic or draftsmanship because they dodge nearly all the mines: the boundary will run
straight as a die to a mine fence, then swerve neatly around
it, leaving the mine property happily exempt from city taxation.

Montana Street is one of Butte's busiest thoroughfares. In one section, one side of this street is in the city limits; the other side, though occupied by several large warehouses and the passenger depot of a major railroad, is not—and the blissful tenants of that side of the street benefit by city sewers, fire protection, and other services but pay no city taxes. You can round a corner in Butte and leave the city, turn the next corner and be back in. This condition does not seem particularly strange to the citizens of Butte and planners despair of remedying it since Montana law provides that before a city may annex a district, 51 per cent of the district's property owners must consent. The property owners in these "islands" are unlikely to consent to added taxation.

The prospectors, and later the industrialists, who ruled Butte stripped the Rocky Mountains of their forests within a radius of fifty miles of the city. After copper was discovered came the horror of open-hearth smelting—the reduction of copper on giant wood and charcoal fires around the city, an operation which blanketed Butte with a perpetual pall of filthy yellow sulphurous smoke, hastening the demise of citizens with influenza or pulmonary disorders and denuding the hills of vegetation. Open-hearth smelting ended when the plant was built at near-by Anaconda ("beautiful," said Pennell, "with the beauty of death!") but the damage had been done. In recent years, however, Nature and relief workers have been bringing grass and trees back to Butte. It's a long job.

Federal help has enabled Butte to clean up the old mine dumps, bring some green back to its residential sections, and improve its recreational and cultural resources. Butte has never gone in much for culture, on a community scale, though in hundreds of mean homes and obscure and dingy bars there live the music and color and legend of a dozen peoples. In Meaderville swing blares from the "Rocky Mountain," and one of the city's masters, feeling his costly liquor, tosses $20 to the orchestra conductor in trade for his baton and leads the band, weaving drunkenly. Out on the "flats" hundreds squeeze into a hot little room, drink their cheap beers, and clamber onto a splintered floor to push each other around to the music of a juke box. Sunday, a miner and his wife and children may picnic at Columbia Gardens, the park given to Butte by William A. Clark. In it are free "rides" for the youngsters and brick stoves where the mother, who has cooked in a miner's hut all week, can cook again after her husband has built the fire. Here are trees and grass, not as dirty and worn as they used to be.

Such cultural efforts as have been made recently appear to have come from the upper levels of Butte society—for Butte has an elite; it even had, forty years ago, a *Blue Book*. That impressive volume, compiled by one John Boyle O'Reilly, set out as do all *Blue Books* to advise hostesses as to which fellow citizens might be bidden to their functions without fear of embarrassment: the ladies and gentlemen whose names were inscribed in his chaste scroll could be depended upon to refrain from the heartier expressions of good-fellowship then popular in Butte social life—such as fights. But, warned O'Reilly very wisely, "the lines have not been too closely drawn." Despite this liberal interpretation of its scope, the *Blue Book* was not a success: it appeared but once.

Butte's only recent cultural development of importance was sponsored by its Junior League, whose eager maidens, aware of the city's artistic possibilities and ashamed of its cultural lag, established a municipal art center and later turned it over to a nonprofit community organization and the Federal Art Project. Butte also has a concert association, similar to that in many cities of the hinterland. Though it is only fifty miles from the scene of operations of the Vigilantes, it has no historical museum nor any other kind save for the outstanding mineral and gem display in the State School of Mines.

Housing is poor and expensive. About 53 per cent of the residential units are substandard; nearly half of all dwellings lack private toilet and bath. The preponderance of single men encouraged construction of multiple-unit dwellings and discouraged family homes with yards. A United States Housing Authority project, completed within the last few years, has alleviated some of the worst conditions but could aid only a comparatively few families.

Wage scales of Butte building-craft unions are 20 per cent higher than in seventy other selected American cities. Living costs are slightly higher than average, lumping them all together; some goods and services, such as clothing maintenance, personal care, and household operation, are much higher than average. All of Butte's utilities, even water, are privately owned and service is costly compared with other cities. A Miles City, Mont., newspaper man once essayed to describe Butte's economy in a sentence: "In Butte everybody goes around happily 'sticking up' everybody else; and they think they have prosperity!"

About fifteen years ago, a Bureau of Mines review of conditions in Butte commented: "It is usual in American mining districts for towns to begin as camps and progress into cities. Butte has reached the latter stage, and if there remain reminders of the old days . . . it is a matter which local public pride may be expected to correct year by year." But public pride in Butte is an unpredictable and ungovernable force, occasionally virile and well directed, occasionally going off on a tangent quite understandable to Butte but mystifying to more staid communities. Butte was proud of and admired, for instance, one Jerre Clifford, of whom the mayor's own newspaper said in eulogy: "He was one of the really big men Butte has produced; many are the men in all walks of life whose burdens have been made lighter by his benevolence and kindliness." Clifford was Butte's biggest gambling operator and owner of a statewide lottery, but according to Montana standards he was an upright and a generous man. He made money, spent it, and gave it; and more than that, plus rudimentary honesty and affability, Montana asks of no man.

The city is shamefacedly proud of its periodic outbursts of maniacal exuberance, as when students defy police bans on pre-game demonstrations, mass in little groups on obscure streets, and converge on the business district in a rioting mob of three thousand, routing the police with rotten eggs and looting a few candy stands. City officials are angry but secretly appreciative of the students' ingenuity; for the vandalism they blame older rowdies, graduates of Butte's once-notorious "overall gang," long since broken up.

But it is not mass movements which stick in one's memory as most closely associated with Butte: it is rather the stories of the heroic, foolhardy or pathetic individuals whose exploits have built the biggest mining camp's legend and still are building it.

Thus—hero: "American George" Chubb. . . . During a circus parade an elephant was maddened by stepping upon a fallen live wire, and charged the crowd. Miner Chubb, who never had seen an elephant before, leaped upon the berserk beast's trunk, was swung dizzily from side to side of the street; finally, clinging to the trunk, helped to beat the animal into submission with a club handed to him from the crowd. A few years later "American George" placed twelve dynamite shots in a drift while his partner started up a chain ladder. Before Chubb could get up the ladder the shots began to explode prematurely and he tumbled back into the winze. The ladder was beyond his reach and Chubb screamed to his partner to toss it down to him; but the partner, afraid to venture near the shaft, cowered in safety while blast after blast flung Chubb's body from wall to wall until it had been pounded to dust. The partner, shunned by all of Butte, crept nightly into a dark corner of a grimy bar and drank himself to death in a year.

Clown: "Colonel Buckets," race-track tout. . . . Illiterate, he was nevertheless persuaded by practical jokers to file in the primaries for lieutenant governor of Montana. Most of his campaigning was done in Butte's most disreputable sections: it was said that his was the first political campaign in history to be conducted entirely at night. He was induced to hand out on the street cards advertising a cure for waning manly vigor, under the impression that they were campaign cards for himself. "That's my platform," he told each shocked or incredulous recipient. Overcome by his labors getting out the vote, the "Colonel" was lost for three days after election. Butte was not particularly surprised to find that he received 12,632 votes—not, fortunately, enough to win.

Fool: an unnamed boy. . . . In strike time, cold spotlights pierced the night sky and grim gunners beside them watched pickets in the street below, playing horseshoes by the light of an ancient arc. Deep in the earth water rose and the scabs pumped frantically—for in the big 1934 strike the miners "pulled" the engineers and maintenance crews too. Suddenly a youngster slipped away from the horseshoe game's audience, seized a chain and risked his life by tossing it over a power line, releasing his hold an instant before it settled down on the wires. A flash crackled along the line, sparks from the

chain bombarded the pickets, the pumps stopped. Desperate
bosses called electricians; when they came, women and children pelted them gaily with rocks while the miner pickets,
peaceably inclined, remonstrated.

Hero, clown, and fool; these are the men who have made
Butte, these and that ordinary miner whom we left, several
pages back, picnicking with his family at Columbia Gardens.
After the picnic supper they will herd aboard a bus and ride
through the clamorous night of their city up some precipitous
street to their dreary, crowded, dingy home. The girls on the
"line" will have drawn their painted rockers to the windows,
the bars and streets will have begun to fill up: for the mines
are working again and it's an all-night city in good times. But
if the mines were closed by a strike, uneasy peace would
settle over the avenues, picket lines would begin forming
at the mine gates and the company's guards would inspect
their weapons.

Busses roar noisily through the streets and planes roar overhead, and a drunken driver may hurtle into Broadway from
the Meaderville road, maiming a pedestrian. The police will
get him, but it will be hard to convince a Butte jury: life is
cheap here.

Then it is nearly dawn, and the darkness lifts from the
edges of the encircling peaks. In strike time the pickets leave
in relays for coffee and the guards loosen their grip on their
guns; the searchlights go out. But now the mines are running.
. . . A few men sidle out of the green gateway to the line,
turn up their coat collars, clump off to cheerless rooms; a few
drunks are ejected from bars; if the town is "open," janitors
are cleaning up in Curley Darragh's Arcade. ("If he isn't at
the Arcade, he isn't in Butte.")

At last, Butte sleeps.

Puncher,

XI. THE GRASS WAS FREE ..

CONFLICT is the first essential of drama. Thus invariably the most dramatic, most glamorous period in the history of any plains state is the era of the "open range."

Yet the searcher after economic and social forces in a regional history at first glance might find this conflict tawdry and the "romantic" industry about and within which the savage battle raged a somewhat ruffianly business. He would find that the initial "capital goods" of the range industry was second hand: broken-down, footsore oxen from the emigrant caravans—and the commodity upon which it built its prosperity, the longhorn steer, an ungainly, unloved freak of the animal world. The range itself, this student would discover, was usually commandeered and frequently stolen outright. The industry's entrepreneurs were often unscrupulous and greedy; their enterprises were brief and bloody struggles against Nature, beast, and man.

But no matter how skeptical might be this scholar's approach, he could hardly conclude his study without having succumbed in some degree to the indubitable romanticism of his subject. And he might end up by buying himself a pair of high-heeled boots and hurrying west. They have been known to do it.

Judged by modern economic practice, everything about the range industry was fantastic. Men hazarded fortunes and often their lives on a meteorological and biological gamble: their herds must increase 20 per cent or more annually because the normal annual loss would be 10 per cent, and in bad winters might be 40 per cent or even 90 per cent. Men born in mansions and graduated from the nation's greatest universities were content to gamble thus, and to live, while the game was played out, in caves dug out of cliffs, or in sod huts, or in dingy log cabins. Other cultured, kindly gentlemen could direct and participate in the mass killing in cold blood of other men—part of the game and essential if one were not to be dealt out.

And a great industry was built up and flourished briefly by undisciplined and heedless exploitation of a resource it did not own and upon which it had virtually no legal or moral claim.

Granville Stuart, a Virginian of Scotch descent, was one of the first in Montana Territory to engage in the beef business; in 1860 he brought in some lame oxen from Fort Hall, Idaho Territory, on the Oregon Trail, fattened them in western Montana, and a year later drove them back to be resold or traded for more "lags." Oxen were merely work cattle; turned out to grass and not worked, they became beef steers. The beef market in the mining camps was excellent and the industry grew rapidly. In 1866 Nelson Story drove in 600 head of longhorns from Texas over the Bozeman Trail— the first Texas drive. Six years later the first Montana Territory brand book was issued by the clerk of the supreme court in Virginia City. It contained 245 brands; in later years there were to be 70,000 brands on Montana grass.

By 1880 overcrowding had already become a problem in the western part of the Territory and in that year Granville Stuart pushed over the divide from the Deer Lodge country to bring the first herd into central Montana. Within five years he was again hunting new range. "It would be impossible," he wrote later, "to make persons not present on the Montana cattle ranges realize the rapid change that took place in two years." He continued in his *Forty Years on the Frontier:*

In 1880 the country [central Montana] was practically uninhabited. One could travel for miles without seeing so much as a trapper's bivouac. Thousands of buffalo darkened the rolling plains. There were deer, antelope, elk, wolves and coyotes on every hill and in every ravine and thicket. In the whole Territory of Montana there were but 250,000 head of cattle, including dairy cattle and work oxen.

In the fall of 1883 there was not one buffalo remaining on the range and the antelope, elk and deer were indeed scarce. In 1880 no one had heard tell of a cowboy . . . and Charley Russell had made no pictures of them; but in the fall of 1883 there were 600,-000 head of cattle on the range—the cowboy, with leather chaps, wide hat, gay handkerchief, clanking silver spurs and skin-fitting high-heeled boots . . . had become an institution.

The cattle business in western Montana, the mountain and valley country, had been conducted largely on the eastern pattern—small herds on farms. But in central Montana the grass was free: it belonged to the people of the United States. The great herds on this last stand of the open range grazed upon millions of acres to which the herds' owners had no right other than the fact that they got there first, a "squatters' " right which was given recognition of sorts in 1877 in the curious law of "customary range." In many instances, owners of 30,000 or 40,000 head of cattle owned not one square foot of the land those cattle used, nor even the land upon which their ranch buildings stood.

Along toward the end, one Montana company was shipping more than 9,000 head of cattle annually to market; its herds, more than 30,000 head, had a quarter million acres of range. And at that time this company owned just 450 acres of land.

But no inference should be drawn from this that the vast grass empire was stolen. Many of these companies would have bought land, or leased it (and some did lease, in Canada), had it been possible for them to do so; the basic fault was not theirs—it lay in political maladministration of the public lands, a long and disheartening history of occasionally corrupt, more often stupid bureaucratic bungling.

Much land was stolen: some from the Indians, who got even
—as we shall see later in this section; some from the people
of the United States, who did not—this by means of illegal
fencing of the public domain, fraudulent homestead entry,
dishonest manipulation of land grants.

But the central Montana range was merely commandeered,
expropriated. If it was to be utilized, this had to happen: for
it was not surveyed and could not be bought. Until 1888
everything to the north of the Missouri River was Indian reservation, as was much of the area south of the Yellowstone.
Between these two rivers lay a "no-man's-land," subjected to
continual Indian raids, blizzard-swept, infested with wolves
and outlaws—but a paradise of free grass.

To acquire a portion of this empire, the stockman merely
inserted a notice in the nearest weekly newspaper (and it
might be hundreds of miles away) listing his brand and
establishing by personal decree the extent of his range, bordering it upon creeks or familiar landmarks such as buttes or
dry coulees. The same definition of his domain appeared
under his brand in the state's brand books.

There then arose the problem of maintaining his dominion, of holding off the "grass pirate" who sought to edge in
upon his range. Whereupon into the Montana statutes went
the law of the "customary range"; it stands to this day, al-
tered only to the extent of removal of the minimum penalty
for violation. Section 1 of this law, adopted in 1877, prohibited branding of another grower's cattle but provided no
criminal penalty for this offense, setting out merely that it
should constitute grounds for civil action for recovery of damages three times the value of the cattle involved.

This failure to make outright rustling and brand blotting
a criminal offense was easily explainable. With herds grazing
in common on unfenced range, such an offense was too hard
to prove for the Territory to undertake the task with its very
limited law enforcement facilities; calves frequently were
misbranded by accident and this would provide opportunity
for a vindictive cattleman to send a neighbor he disliked to
prison. So instead burden of proof was left upon the stockman
directly concerned.

On the other hand, this weakness of the statute undoubtedly contributed to the cattlemen's later impatience

with legal procedure and their adoption of the Vigilante system to rid the Missouri badlands of rustlers.

Section 2 of the law, however, sought to make up in part for the impotence of the first paragraph; it was this section which established the principle of "customary range." It read:

Any person who shall drive, or cause to be driven, any cattle, horses, mules, sheep or swine from their customary range without permission of the owner thereof, shall be deemed guilty of a misdemeanor and on conviction thereof before any justice of the peace in the Territory of Montana may be fined in any sum not less than five nor more than one hundred dollars, and may be imprisoned in the county jail not less than ten days nor more than ninety days, or both.

This law, intended to discourage alike the rustler and the "grass pirate" who would shove the first-comer's stock off the range to make room for his own, has been a colossal headache for Montana justices of the peace for more than half a century. It attempted to establish a proprietary right for a private individual upon public property; and though it is still on the books, its constitutional validity is at least questionable. Countless times disputatious neighbors dragged each other before harassed justices and brought charges of violation of the "customary range," a term so broad as practically to defy definition, considering the recklessly migratory habits of range stock driven hither and yon by rain, drouth, lightning, fire, mosquitoes, poisonous weeds, or sometimes just a bad smell. More than one exasperated judge threw a case out of court because the only way to settle it was to get the opinion of the cattle themselves.

But there were other ways to hold one's range; and the most effective of these, at first, was the roundup boycott. Outfits whose "customary range" had been invaded announced publicly that they would not "work" the newcomer's cattle, that he would not be permitted to participate in the common roundup. Thus John H. Conrad of Fort Benton was socially and economically ostracized when he brought a herd onto range claimed by the Niobrara Cattle Company in central Montana in 1885. The local association of cattlemen adopted a resolution:

WHEREAS, The custom of disregarding the prior rights of others on the range is becoming frequent, annoying and damaging in a high degree to range interests . . .

RESOLVED, That we discountenance such actions [as Conrad's] as unfair and injurious to the best interests of the country and that we refuse to recognize or work with any parties infringing upon the prior rights of others by turning stock on a range previously occupied, and be it further

RESOLVED, That we refuse to work with or in any way handle the cattle of the said J. H. Conrad.

The resolution was widely published, and Conrad, one of the first to be thus publicly stoned, took his herd elsewhere.

This extra-legal appropriation of the public range was greeted somewhat incredulously in Washington, where the General Land Office Commissioner commented:

In certain localities in Montana the cattlemen have taken exclusive possession of extensive tracts of grazing lands and hold them by publishing periodically notices that the ranges are full and that no more cattle will be allowed to go on the lands, and by making away with the cattle of other persons found there and driving out all settlers.

Before Washington got around to doing anything about it, however, the roundup boycott had lost its effectiveness. Later interlopers, not as susceptible as Conrad to moral suasion, left their cattle on the disputed range, and far from being dismayed by the boycott, conducted their own roundup—*before* the common roundup began. The established cattlemen could not discipline the newcomer unless he shared membership with them in the general roundup, which divided the unbranded calves among the members according to the section of the range where they were found, or sold them and divided the proceeds. The "sooner," rounding up alone before his neighbors' riders got on the range, could gather up all the mavericks for himself. And he could do worse: in his early roundup he could seriously impair the value of his truculent neighbors' stock. Cattle must not be run more than absolutely necessary, because running cuts down flesh, and flesh is money. And to run them in the early spring when they have not completely shed their heavy winter coats not only seriously reduces their weight but sometimes costs their lives.

Thus the roundup boycott died when it was realized that the "pirates," social outcasts though they might be, were profiting exceedingly, as did the settler upon whose strangely prolific cows Granville Stuart commented:

Near our home ranch we discovered one rancher whose cows invariably had twin calves and frequently triplets, while the range cows in that vicinity were nearly all barren and would persist in hanging around this man's corral, envying his cows their numerous children and bawling and lamenting their own childless state. This state of affairs continued until we were obliged to call around that way and threaten to hang the man if his cows had any more twins.

Not until 1895 did Montana legislators catch up with the "sooners" of the roundup. In that year it became illegal to brand on the open range between December 1 and May 1; but by then it was too late—there was little open range left.

Despite such setbacks, the Montana cattlemen continued to defend with fanatical conviction the theory of the "customary range," surely one of the most incongruous principles ever to win even temporary place within the framework of American free capitalist enterprise. The range industry came to regard any attack upon the principle as barefaced outlawry or theft of a God-given resource—even though the attacker's right might be as valid, legally, as that of the entrenched range interest.

And finally, after the law, moral suasion, threats, and even a few shootings had failed to check this tidal wave which was engulfing their "customary range," the cattlemen built a fence around it.

Federal reaction was as prompt as it had been tardy before. Land office attorneys streamed into federal courts with complaints. By 1887 somewhere near 250,000 acres of public domain in Montana had been illegally inclosed within barbed wire, President Cleveland had ordered every foot of it torn down, and big names in the range country were standing angrily before federal judges being scolded. The Swan Land

& Cattle Company, organized in 1883 with Scotch capital, had purchased 500,000 acres of Northern Pacific railroad land grant (alternate sections) and had put up 130 miles of illegal fence. United States production of barbed wire tripled between 1880 and 1890, and from the reports of land office registers to the Commissioner in Washington, it appeared that all this increased output had been unrolled in Montana.

In 1887 the Commissioner reported 135,000 acres down, at least 85,000 to go. His task had been complicated by the ingenuity of the stockmen. Edward Cardwell purchased a railroad grant composed of the odd sections of a Yellowstone county township, and with the connivance of the owners of even sections on the outside edges of the township line, he built a fence inclosing the whole township—and incidentally numerous sections of public domain. The courts held the inclosure illegal even though all the fence was built on private land. Cabot Thomas left one opening in his fence on the shore of a lake and another opening across an impassable coulee, contending the fence therefore did not constitute a complete inclosure. The circuit court decided it did.

The government's war upon illegal fencing continued into the 1900's, and even today an occasional instance crops up, but the practice boomeranged against the cattlemen and it declined in popularity after the disastrous winter of 1886–87. Cattle which prior to that winter had drifted with the storms and had sometimes reached range blown free of snow, piled up instead against the new fences and starved or froze to death.

It was a practice of cattlemen, as soon as they arrived on a new range, to announce portentously that that range was in imminent danger of becoming overcrowded. Perhaps it was this early crying of "Wolf!" which caused the stockmen's later warnings, when they really were justified, to go unheeded.

Throughout the '80's the range industry wrangled over proposals to permit leasing of the public domain for grazing. Such schemes were denounced as class legislation because they would enable the corporate livestock interests to prevent settlement and crowd out the small cattle operator. The Montana Stock Growers' Association changed its position several times, depending upon which faction controlled its convention, and the state's congressional delegation was told one year to seek a leasing system, the next year to defeat it. The lines were never clearly drawn, for large operators whose range was not yet menaced would combine with the "nesters" to beat down any proposal that they pay for it, and other big companies, recognizing the inevitable, sincerely opposed a step which they said would make for hostile division of classes in the west.

But though stockmen might shy away from a lease system which was essentially undemocratic and sure to make trouble, most of them would use almost any other means to acquire range. According to John Clay, pioneer stockgrower and commission man, there was "scarce a ranchman in the west who has not transgressed the land laws of the country." Homestead laws were flagrantly violated, often with the aid of corrupt local officials, especially the Desert Land Act, which required the entryman to construct an irrigation system, and the Timber Culture Act, which required him to plant trees.

A handful of dispirited saplings stuck in the ground where there was no chance for them to grow (and, indeed, sometimes dead before they were planted) often enough constituted "proof" under the latter law. Desert land homesteaders would turn the spring runoff into trenches a few inches deep and obtain affidavits attesting to the fact that the land was being "irrigated." A prominent pioneer citizen of Great Falls had himself dragged in a rowboat by a team of horses through a dry ditch; witnesses testified they had seen a boat traversing the ditch.

Most of these fraudulent entries were the result of the stockmen's effort to control water sources, even more important than the range itself. In 1888 the Miles City land office register reported to the Commissioner that ten entries covering 6,000 acres had been made by various individuals on behalf of one big cattle company. It was not uncommon for a cow outfit's whole staff—foreman, riders, down to and including the cook—to arrive in town and invade the land office en masse to "take up homesteads."

It cannot be argued, of course, that the government should knowingly have permitted the expropriation of public property implicit in such illegal land entries and illegal fencing, and the arguments against leasing were valid enough; yet, granted hindsight today, we can see that it might have been better had the government winked at the law violation or overcome its repugnance to class legislation sufficiently to permit leasing.

Because the stockmen in possession of the range, unable to fence, lease, buy, or homestead, had only one way left to hold it: stock it to the limit. And so cattlemen and sheepmen themselves destroyed the industry. Newcomers could not be kept out altogether, and a range stocked to the limit soon became a range hopelessly overgrazed. When this point had been reached, one enemy neither the stockmen nor anyone else could lick—Montana weather—descended upon the range and blotted out the herds almost as if they had never been.

Three rivers—running west to east and throughout much of their course virtually parallel—segment Montana. Each of them has formed a boundary and a pattern for the open range, and each, like the divisions of a sundial, has recorded a period in the industry's brief life.

South of the Yellowstone was Indian country, so the early Texas herds swam that river and were bedded down on the great central Montana range between it and the Missouri. North of that meandering muddy stream was more Indian country, and cutting through it, near the Canadian border, was the Milk River. It was to be the cattleman's last frontier: when the herds crossed it, as they did in the '90's, they went to their doom on the bleak, shelterless prairie of northern Montana and southern Canada, and the story of the range had ended.

Dust hung low over the central Montana badlands of the Missouri River in the summer of 1885 as 100,000 head of cattle streamed onto that range to join the hundreds of thousands already there. President Cleveland had canceled the stockmen's leases on Indian Territory—Oklahoma—and 200,000 head had been forced onto the already overcrowded ranges of other Territories. Texans cursed. "We been votin' Democratic ever since the War between the States," one of them complained to a Montana comrade, "an' the first time we get a Democrat in as President, look what the sonofabitch does to us!"

A few of the cattlemen did more than curse: they hastened to Washington and complained directly to Cleveland. "Gentlemen," he replied imperturbably, "you have been given a certain time to get your cattle out of Indian Territory. Much of that time has now passed. I suggest that you get home and get them moving!"

Then there were the sheep. In the two or three years prior to 1885 the number of sheep in Montana trebled. Sheep first came into the Territory in the '60's, and in 1870 there were 2,000 head. Fourteen years later there were 500,000 and two years after that, almost 1,000,000. By 1893 Montana's sheep numbered 2,225,000 and by 1900 more than 3,500,000.

As this new horde of cattle and sheep moved in on them, stockmen in central Montana clamored for opening of the Indian reservation to the north, but this did not come until 1888. In the meantime, desperate operators moved thousands of head over the Missouri onto the Indian lands anyway, for there lay millions of acres which the Indians did not use, grass untouched since the buffalo had gone; and the cattle faced starvation. This move was easy for a cattleman who happened to have married an Indian woman, and there were many of these, including Granville Stuart. (But when the reservation was opened in 1888, a new law decreed that no white man could hereafter acquire any rights on Indian lands by virtue of marriage into the tribe.)

More cattle streamed across the river and north into Canada, where grouped townships could be leased. A quarter million head crossed the Missouri and the Milk, headed for this new and unfamiliar range. Some of the old-time cattlemen quit rather than cross the Milk River. "I did not like the country and would not move over there," Stuart commented tersely in his memoirs. His partner took over the herd.

So passed the mirage which had charmed and deluded the lords of the grass—the illusion of "customary range."

A Montana cattleman, riding his range one day, found a sheepherder camped upon it, with his flock. He ordered the herder to get off. Returning the next day, he found the lamb-licker still there. Again he demanded that the interloper quit his range.

The herder looked up calmly at the mounted stockman. "You own it, pardner?" he asked.

The cattleman admitted that he didn't. "But it's my range," he retorted, "and I want you off!"

The herder got up slowly, drawing a Winchester rifle from the ground as he did so.

"Listen, friend," he said quietly. "I just got out of prison after shooting one sonofabitch like you, and I'd just as soon go back for shooting another."

The cattleman rode home. "Looking into the barrel of that gun," he told this writer many years later, "you know, I realized for the first time that I didn't own that range. . . . And, by God, I didn't even have a gun on me!"

XII. SEVEN GOOD INDIANS

The Indians of North America made their last stand in Montana and just across the line in the western Canadian territories. The '70's and '80's were a savage time: nearly two full decades of guerrilla warfare in which few men died but hundreds of thousands of dollars' worth of settlers' property— their cattle, horses, and homes—disappeared. In the winter of 1880–81 Indian depredations in just two Montana counties cost the stockmen $60,000 worth of cattle.

The central Montana range, "no-man's-land" heretofore referred to, lying between two great Indian reservations, was under constant attack throughout this period by tribal war parties, embittered or encouraged by the government's criminally inconsistent Indian policy: one of brutal severity one year, maudlin sentimentality the next.

And the Indian memory is long. Perhaps in those disorderly decades the eastern Montana tribes were getting a little of their own back from Sir St. George Gore and Maj. Eugene Baker.

Sir St. George Gore was an Irish bachelor baronet who came to Montana in 1855 with a few fellow "sportsmen," some métis and Indian guides, about 40 servants, 112 horses, 24 yoke of oxen, 14 dogs, 21 carts, and 6 wagons. The caravan set out from St. Louis, wintered at Fort Laramie, Wyoming, and arrived on the Montana plains in the spring. In violation of his visitor's passport, he established a trading post in the Crow country, providing his reluctant hosts, among other things, with guns and ammunition. For two years the Irishman and his companions hunted on the prairies and in the mountains of Montana Territory.

Hunting was good. "The Indians," reported A. J. Vaughn, Indian agent, to his superior, "have been loud in their complaint at men passing through their country killing and driving off their game." And well they might have been, for Vaughn tabulates the "bag" of Sir St. George Gore, sportsman, as "105 Bears and some 2,000 buffalo, elk and deer."

Sixteen hundred of these slaughtered animals, Vaughn said, the Irish baronet admitted he had had no use for, "having killed purely for sport." "What can I do," Vaughn added, "against so large a number of men coming into a country like this so remote from civilization, doing & acting as they please, nothing I assure you beyond apprising you of the facts on paper."

When he wrote the report, Vaughn was on his way to the Crow country where St. George Gore's sporting spirit had taken its heaviest toll, and the Indian agent underscored his view of the expedition's effect upon his charges in this closing sentence:

"Should I return from the Crow country safe I will avail myself of the earliest opportunity of apprising you of all the particulars of my trip."

For the next thirty years the Crows were the most relentless and most cunning of the tribes which preyed upon the white man's herds.

At dawn one January morning in 1870, weather 40 below, Maj. Eugene Baker and his Second United States Cavalry came upon a camp of Piegan-Blackfeet on the Marias River in central Montana. Baker and his troops were hunting Mountain Chief, a hostile Piegan chief who had murdered Maj. Malcolm Clark, a retired fur company agent.

The camp which Baker discovered so suddenly that morning was that of Heavy Runner, a friendly Indian, and its lodges were full of smallpox victims, with all the able-bodied braves off on a hunt. Baker for some reason assumed, without inquiry, that it was the camp of Mountain Chief. On his order and without warning to the tepees' sick or sleeping inhabitants, the troops fired into the cluster of lodges. One hundred and seventy-three Indians died in the unprovoked slaughter; twenty more were wounded. Some histories say the first to fall was old Heavy Runner himself, who had come forward with the papers proclaiming his loyalty and friendliness to the United States Government.

The War Department ordered an "investigation" of Baker's barbarous conduct. He was exonerated by his superior officers in this inquiry.

More than a fourth of the Territory of Montana and much of Dakota and Wyoming had been ceded to the Indians in 1868. The Bozeman Trail was closed and Fort C. F. Smith, established to protect it, was abandoned. Some cattle came in over the old mining trails in western Montana but immigration virtually ceased for eight years, until the state was "reopened" after the Custer massacre. In the meantime, hundreds of white settlers in the country and dependent upon Fort C. F. Smith were forsaken; within two weeks after the treaty was signed the tribes were on the warpath, slaughtering the settlers with guns and ammunition which had been provided by the government to induce them to sign the treaty.

The Indians were scolded and a "promise" was exacted from them that they would remain on their reservations. Their new agents, mostly political appointees from the east, were supposed to be responsible for them. Maj. Martin Maginnis, the Territory's congressional delegate, thus described the agents:

They will take a barrel of sugar to an Indian tribe and get a receipt for ten barrels. For a sack of flour the Indians sign a receipt for fifty sacks. The agent will march three hundred head of cattle four times through a corral, get a receipt for twelve hundred head, give a part of them to the Indians, sell a part to a white man, and steal as many back as possible.

The Indians were well aware of the fact that they were being cheated and that their agent, representative of the great government with which they had signed a treaty, was a thief. If that was the way the white man did business, the Indian could accommodate himself to such methods; and he did so, rapidly. Besides, theft of horses was an honorable Indian pursuit and always had been. It was unreasonable, in the Indian view, to ask that the popular practice be abandoned.

Agents apparently shared this opinion, for they permitted raiding parties to leave the reservations continually, and showed no particular interest when these parties returned with greatly augmented strings of ponies, many of the additions bearing white men's brands.

Raging cattlemen demanded better military protection. An army fort had been established on the Helena-Fort Benton

Trail at Fort Shaw to protect bullion shipments from the mines, and soldiers were stationed in little groups in unfortified villages, but the stockmen's opinion of such protection can be read in Granville Stuart's diary comment upon the garrison in the town of Martinsdale:

There are thirty soldiers stationed here, and it is a good safe place for them as there are some settlers below to keep the Indians off them and the big spring roundup of cattle is commencing and there are fifty men camped here who will work down the river fifty or sixty miles, so the soldiers are reasonably well protected.

Another post was finally established, in response to the clamor, on the Missouri cattle range—Fort Maginnis at the foot of the Judith Mountains; but the exasperated cattlemen soon found that the presence of the soldiers had increased, rather than diminished, their troubles. Stuart found it convenient to have a post office and telegraph station near his ranch house, but he was no little annoyed when his best hay meadow was arbitrarily included within the military reservation, and his opinion of the troops did not change. Montana old-timers testify today to the hostility of the cattleman and cowboy toward the United States Army, and within the older generation a derisive attitude toward the federal military is still apparent.

Many army blunders contributed to this. Soldiers earned the instant enmity of the cowboys when they betrayed their utter inability to handle cattle and in their efforts to take care of the forts' beef herds stampeded those of the neighboring ranches. The arrogance with which army officers met the protests against such inefficiency alienated the cowboys' bosses, and feeling mounted when the army proved ludicrously incapable of meeting the menace of Indian raids or those of white outlaws.

In the very few instances in which troops actually recovered horses stolen by Indians and captured the culprits, the commanding officer insisted upon taking not only the thieves but also their loot to the reservation from whence the Indians had come. The astounded cattlemen pointed out that the army merely was providing a military escort for the criminals: horses or cattle, once on a reservation, were lost forever. The army brushed aside such protests, and for a time, until convinced it was futile, stockmen ran a comic race with the military; but they found that no matter how rapidly the owner got to the reservation to claim his property—no matter if he were there already, waiting when the unchastened redskins arrived with their federal bodyguard—his horses vanished before he could get his rope on them.

Nor was the social life of the forts one which would enhance their value in the eyes of grumbling neighbors. A column in the weekly *Mineral Argus*, newspaper in the mining town of Maiden near Fort Maginnis, was given over to notes on life in that cultural center. This seemed to consist largely of amateur readings, gala balls, and experiments in the drama. Occasionally a cavalryman fell off his horse; one broke his neck and there were solemn obsequies. The pretty routine was varied by visits to near-by "Whiskey Gulch"—now Gilt Edge—because Mrs. Rutherford B. Hayes, ardent dry, had prevailed upon the War Department to ban liquor from military reservations. And the routine was unaltered when an attempt was made by the Missouri badlands outlaws to hold up an army paymaster, who was saved, with the army's money, by the runaway team though the driver was shot.

The army did nothing about that, and it did nothing about the incessant raids of Indians and outlaws. The cattlemen demanded that Indian agents be instructed to cease giving permits for tribesmen to leave their reservations; the request was refused. They then demanded that troops cooped up in various forts be regularly stationed at points along the trails used by the Indians on their raiding jaunts, as a warning to the marauders and for better pursuit. This demand, too, was rejected; but the War Department notified them that they might "report" any Indians on their range known to be raiding.

"Blessed privilege," commented Granville Stuart sourly; and he recounted the plundering of one ranch and the consequences:

Buchanan rode thirty miles to Fort Maginnis and reported his losses, which required one day. The commander telegraphed to his superior officer, stationed at Fort Benton. He telegraphed to the commander of the division at Fort Shaw and he to the commander of the department of the Missouri at Fort Snelling, Minnesota. By the same roundabout way the order came to send a detachment of cavalry from Fort Maginnis after the Indians. The order was received just eight days after the cabin had been plundered and the horses driven away. Where were the Indians?

One cavalry unit, recovering thirty stolen horses, started with them, and the Indian raiders, to the reservation. Eighteen of the horses had been so hard-ridden by the Indians that they could not keep up with the grain-fed cavalry mounts. The troopers thereupon shot them and left the carcasses beside the road, although with a few days' rest, good grass, and water they could have recovered. Montanans decided, said Stuart, "that it was harder to recover their property from the military than from the original Indian thieves."

But Montanans in the '80's could not be thus put upon for long; a showdown with the army was inevitable, and it came. One day a party of Piegan raiders which had stolen sixty horses rode by accident into an army encampment and fled, leaving the horses. The army proposed to return them to the Crow reservation, though the owners, pursuing the thieves, had arrived to claim their property, and despite the fact that the raiding Indians were Piegans, not Crows.

A cavalry detachment, fully armed, set out with the sixty horses. At the Granville Stuart ranch William Cantrell, a stock detective employed by the ranchers, and two Stuart cowboys, all with Winchester rifles, intercepted the troop and demanded the horses. The lieutenant in charge refused, and Cantrell raised his rifle. The cavalry officer, though he was backed by half a dozen fully armed men, yielded up the horses instantly and took his men back to the fort.

Nothing more was ever heard of that incident. It was the last attempt of the army to hold or to return to a reservation a band of stolen horses.

Newspaper comment in those days of limited "coverage" was always terse and vigorous. There was, for instance, the tantalizing item in the *Mineral Argus:* "Fort Benton has a haunted house." Just that, and nothing more. Similarly laconic was a bit of "suburban" correspondence on November 27, 1884, which indicated how the stockmen, strictly on their own, were doing. The "Cottonwood correspondent" reported: "The Crow Indians are raiding the Musselshell for horses." Ten days later the *Argus* carried the correspondent's "follow story"—a succinct line: "There are seven good Indians on Cottonwood Creek."

Today's maps, some of them, show a gulch in the Musselshell country known as Seven Blackfoot coulee. It is reputed to have been so named because one morning in 1884 a passerby was startled to find, swinging from the branches of some cottonwoods on the coulee's slope, the bodies of seven Indians.

It is too late now to determine whether the *Argus* correspondent, who said they were Crows, or whoever named the coulee erred in their tribal designation; nor is it very important. The only thing that mattered to the cattlemen was that when last seen the seven Indians were "good."

But Sir St. George Gore and Maj. Eugene M. Baker, U. S. A., died in bed.

XIII. NINE HOLES IN RATTLESNAKE JAKE

The Missouri badlands of central Montana, now incorporated within the Fort Peck Game Reserve, constitute a spectacular, unearthly realm which remains to this day, save for uninhabitable deserts, one of the loneliest areas in the United States.

Within a few years the water backing up from the new Fort Peck Dam will flood much of this section. Few living Montanans have seen this magnificent wilderness, for few have ventured into it since the days of Missouri River steamboat travel. It is not an easy country to reach, and it is little more hospitable today than it was fifty years ago. Even the swarming homesteaders, who plunged their plows into hillsides so steep they could not harvest crops from them, did not dare to match their puny enterprise against the loneliness of the badlands, though parts of the region, more accurately designated as the Missouri "breaks," are well-watered and fertile.

Here are cliffs so sudden and precipitate that cattle, reaching for tempting clumps of grass, have tumbled hundreds of feet to death; here are hundreds of thousands of acres untenanted by man or domestic animal, and scores of townships without a town, or even a house. In the badlands' extent of more than one hundred fifty miles, there are but four roads and three of them are barely passable trails. The fourth, a fairly good auto route, crosses the river by ferry; it is the only crossing in all that lone land.

The trails are old wagon roads which get down to the river somehow—twisting along in an old water course or plunging wildly down an extended buttress of a long butte. Scrub pine, spruce, and cedar are scattered in the purple-shadowed coulees and on the hundreds of isolated hills which start up suddenly from the vast canyon floor; the sun, soon gone, rekindles briefly the centuries-old color in pre-glacial cliffs, and a distant mountain range turns violet, then black, against the blue-green sky.

Here in the Missouri "breaks" in the early '80's an organized company of renegades, ex-buffalo hunters, ex-wolfers, fugitive southern bushwhackers, murderers, and a handful of ne'er-do-wells who bore noted names in Montana, established their headquarters. So complete was their command of the area that for several years law-abiding ranchers did not dare to venture in; and so far as available records indicate, no detachment of United States troops, though one was stationed but a few miles away, ever went near it.

First settlers along the Missouri were the half-breed trappers, who feared nothing on earth. Wolves, bobcats, mountain lions, and coyotes swarmed there, and some still inhabit that country; but there were compensations. It was the best game region in Montana, and fur-bearing animals were reasonably plentiful. (Trapping never attained in Montana the dimensions as an industry that it did in other better-timbered, better-watered western states.)

Mackinaws, keelboats, and pirogues were built at the forts (trading posts) or in little shipyards along the Missouri by men who had learned their trade on the upper Great Lakes or in service of the Hudson's Bay Company. They bore heavy fur loads down the Missouri to the market at St. Louis, and until the coming of the steamships, brought traders' goods and supplies back upstream.

After the trappers came the woodchoppers, whose little yards along the river supplied fuel to the steamboats. Their life was brief and their impress upon Montana history insignificant; any able-bodied man could chop wood, and their only role in history appears to have been their frequent assassination by marauding Indians. The first steamboat reached Fort Benton in 1860; in 1880 the Utah Northern Railroad, a branch of Jay Gould's Union Pacific, entered the territory and the era of river transport had ended. The last freight to arrive by boat was unloaded at Benton in 1888.

As the woodchoppers moved out of their cabins, the wolfers moved in. In contrast to their inoffensive and undistinguished predecessors, the wolfers were perhaps the toughest lot of men the west has ever known—tougher, even, than the buffalo hunter.

Every Indian on the plains hated the wolfer and would, if he could, kill one on sight; yet it has been said that few were ever shot from the front—a tribute to their remarkable marksmanship. Indian hostility grew out of the fact that the poisoned bait left by wolfers, and their traps, killed the Indians' dogs, occasionally their ponies, and sometimes the Indians themselves. War parties would go out of their way to "get" a wolfer; and if they missed him they would steal all his possessions, including his horses, burn his cabin, even hunt out his traps and wantonly destroy the skins of the animals he had caught.

Wolf pelts became marketable in the '70's and from then until the end of the range era and the appearance of government hunters, the wolfer was a familiar figure on the plains and in the saloons of cowtowns. He was usually thin, bearded, inclined to surliness, and (if in town) drunk. "It was a hard and perilous life led by these intrepid men," Stuart declared, "but all the more attractive to them because of the dangers encountered." He continued:

They usually traveled two together for company and for greater safety . . . A good season was often very remunerative, netting from two to three thousand dollars. The money rarely did him much good, as the wolfer usually came to a trading post, disposed of his skins, and then joined in a wild carousal, drinking and gambling until the money was all gone.

The Territory adopted bounty laws in the '80's, offering first $1 and then $2 a head but adding, with characteristic Montana fiscal recklessness, a nickel for each gopher. Children quit school and ranch hands quit work to trap gophers; thousands were turned in, the Territory could not pay and the law had to be repealed. Wolf depredations increased immediately, but this was attributable in part to the fact that settlement had begun in Assiniboia, now southern Saskatchewan, and the wolves were being driven south into the Montana badlands.

A state bounty law was passed in 1895, providing for payment of $3 a head. In the six months of that year in which the law was effective 3,000 wolves and nearly 12,000 coyotes were killed. In 1899 the legislature increased the bounty on wolves to $5; about 6,000 wolves and 22,000 coyotes were killed. The toll of the gray killers continued, however, to be serious; in 1905 the wolf bounty was doubled and in 1911 raised to $15.

There were enough wolves left in the second decade of this century to harass homesteaders considerably, but today they

have been virtually exterminated, chiefly through the efforts
of federal hunters employed by the Biological Survey. The
last of the great wolf raiders were Old Snowdrift and his mate,
Lady Snowdrift, whose prowess and cunning were such that
they earned Montanans' grudging admiration. In 1921 Stacy
Eckert, a forest ranger, found their den and took seven pup-
pies, one of which he trained and which later, as Lady Silver,
appeared in the movies with the famous dog Strongheart. In
the next two years, Don Stevens, a government hunter who
became a newspaper man and this writer's boss, killed Snowdrift and his mate. The male was the largest wolf ever killed
in central Montana.

The effectiveness of government hunters indicated that
there was some basis for the criticism of the wolfers on the
ground of tenderness toward their quarry—and an eye to
business. The bounty law grew out of the discovery that as
long as the sale of wolf pelts was the only reward, wolfers were
inclined to spare the pups to be sure of a continuing livelihood. Cattlemen, however, who bought staghounds and
hunted down the marauders, felt no tenderness toward the
whelps; a slaughter with six-shooters when a den was found
was a cowboy sport.

Rocky Point, Montana, was a wolfers' town, a cluster of
adobe-chinked log huts on a high bluff above the Missouri.
Along with near-by Carroll, it had flourished briefly in the
'70's while an effort was under way to make Carroll a rival of
Fort Benton as head of navigation on the Missouri: seventy
miles east of Benton, its use would have avoided navigation of
a shallow and tricky channel and lengthened the shipping
season. But Fort Benton was too well entrenched; although a
good trail was established from Carroll to the gold camps and
Fort Maginnis erected to protect the route, the new town
languished.

Probably at no time did Rocky Point's population exceed
seventy-five, but the community was a popular hangout for
wolfers, trappers, and the furtive vagrants of Indian country
—for just across the river was the great northern Montana
reservation. In the badlands coulees near the village were the
log cabins and dugouts of traders of illicit whisky for the
Indians; in Rocky Point itself there was a "hotel," where

meals could be obtained, a trading post, and a saloon or two.

Never a very nice town, Rocky Point's character changed markedly for the worse as Missouri River navigation dwindled. Gradually the little cabins in the lost coulees began to be taken over by a new class of men, and in the saloons of Rocky Point and a couple of other badlands settlements devious plots were hatched.

These men were cattle rustlers and horse thieves. Unlike such gentry in other western states, the Missouri badlands company were organized, tough, efficient, and courageous. Their operations in the early '80's had grown to where they covered portions of three Territories—Montana, Wyoming, and Dakota—and extended into southern Canada. Their raids (mostly upon horse herds, for horses were readily marketable, could be moved more swiftly, and handled more easily) were not haphazard affairs for individual enrichment but strategic excursions for the common gain, usually based upon information acquired from sympathizers or hirelings in respectable trading centers such as Fort Benton.

Their tactics were straightforward and effective. There was no bribing of peace officers or collusion with dishonest ranch foremen, as in the modern western movie; instead there were swift night raids and withdrawal to the shadowed badlands, wherein there were no peace officers and where ranch foremen dared not venture. There, in corrals deep within secret canyons, brands were "blotted," weary horses conditioned, and the stolen herds shuffled so as to make recognition more difficult. Night drives followed: Montana horses to Dakota, Dakota horses to Wyoming, Wyoming horses, smuggled up through the Yellowstone badlands, to Canada; Canadian horses (including some bearing the royal brand VR) to Montana. . . .

There is no way today to determine the toll of these relentless raiders, save in the memoirs of old-timers and in the newspaper reports of their attacks. Granville Stuart speaks of the loss, while he was absent on roundup, of a valuable stallion and a number of other horses, none ever seen again; and of 24 beef steers slaughtered by the rustlers and left to rot in a coulee when their scouts reported a cowboys' camp between them and their objective.

There are frequent references in newspapers to loss of 10

to 12 head from the big strings of major range operators; in some instances 30 or 40 head, a small rancher's whole string, would vanish in a single raid.

At first the ranchers could determine easily whether their losses were attributable to Indian or white thieves. Indian horses were all unshod, whereas usually some of the outlaws' mounts had shoes; Indians raided in large parties and left many tracks, the whites split up and moved in very small groups. Soon, however, the white rustlers learned of this checkup and modeled their operations on those of the tribes, further complicating the problem for the vengeful cattlemen.

By 1883 the situation had become intolerable. In addition to the mounting horse thefts, cattle losses on the Montana range to rustlers alone were approximating 5 per cent annually; and cattle and horses on this range were worth $35,000,000.

Stockmen attempted to persuade the territorial legislature to pass a bill providing for inspection of brands and registration of all cattle and horses driven out of the state, and establishing other safeguards. The bill failed, partially because of the hostile attitude of Governor Crosby, a New Yorker, who according to Stuart was "a delightful person to meet socially [but] . . . had spent most of his life on the staff of various generals of the army and in Europe and was entirely out of harmony with his surroundings in Montana and unfamiliar with . . . the needs of the Territory."

There was clamor at the meeting of the Montana Stockgrowers' Association in the spring of 1884 for direct action. Stuart warned that the outlaws were intelligent and ruthless and their badlands strongholds were fortresses. He and some other cool heads counseled caution and succeeded in preventing an outright declaration by the association in favor of lynch law. In view of what later occurred, this action by Stuart, who was one of the chief sufferers from the rustlers' depredations, undoubtedly was intended merely to keep the association itself "in the clear." This association included in its membership Theodore Roosevelt, ranching in North Dakota; Russell B. Harrison, son of a subsequent President of the United States; and the Marquis de Mores, French nobleman who established a packing plant at Medora, N. D. Roosevelt and the Marquis, said Stuart, were all for "cleaning the rustlers out."

Stuart's foresight saved the association from the disgrace which befell the Wyoming cattlemen's organization as a result of its role in the Johnson County war of 1892. Two days after the Wyoming association ended its convention that year, a trainload of gunmen and operators of big cattle spreads headed north from Cheyenne to "clean out the rustlers" in Johnson County—climaxing a long battle over range between big and little ranchers. At Casper they left their special train and rode on, and surrounding the K C ranch (where the post office of Kaycee, Wyo., is now located) they trapped and killed two of the alleged rustlers. A passing rancher, however, had spread the alarm and two hundred Johnson County farmers and small ranchers rode to the attack. They outnumbered the "invaders" four to one and had them hopelessly besieged on a friendly ranch when troops summoned by the governor arrived to end the "war." One of the "invaders" had been killed and three wounded. They were escorted back to Cheyenne and indicted but never tried.

Apparent failure of the Montana association to act in 1884, however, encouraged the badlands outlaws. In the month following the meeting, when most cattlemen were absent from the ranch houses on spring roundup, the rustlers combed the country and filled their corrals with stolen horses. So Stuart called a meeting at his ranch near Gilt Edge which was attended by stockmen, their most trusted cowboys, and the stock detectives employed by the association. No memoir tells what transpired at this conference, but from it emerged a determined little company which came to be known as "Stuart's Stranglers." Stuart himself preferred to call it a "Vigilance Committee." It had fourteen members.

It was months before news of the "Stranglers'" campaign was taken seriously in the Territory; by then the campaign was over. Weeks more passed before word of it reached "outside"; newspaper treatment of the story was in inverse ratio to the journal's distance from the scene: thus the tale was deprecated in the *Mineral Argus,* published a few miles away, and "played up" in Calgary, Alberta, hundreds of miles north. The *Argus* did its best, however, to report the engagements in the little war; it was handicapped severely by the disinclination of the participants toward publicity and the hostility of both sides toward war correspondents. Also it editorial-ized vigorously: "The most speedy and safe cure is to hang them [horse thieves] as fast as captured."

A few days after the meeting in Stuart's home, a rancher who had attended it caught two rustlers red-handed running off seven horses belonging to his neighbor. One of the outlaws fired at the cattleman, and strangely enough missed— this mishap was blamed on a plunging horse. He was promptly shot dead by the rancher, and his companion was captured and put in a stable "under guard." That night the "guard" was overpowered, the horse thief removed by a posse of Stranglers and hanged. On his coat was hung a card with a simple legend: "Horse Thief."

The badlands colony was not immediately alarmed; frequently isolated members of their tough company had run afoul of little bands of cowboys and had played out their hands at the end of a rope. But six days later another of their number was caught, allegedly with two stolen horses in his possession, taken to the Stuart ranch and held overnight, and hanged at dawn. Again a card on the victim's coat read "Horse Thief." This was Sam McKenzie, half-breed ex-wolfer accused of being one of the fastest and cleverest of the badlands bravoes; in addition he was described as "refined" in appearance, handsome, and silent. Sam's friends began to sit up and take notice.

The next engagement brought the war out into the open, somewhat to the chagrin of both factions; and the Stranglers themselves were not officially in on the kill. It was the most spectacular incident of the whole range period in Montana and has not been accorded the place in western history it deserves. It made the eastern newspapers, however, and is still commemorated by an occasional celebration in Lewistown, scene of its occurrence. The celebration is called, accurately, "The Shooting of Rattlesnake Jake."

"Rattlesnake Jake" Fallon and "Long-haired" Owens were wanted in half a dozen towns in at least four Territories. Notorious as rustlers throughout the northwest, they were suspected of being killers as well; and in appearance they were badmen so bad that they could fit only into the pattern of the earliest movie serials: no modern producer, fantastic as some western extravaganzas may be, would believe them. Today's film fanciers, viewing westerns cynically or not at all, or else educated to the belief that desperadoes are good-hearted fumbling Wallace Beerys, would dismiss these two as absurdly overdrawn, as caricatures. They were overdrawn, and so was their finish. . . . It was bad theater, but it packed a punch.

Owens' dirty, unkempt black hair hung down over small, shifty, green-gray eyes. Rattlesnake, according to Granville Stuart, "was not quite so evil-looking as his pal, although he was far from prepossessing." Stuart saw the men camped the evening of July 3, 1884, near a neighbor's ranch, and reported to his "boys." The Stranglers decided the pair planned a raid on the neighbor's horse herd while he attended Lewistown's Independence Day celebration, and set out to get them.

The outlaws had decided to spend a few hours in Lewistown too before getting to work, so the Stranglers trailed them there. Rattlesnake and his pal were more than just armed: they were virtually commissioned like men-of-war. Each had two .44 Colt frontier model six-shooters and a hunting knife in his belt, and each carried a Winchester rifle. Thus burdened but not seeming to mind it, they stalked clanking into Crowley's saloon and had a few drinks. (If Montana range town tradition has not changed, about every third drink was on the house; their "few" were probably a dozen, "straight" of course).

Leaving the saloon, the desperadoes mounted and rode to the race track. They bet heavily on the last race, and lost. Their dispositions, never too good, thereupon took a sudden turn for the worse; and at this inauspicious moment a parade participant named Bob Jackson who was dressed in the costume of Uncle Sam chose to walk past them.

For some unaccountable reason, reported Granville Stuart, Jackson's appearance was offensive to Owens. Perhaps, like many a rebel and anarchist westerner, he was annoyed on principle when he saw a symbol of government. At any rate, he tapped Jackson on the head with the butt of a six-shooter, and Uncle Sam sat down.

Owens then turned his gun around and amused himself and Jake (and apparently some like-minded spectators, for no one interfered) by forcing Jackson to grovel and crawl in the dust like a snake, dirtying his costume. Tiring of this, Owens suggested to his partner that they clean out the town, and the two rode back to the business district firing their guns in the air.

Up to this time the Stranglers who had trailed the pair to Lewistown had not interfered. They had been instructed to shun public brawls, and probably they were hoping that their quarry would soon recall the waiting horse herd and get out of town. Then things began to happen so quickly that the whole incident was taken out of the Stranglers' hands.

Owens and Jake, who had stopped in Crowley's for a few more drinks, swaggered into the street with guns in hands and prepared to mount their horses. Jake dropped quickly into his saddle, but Owens saw a Lewistown citizen named Joe Doney standing in the strangely deserted street watching them; and for some reason he began to walk toward Doney, a pistol in his hand. Doney, no man to take chances, pulled a .22 revolver from his pocket and fired twice, wounding "Long-haired" in the stomach and the hand. He retreated into a store as Owens, despite his wounds, picked up the gun he had dropped and returned the fire.

The store was full of men who had come from the race track or from the street and armed themselves with the merchant's stock of Winchesters. They began shooting at Owens, and, mortally wounded, he staggered up the street toward Jake. The latter was having his own troubles; he was still mounted, but a rifle shot from the saloon, where some marksmen had also taken up positions, had struck him in the side.

Rattlesnake Jake saw that his pal would not be able to reach him. Now it has been said of many a desperado that he would risk his life, or give it, for his comrade; and many of these legends have been debunked. . . . But Jake did it. He turned his horse and rode back into the stream of bullets coming now from both sides of the street, and dismounted beside Owens.

It was now apparent that both men were fatally hurt, but the firing continued and was answered, shot for shot. The outlaws stood in the middle of the street, with no shelter, directly in front of a tent which had been set up for the Fourth of July by an itinerant photographer. (After the battle was over he got one of the greatest news picture scoops of his generation.)

Calmly the rustlers fired, reloaded, fired. "They's so much

lead in 'em they can't tip over," said one of the citizen rifle-men.

Two foolhardy young men attempted to cross the street; Jake dropped them both instantly, one grazed in the head and little hurt, the other dead with a bullet in his brain. (Jake was following an old frontier custom, shooting for the head.)

Owens, on his knees and crumpling fast, let go his pistols and reached for his rifle. A bullet got him in the head and he dropped; at the same instant a slug tore into Jake's chest and he, too, went down. The citizens then ceased firing, but the two outlaws pulled their triggers as long as life lasted, firing into the dirt for a minute or two.

Marveling townspeople surrounded the bodies and peered at the wounds—nine in Rattlesnake Jake, eleven in Long-haired Owens. An inquest was held on the spot, the some-what hysterical photographer took their pictures, and the pair were promptly and unceremoniously buried.

Few today would grudge the badmen the measure of im-mortality afforded them by Lewistown's celebration. Two brave men who finished with their boots on set a mark for their criminal comrades to shoot at.

Events moved swiftly now; the Stranglers decided the time had come for the cleanup. The night of that same July Fourth they called upon Billy Downs, who was "holed up" in a cabin at the mouth of the Musselshell with another outlaw suspect known as California Ed. Twenty-six stolen horses were in Billy's corral, and in his stable was found a stack of fresh hides bearing the brand of a prominent cowman. Billy and his partner, taken by surprise, offered no resistance. They were escorted to a near-by clump of cottonwood trees and hanged.

There was danger now that delay would permit the alarmed rustler gang to become too well prepared, or even to flee; so the night of July 7, after a strategy conference at the Stuart ranch, the Stranglers rode for the first time into the badlands.

At a woodyard on Bates' Point, Missouri River, fifteen miles east of the mouth of the Musselshell, there lived an old man named James with his two sons. This isolated camp was a favorite hideout of the horse thieves and served as headquarters for one John Stringer, reputed captain of the band. "Stringer Jack" was young, tall, very good-looking, and in the words of his most implacable enemy, Granville Stuart, had "a pleasing personality."

Nine Stranglers, according to Stuart (other sources put the figure as high as twenty) laid siege to this rendezvous. Although both sides must have expected this engagement, neither, apparently, made the proper strategic preparations. Stringer Jack had called a conference of his men but had not anticipated attack so quickly and had failed to post guards; he had never needed guards before. His foes were not sufficiently familiar with the layout of his place and failed to make ample provision for "covering" the whole establishment.

The Stranglers came in sight of the woodyard before dawn and took up their positions. Before them lay a cabin, a large log barn, a pole corral connecting the two buildings, a couple of ramshackle outhouses, and—nearly a hundred yards from the cabin—a wall tent built of poles and wagon sheets (tarpaulins). The Stranglers assigned only three men to this tent —a mistake, though it cost the attackers no lives.

Shortly after sunrise old man James emerged from his cabin, unarmed. A Vigilante rose from his hiding place and demanded that James open his corral, drive out the horses it contained, and surrender himself to the besiegers. He opened the corral but instead of surrendering, made a break for the cabin. He was fired on but not hit, and got inside. Now from portholes which had been cut in the cabin walls on all sides came a defiant volley of rifle fire.

Stranglers who had stood up to watch the fun took cover quickly and answered the fire. They had no way of knowing how many men the cabin contained (there were five—James, his two sons, two others) but they knew them to be good marksmen.

This type of siege was hopeless, but the firing continued. Meanwhile the three men left to guard the tent found themselves in serious trouble as its occupants spilled out, shooting as they came—and there were six of them. The Stranglers, however, had the advantage of the higher position and escaped unwounded, dropping behind a natural breastwork while the outlaws tried to get into heavy brush.

One of the men who had been in the tent was Stringer Jack. As he made a break from the bushes, seeking a better vantage point from which to sight his attackers, he was killed. Another of this group was Dixie Burr, son of one of the army road engineers who had accompanied Captain Mullan on his trail-breaking expedition to Montana in the '50's, and nephew of Granville Stuart. He was wounded but made it to an abandoned well and hid until dark, when with three others, two of them wounded, he escaped downriver on a raft.

The siege of the cabin continued most of the day. Finally, after several attempts, two Stranglers succeeded in setting fire to it and its five defenders died in the flames, perhaps of their wounds or perhaps by their own hands. None of the Stranglers was killed and none seriously wounded.

One man, Paddy Rose, who had been in the tent, concealed himself in a coulee and after dark made his escape, wounded, on horseback. He reached Fort Benton; he also was a member of a prominent family and in the river city obtained treatment for his wound and was helped to reach Canada.

But four men had escaped downriver, and the Stranglers were determined that they should be caught. The United States cavalry, which all this time had been shooting at its tin Indian targets on the parade ground at Fort Maginnis, was appealed to. After all, these men, or some of them, had been implicated in the attempted holdup of the army paymaster. The fort's telegraph facilities broadcast the fugitives' descriptions, and at Poplar Creek Indian agency, about two hundred miles east on the Missouri, the fugitives were picked up by Indian police.

A deputy United States marshal set out to get them, after recruiting a posse in the neighborhood of Fort Maginnis and therefore, oddly enough, from among the membership of the Stranglers. The marshal and his posse returned to report solemnly that they had been overpowered by a masked band at the mouth of the Musselshell and that their prisoners had been taken from them, hung from a log placed between two cabins with an end resting on each roof, and cabins, log, and bodies burned.

Said the *Mineral Argus* curtly: "Eastern Montana is rapidly reducing the number of horse thieves."

About 300 head of stolen horses were recovered by the Stranglers in a couple of months. James' corral at Bates' Point alone had held more than 160 head when the Stranglers' final attack was staged. After Stuart and his neighbors had taken their own horses out of this bunch, the 69 remaining head were held at Stuart's ranch and he advertised for their owners to come and identify them. The "Vigilance Committee" quietly dissolved.

Estimates of the number of men killed in the cleanup of horse thieves vary from 19 to 75. Interviewed by a newspaper in Calgary, Alberta, F. S. Stimson, manager of the Northwest Ranch Co., reported 38 men had been killed. Stock prospects in the Musselshell country had improved remarkably as a result, he said. "Some recently elected deputy sheriffs are raising a howl about it, but the general opinion is that as far as stock interests are concerned, the hanging was a great success."

The *Mineral Argus,* deploring wild rumors, thought even 17 was "placing the number [of victims] a little too high." However, it held that the campaign had succeeded. "Infrequent report of losses of late is tangible evidence of the horse thieves' exodus to healthier climes. Suspicious looking parties have been seen descending the Missouri in small boats and adopting other means of flight."

Other Montana papers took up the cudgels for the stockmen as criticism of their extra-legal tactics grew. (Montana had gone a long ways from its Vigilante period.) Thus the *Rocky Mountain Husbandman,* speaking of "the severe measures adopted recently by the stockmen of eastern Meagher county," defended the Stranglers earnestly:

They were the most efficient and thoroughly organized band of thieves that has probably ever existed in the west . . . Mob law is certainly to be abhorred, yet when we consider the great annoyances that the people have been subjected to, we cannot censure them for thus summarily dealing out justice without awaiting the inefficient, slow action of the law.

Less than a month later the *Husbandman* went still further, calling upon citizens who had not participated in the campaign to dig into their pockets and help pay for the costs:

To carry on this campaign, which has occupied the entire summer, has necessitated a great deal of privation and the endurance of many hardships, sleepless nights, living on half rations, swimming streams, etc., and has cost from $3,000 to $5,000 in cash, and since every stockman in the Territory has benefited, all should contribute something toward reimbursing the men who have furnished the money . . .

The article went on to rebuke sentimentalists who protested the summary elimination of the outlaws, and insisted the campaign was not a "wild, misdirected raid governed by the caprice of cowboys." Some concern was noted lest "people residing in the States" get a wrong impression because they might have read how cowboys "sometimes enter a peaceful community and paint the town red."

Nevertheless, the critics would not be stilled, and their outcries were encouraged, undoubtedly, by interests hostile to the stockmen—particularly the miners who had been warring with the range interests for political supremacy.

Stuart, who had expected criticism, appears to have been wisely silent, waiting for the tumult to subside. A rival range operator, James Fergus, at first took it as a joke. Arriving in Helena in the fall of 1884, he was quizzed by reporters about the cleanup, and was quoted by them as saying he had persuaded his neighbor Stuart to send his cowboys to shoot Democrats and thus enable him to bring about his own election to the territorial legislature. (Fergus was a Republican, Stuart a Democrat.) "They got rid of 22 before I left and probably have got rid of the other 18 [the county had a Democratic majority of 40] by this time," said Fergus. "When Granville found out what he had done he was taken sick and is still sick and I don't think he'll ever come out of it." Stuart was, as a matter of fact, ill at the time of what the *Mineral Argus* called "mental exhaustion."

Fergus was sharply criticized by the *Mineral Argus* in his home territory for his ill-advised joke; the *Argus* and its subscribers were beginning to squirm. "If this is the way a sojourn in Helena affects Mr. Fergus's idea of wit," the paper commented angrily, "he had better come home."

Fergus soon found, too, that it was no joke. A couple of months later he issued the most sharply worded statement of any to come out of the "horse thief war," detailing the stockmen's troubles with distant and dilatory courts in which offenders, after being hauled two hundred miles, were acquitted for lack of vigorous prosecution or failure to obtain witnesses, and concluding with a threat:

Sympathizers who are more or less "tarred with the same stick" will be watched and their names placed on record. It would be well for such to understand that the hanging, etc., of horse thieves has not been done by bands of lawless cowboys, but was the result of a general understanding among all the large cattle ranges of Montana.

Stuart, who despite Fergus' jocular prediction had recovered his health, probably wished his neighbor would shut up. This statement of Fergus' was the first to disclose the fact that the campaign grew out of an agreement among the cattlemen and was not, as had been supposed, a spontaneous uprising of exasperated operators on the Musselshell range.

Nevertheless, the next Montana legislature adopted the inspection measures which had been demanded by the cattlemen. Criticism of their action persisted; in later years there were a few shootings when the epithet "Strangler" was hurled at some participant in the campaign. But the Missouri badlands were rid of desperadoes.

One man who participated in some of the Stranglers' councils, though he was then only a boy, is still living (1943). He is Charley Stuart, half-breed son of Granville, and his country is still the badlands.

Granville Stuart, for all that he led the bloody war against the horse thieves, was a person of refinement and taste. His ranch house library contained some three thousand books and the important current magazines and newspapers, and his home was an outpost of culture in a wilderness. He treated his Indian wife with respect and generosity until her death. After his retirement from ranching he became state land agent, then for a time special United States minister to Paraguay and Uruguay. When he died in 1918 he was Butte's city librarian.

Stuart insisted, years after the "war," that the Stranglers killed no innocent men. Some old-timers think, however, that a few "toughs" who consorted with rustlers but were not actually guilty themselves were caught. There is a story that a half-breed boy, skilled as are so many of his people on the fiddle, was forced to play all evening for the entertainment of the Stranglers and coolly hanged next day. "What of it?" asked the veteran who told this tale. "His being a fiddler hadn't nothing to do with his being a horse thief!"

The Musselshell-Missouri cleanup was only one of several; the pattern was repeated throughout the Territory during the range era, but on a smaller scale. Turbulent Miles City on the Yellowstone decided one night in 1883, after an undesirable character had insulted a woman on the street, that it had stood for enough. The offender was hanged by a quickly formed party of Vigilantes. Whereupon—the same night—an entire block of Miles City business buildings was burned to the ground by enraged comrades of the victim. Miles City's Vigilantes, who had gone home to bed only to be wakened to fight the fire, reorganized in the morning and ran every undesirable out of town—what town there was left.

Looking back on it all some years later, a Miles City newspaper, the *Yellowstone Journal,* summed it up: "With such a community as we had, arrest and punishment for ordinary and usual misdemeanors would have necessitated continuous sessions of courts and vastly increased jail facilities." Under those circumstances, there was of course nothing to be done until the limit of tolerance had been reached. Then the more "law-abiding" folk could always take matters in their own hands and get rid of the bad men. . . .

But that wasn't always easy. Rattlesnake Jake and his kind were pioneers, too—just as much as gentleman Granville Stuart. And there's an unprintable song still extant in Montana having to do with the hardiness of pioneers.

XIV. HOW TO GET RICH ON THE PLAINS

America's robber barons, with the help of costly public relations counsel, finally mastered a technique of propaganda with which to conceal the profit motive in their undertakings. This was not true in the golden age of the trail herds.

On the western range was wealth for the taking, and nobody made any bones about it, least of all the authors of some of the most enthusiastic "promotional literature" ever written, chief among them Gen. James S. Brisbin. His book, *The Beef Bonanza, or How To Get Rich on the Plains,* came off Lippincott's presses in 1881. It was an invitation to high, wide, and handsome looting of a virgin empire.

"I believe," Brisbin wrote, "that all the flocks and herds in the world could find ample pasturage on these unoccupied plains [of Montana] and the mountain slopes beyond." He was wrong about that; but he wasn't the only one. His subsequent conclusion was accurate enough: "The time is not far distant when the largest flocks and herds will be found right here, where the grass grows and ripens untouched from one year's end to another. . . . Montana has undoubtedly the best grazing grounds in America."

His was but one of several volumes which appeared at about the same time and spurred on the "beef rush" to Montana. Questionable motives produced some of these works, their authors having land to sell or some other pecuniary end in view, but Brisbin apparently was driven only by his overpowering desire to tell the world, and especially young men, of this new bonanza—and, incidentally, to sell a book.

His work is crammed with case histories, apparently authentic but of brief duration. His survey of the Territory's possibilities happened to have coincided (as have so many others, unhappily) with a transitory period of good weather. The book appeared on the eve of the first disastrous winter of the range era. There is in it hardly any mention of the tremendous risks which had to be faced by any reader who would venture to "get rich on the plains."

Brisbin cited figures to show that a $100,000 investment

could be doubled "easily" in five years, paying meanwhile an annual dividend of 10 per cent. He reproduced letters from ranchers: one advised his brother that an initial investment of $3,060 would grow to $100,000 in eleven years and estimated starting costs—Studebaker wagon, $100; two yoke of oxen, $150; wages for an Indian herder, $10 a month, and so on. The grass, it was pointed out, was free.

No one denied, not even Brisbin, that the beef business took some capital. Thus it differed from the gold rush; and it attracted a different class of men. Paradoxically, considering the frankly selfish arguments which lured the cattlemen to Montana, little of the outside exploitation which is a theme of this book can be charged to them, or to the sheep raisers. They were for the most part "pilgrims" who remained and were "made into hands." Absentee corporate operation was attempted, it is true, but it failed; after the purifying cataclysm of 1886–87 the remaining big outfits were predominantly of western origin, their owners Texans, Nebraskans, or Coloradans, if not Montanans.

It is hard to say what kept these men in Montana, when so many others had made their cleanup and departed; but the satisfactions of a free and adventurous life certainly cannot be overlooked.

These were genuine. A good deal of rubbish has been written about the era of the open range, but it was truly a time of valiant men, men of all kinds but sharing that one outstanding characteristic. There were men like "Prairie Dog" Arnold, about whom the north country is rich in stories. Arnold came west as a young man, was painlessly separated from his bank roll by card sharpers, and found himself broke in a strange town. He could have wired home for money; instead he snared prairie dogs, put them in cardboard boxes (nobody had ever thought of this), and sold them as "pets" to the first tourists, gullible then as now. Ultimately he became a prosperous rancher, and always took the trail with his riders. One evening he recommended a certain camping place to his crew because of its good spring. One of his boys went to the spring and returned on the run, howling. "There's an Indian's head in that spring!" he complained. "Damn it," said Arnold—an insatiable collector of Indian relics—"I forgot about that head; I put it in the spring last year to peel it and intended to get it out before you boys showed up."

There were men like Pierre Wibaux, member of a wealthy French textile family. He came to Montana in 1883 to start in the cattle business, and made his home in a dugout in a cliff. A year later he brought his bride from New York to a sod hut; there they ate their first holiday dinner together resplendent in full evening dress. The disaster of 1886–87 all but wiped him out, but Wibaux went to France for capital, got it, and started again. He lived to see his herds, "actual tally," number 75,000 head. The community in which he settled was originally given the inelegant name of Mingusville, for its first citizens, Min and Gus; it is now Wibaux. For a time it was the greatest livestock primary shipping point in the west. Near it now, atop a prairie knoll, is a statue of Pierre, who provided in his will that this image should be erected "to overlook the country I love so well."

These men did not shrink from hardship and hard work. On the other hand, they didn't believe in being too fussy about their living conditions. Bill Skelton, first rancher on the Judith, was credited with discovery of a method of sealing one's cabin against the cold without the drudgery of chinking the spaces between the logs with mud. In the summer, Bill found, the draft through the cracks was not unpleasant. As soon as it got cold enough to annoy him, Bill went outside and threw snow into the cracks, then went indoors and built up a roaring fire. As the snow began to melt, Bill let the fire go out and, presto!, ice sealed the open spaces. It worked very well, Bill found, so long as he was careful to adjust the intensity of his fire to the degree of coldness outside.

Old-timers recall Bob Chesnut, who died with a bitter grudge against the government because, although he was the first settler and postmaster in Chestnut Valley, he never could persuade the Postmaster General to spell it right— without the first "t." Bob was reputed to have been a member of Quantrell's bushwhacker troop and to have participated in murderous raids in Kansas; but that didn't temper his insistence upon his rights as a pioneer.

There were scores of others about whose past the less said the better. Numerous fugitives from both sides in Wyoming's

"Johnson County war" drifted north into hospitable, unques-
tioning Montana, guns in their belts. This was in the '90's,
when few Montanans carried guns in town, and the holstered
six-shooter became the mark of a Johnson county veteran—
a bitter, vindictive small rancher, or a gunman who had served
the big cattlemen in that angry contest. Montana legend has
it that within a decade most of these fugitives killed each
other off in barroom brawls or prairie ambushes.

There were a lot of Missourians, Ozark people. Among
these were the Currys, who produced one of the west's most
spectacular outlaws—"the Kid." On July 3, 1901, soon after
he had murdered Pike Landusky, saloonkeeper and deputy
sheriff, to avenge his imprisonment for a minor offense, Kid
Curry and his gang held up a Great Northern passenger train
near Malta, Mont., and escaped with $80,000, mostly in new,
unsigned currency. They hurried to Great Falls, where the
Kid summoned an acquaintance, now a prominent Great
Falls citizen, and asked him to have signatures forged to the
currency, promising "any amount of it" in return for the
service. The Great Falls man refused and fled from the Kid's
room, but he did not inform upon him, though a reward of
$25,000 was posted. The Kid was caught and jailed in Knox-
ville, Tenn., a year later for murdering a policeman, but he
escaped and was never recaptured. Despite the price on his
head he returned to Montana and the editor of the *Great Falls
Leader* received one day—in the mail—a "special" from that
newspaper's correspondent at Malta: "Kid Curry was visiting
here last week."

The Kid moved on, finally, to Patagonia in South America.
There one of the Coburns, operators of the big Circle C outfit, was said to have visited him several years later. Some
stories say the Kid died there; one Montana friend of the
outlaw says he died in Denver. Others insist he still lives.

Even outlaws and killers like the Kid could claim sanc-
tuary and the privileges of traditional Montana hospitality.
The difficulty and occasional dangers of travel made hospitality a cardinal obligation—and sometimes disastrously expensive. Unfortunate was the rancher whose place lay approximately halfway between another range settlement and a
trading post: he had many overnight guests whom he had to

feed. Seldom was anyone, known or unknown, turned away; and though the host might have his doubts about some of his guests, he would ask no questions and mind his own business.

Sometimes the code was violated, however. A group of cowboys stopped one night at a ranch on Rock Creek, expecting to be asked to remain, but the owner said he could not accommodate them and sent them on to the next place— twenty miles away. The cowboys rode off, but returned immediately and scrawled on the rancher's door the purported "Vigilante" sign—"3-7-77" (dimensions of a grave). The next day the inhospitable rancher turned his place over to his son and quit the country.

Distance from the trading centers made neighborliness imperative. There was frequent borrowing from ranch to ranch and the borrowed articles were nearly always returned. Handshakes sealed deals—it was often years thereafter before the principals took the time to make court records of their transaction. The validity of the word was taken as a matter of course, even among outlaws and prostitutes. The latter frequently staked a "busted" cowboy to a new outfit, and few cowboys would cheat a whore. One who did was blacklisted all over the west and the others who had ridden with the same outfit dug into their own pockets to repay his debt.

The difficulties of travel also gave the towns a certain unstable character, like that of a periodic drunkard. They would lie seemingly asleep for months, then burst into sudden metropolitan activity with the arrival of a roundup outfit or a group of ranchers, bent on spending. Stockmen and their wives went to town only two or three times a year, usually with two or more wagons tied together and drawn by four-horse or six-horse teams. Then they would stock up for months. The trip seldom took less than two or three days, so the first day after arrival in town was spent by the men in "relaxation" and the second in recovery from it. Unless he had brought his wife, the cattleman usually forgot or tired of looking for some of the "women's stuff," and this, one old-timer recalled, gave her a topic of conversation for several weeks after his return. The principal items were always clothing, groceries, tools and harness, and medicines.

Included in the groceries was canned milk. Hilarious stories have come down from these years, before the ranchers finally surrendered to their womenfolk's demands and provided milk cows. (Some haven't surrendered yet.) In the meantime there were occasional, seldom successful, efforts to get milk from range cattle. Sam Remington, newspaper man and former rancher, has told of one such incident:

My wife said we had to have fresh milk for her sister's baby so we went out and milked the meekest range cow we had. That milk was no good; the darned baby wouldn't drink it. So we tried the next meekest cow; the milk was O.K. but it took five men to catch her, throw her, hogtie her and milk her—and then we only got about a half a pint. This went on, with the boys stalking the cows like deer, until it got so that any cow on the place, seeing a man, would stick her tail up in the air and run like hell for the woods.

After the milk cows came, the wives dropped their loops on the cowboys again and made them do the churning—an indignity which was bitterly resented and which gave rise to ingenious stratagems such as the rodeo method described by Remington:

We rinsed out a two-gallon whisky keg, funneled the cream into it and tied the keg on a horse behind the saddle. One of the boys got on and rode hell-for-leather for a little while, and by Gosh we had butter! We had forgot, though, about getting it out; so we had to saw a door in the keg. That first batch had some sawdust in it. We used the same system, same keg, for quite some time. Then one summer day the hot sun got to working and the damn keg blew up and plastered the rider and the horse with foaming cream. The women made a fuss after that and we had to quit. It had got kind of hard to catch a horse for churning, too.

The towns which served these ranchers were neither moral nor cultured, though one of them did have a Franklin Literary Society. Fort Benton's sidewalks were at times so thickly carpeted with discarded playing cards that it was difficult to see the wood planking. This historic village and others were frequently "shot up" by cowboys in for a carouse, but little damage was done and the deliberate vandalism which eastern visitors blamed on the cowboys usually was the work of outlaws or criminals.

When roundup was over, the towns went on their spree. Cowboys bought new outfits for the dances and the women got out their tight-waisted dresses with bustles, puffed sleeves, and floor-length, full-gathered skirts over two ruffled, lace-trimmed petticoats. No girl dared refuse to dance with a cowboy; it was a deadly insult. The music was usually provided by a reed organ or piano and a violin, and the musicians frequently were the half-breeds, famous fiddlers. The dances were squares, circle two-steps, schottisches, Highland waltzes; occasionally—borrowed from the popular "breed" dances which the whites often attended—there were French jigs, the minuet, and the beautiful but intricate and exhausting *varsovienne*, a Polish folk dance which reached America by way of the French court and French Canada. Dances invariably lasted all night, as they still do in the mountain country; this was partly because there was little entertainment on the frontier and it took a long time to work off the participants' steam, and partly because roads were so poor that dancers arrived late and night travel was unsafe.

The hotels had dirt floors usually and their guests often supplied their own bedrolls. Wood was scarce and fuel, even in the towns, was often "buffalo chips"—dried cow manure. Women at first were reluctant to eat food cooked over such fires, but got over that squeamishness when they got hungry enough.

It was significant that throughout the Montana range period, one of the best-known and most warmly regarded citizens of the Territory was a hotel operator and cook—Mrs. A. R. Barrows, keeper of the inn at Ubet. This was a stage station established in 1880 by her husband. It took its name from his ejaculation, "You bet!" when asked if he could think of one. Announcement by Mrs. Barrows of a special dinner was big news for the papers and her place would be packed to the doors. The *Rocky Mountain Husbandman,* on November 13, 1884, hailed such a treat under the headline "Fun at Ubet": "Mrs. Barrows has returned from a visit to the States, and proposes to give a Thanksgiving party at Ubet. This means an orthodox feast—fat oysters, turkeys, etc., and a whole lot of fun."

Some of the difficulties under which Mrs. Barrows worked may be guessed from the fact that ranch eggs at this time cost a dollar a dozen. Apples, when available, were 25¢ to $1 each. John R. Barrows, her son, described another Thanksgiving dinner when all the ingredients for an "orthodox feast" were lacking, so his ingenious mother prepared substitutes: "pork sausage" was manufactured from salt pork and chopped elk meat, apple cider from dried apples and whisky. "The sausage," he reported, "was declared by men who had not tasted pork sausage for years to be unexcelled."

Mrs. Barrows' hotel had floors, and even supplied bedding. But even the most motherly and efficient innkeeper was helpless to regulate Montana's erratic weather. Her son tells of a traveling salesman's experience during a sudden autumn blizzard in which, though safely in bed, he thought he had nearly frozen to death:

He piled his clothing on the bed and lay there, sleeping a little and shivering much, until he heard sounds of life below. He came down and . . . found a radiant stove humming with newly supplied fuel, and in front of the stove the driver of the Billings stage, who had been facing the blizzard for seven hours. He had removed his heavy wraps and was standing by the stove endeavoring to thaw out the icicles which had frozen his mustache to his chin whiskers, for he was hungry, and until the ice barrier was removed he could have no satisfactory contact with breakfast. The salesman took one look at the ice-bound stage driver and exclaimed, "My God! What room did you have?"

Women were scarce and precious—even those who, unlike kindly Mrs. Barrows, were hardly ornaments to their communities. There was, for instance, agile Josie Walker, waitress, a popular belle of Livingston. Josie's sweetheart, who was in Butte, sent her clothes and money wherewith to travel to the mining city and wed him, but another lover was with Josie when she received the trousseau and the cash, so she left Livingston with him instead. He was careless enough, however, to interrupt the "honeymoon" for a brief business trip, charging Josie to await his return; but Josie waited for no man: she moved on with a third admirer who appeared, oddly, at just the right moment.

It did not pay to be too particular, nor could one be a stickler for the conventions. Miles City was founded in 1877; a year later a minister showed up and performed a belated wedding ceremony, a mass affair uniting one hundred couples. Often weddings were longer deferred than this, which has caused newspaper men acute embarrassment in modern times when, in writing old-timers' obituaries, they have come upon glaring discrepancies between dates of marriages and ages of progeny.

Montanans' humor of the period was inclined to be cavalier in character, if not downright bullying—a throwback to the coarsely guffawing knights of the Middle Ages, men of action, too. Cowboys one night abducted a whole theatrical troupe in a train holdup at Shelby and forced the frightened company to give them a "command performance." The Great Northern Railway, sternly disapproving, hired Pinkerton detectives to hunt down the culprits but without success; the jokers were sure of a welcome at any ranch house and most of them lived out their lives in Montana after simply changing their names.

Even the women were short-tempered and direct of habit when they considered themselves affronted. The *Meagher County News* reported one interesting incident in January, 1891:

It was reported here this week that a woman named Mrs. Scott horsewhipped Mrs. Belle Blazer, the school teacher in Castle, and was fined $5. The story is that Mrs. Blazer punished Mrs. Scott's boy for misconduct at school at which the mother got offended, and waylaid the teacher on the street and horsewhipped her. Mrs. Blazer is one of the best teachers in the county and at one time held the responsible position of superintendent of schools, and it is a shame to Castle to have such an occurrence happen. The boy is said to be a worthless youth and was undoubtedly deserving the punishment.

Study of that excerpt and others in the pioneer Montana press convinces the reader that a great deal has gone out of American journalism. The early-day editors pulled no punches, and although their comments might seem oddly casual, the facts—or as near as they could come to them— were there. Witness this remarkably condensed story in the *Rocky Mountain Husbandman* in November, 1884: "Two men, Jones and Valentine, went hunting in the Highwood neighborhood. Jones returned, with some game, but Valentine has not, and it is suspected that Jones has murdered him."

Such stories are innumerable and perhaps pointless; nevertheless out of them has grown the tradition of the gay and reckless time, the era of the open range. And analysis of the effect of this contribution to the national spirit could fill many books.

The livestock bonanza did encourage the notion that the west was a region of great wealth to be had for the taking, and yet most of the men thus attracted to it remained to become fanatically loyal citizens.

Again, why did they stay, when so many others had taken their riches and gone home?

A clue to the answer may be found in the fact that the open range period is undoubtedly the most "popular" in American history, although it covered, at the most, but thirty years of the two centuries which that history embraces. It is immortalized in novels, in scores of magazines which devote their entire contents to it, and in films. The romantic story of the plains has thrilled all America. It brought youth again to that portion of our country which had begun to settle down: Iowa, Minnesota, Nebraska—even Texas—had not been, after all, the last frontier. They were spacious, yes, and there were riches in their soils; but their trees were thick and tall now and left but a little window through which to glimpse the sky. Grandfather, who planted some of those trees, had known freedom and adventure; but now he had become stodgy, inclined to dourness and contempt for the dreams of youth. . . .

Those who came to "get rich on the plains" stayed, even if they never did get rich, because they had what millions of Americans seek when they read "westerns" and attend cowboy movies. They had a hell of a good time.

XV. KISSINEYOOWAY'O

The best Montana stories deal with the erratic and unpredictable character of Montana weather.

Cowboy "Teddy Blue" and his Texas partners asked an old bullwhacker about Montana's climate. "I'll tell you what kind of a climate it is," he responded. "You want a buffalo overcoat, a linen duster and a slicker with you all the time."

Then there is "Lying" Babcock's story of how Dave Hilger broke his leg, repeated by John R. Barrows in his autobiography, *Ubet*. Hilger, lacking harness, made four tugs for his wagon out of a green buffalo hide, hitched up the horses, and started to town. Midway he was caught in a sudden rain—one of those roaring tumultuous storms which blot out the prairie sky and the landmarks and fill the gullies with "flash floods."

The wagon was rapidly filling with water, so to avoid drowning in it, Hilger got out and walked beside his horses. Arrived at his destination, he was startled to find that his wagon was nowhere in sight; but let "Lying" Babcock finish:

His tugs were tight, and he knew at once what had happened. The rawhide had stretched! The tugs had been heavy and well-furred; now they were no bigger than a lead pencil and the hairs were about two inches apart.

Well, Dave started back in the rain to hunt for that wagon. He had followed those tight tugs for about a mile when the storm broke up and the sun came out with a fresh drying wind.

He stopped to take off his slicker and that blamed stiff-tongued wagon came up and ran over him!

The cold is right sudden, too. . . . Cowboy artist Charley Russell used to tell about his friend who left the poker game downtown in Great Falls and started home afoot one winter night. He froze plumb to death, instant, said Charley, on a corner about a block from the poker game.

At that point in the story, Charley's interlocutor would remark that that was a terrible thing.

"Hell, no!" contradicted Charley. "He come in handy. We

hung a lantern on him an' used him for a lamppost all winter."

Even today some old-timers will insist, speaking of the range era: "It would have been all right, if it hadn't been for the weather."

Always and eternally, the weather: always in Montana the bitter conviction that its vagaries are exceptional and malevolent, though they were so unexceptional and periodic that they ruined, impartially, cattlemen, sheepmen, and wheat raisers.

But most of the veterans will say that the weather could have been contended with successfully—never conquered— had it not been for the settlers cluttering up the range.

That is not the whole truth, either. No industry which functioned as haphazardly as did that of the range could have long endured; nevertheless, the weather came along at the right moment to finish a job begun by other elements, and then so terrible was its onslaught that it was easy to credit grumblings of supernatural malice.

In less than thirty years of cattle drives to Montana from the southwest, more than thirty-five thousand Texans rode into the state. A large share of this number turned right around and rode back, shivering. The inability of the Rio Grande cowboy to withstand Montana's winters was the subject of countless cook wagon jokes, songs, and barroom brawls.

But in the end the Texas cowboy had a free choice: stick it out in Montana until he was acclimated—and at considerably higher wages than he got in Texas—or pack his war bag and go home. The Texas longhorn was not so fortunately situated. Hundreds of thousands of these poor beasts stumbled off the gale-swept plains to die by frozen streams, or staggered on trembling legs into concealed drifts at the heads of coulees, there to be held fast while they slowly starved; or they pushed each other under the ice of the rivers in their frantic stampede to drink at the treacherous air holes.

The wasteful sacrifice of animal life on the open range is hard to credit today. A 10 per cent winter loss was "normal" in Montana; thus a cattleman running 10,000 head could consider his operation reasonably successful if he did not lose

more than 1,000 head each winter, though each of these animals had a potential market value of about $50!

The winter toll was heaviest, of course, among the calves,
and especially those trailed in that same season from the hot
plains of Texas. These losses were increased by the fact that
during their first winter on the range the Texas dogies would
stand around the ranch house and bawl for their food instead
of going out and rustling it for themselves. "This practice is
not encouraged" [by feeding], a Miles City newspaper commented callously. "It is hoped they will absorb enough cow
sense to go out on the range and eat." Most of them did,
when they got hungry enough.

The cattlemen could do little to reduce the 10 per cent
loss ratio. Half of it might be attributable to wolves and
rustlers, and a constant war was waged against them; but the
other half could only be offered on a sacrificial altar to the
gods of storm, who would not be placated thereby, either.

Nor was it only winter weather which gnawed at the cattleman's profits. Summer drouth, because it meant a shortage of
feed, invariably meant heavier winter kill. There were heavy
summer losses, too, through consumption by the stock of
poisonous plants which they would not touch when there was
sufficient grass. And drouth brought fire.

Nothing in Nature is as terrible as a prairie fire; not even a
blizzard. Where such a fire had been, nothing could live; and
out of such disasters grew the legends of country so desolate
that magpies flying over it had to carry their own provisions.
Gophers would come up from their cool chambers and starve
to death in the ashes. Game which escaped the holocaust
would start a long and hungry trek to find water, grass, and
brush, and die before finding them.

Grass fires moved with the speed of the wind. Only the most
terrible forest fires, those which are "crowning"—flame leap-
ing from treetop to treetop—can do that; and forest fires,
usually in rough country, pause due to shifts or breaks in the
wind. The prairie fire did not pause: it swept on at forty or
fifty miles an hour, faster than a horse could run, widening its
front all the while, a low wall of flame above which rolling
masses of black smoke heaved in the wind and then spread
to curtain the sky for weeks.

Such a fire would force a range operator to move thousands of head from their customary grazing grounds to a new district strange to him and his stock and perhaps already precariously near overstocking. On his old range no cattle could subsist until the new grass came in the spring; and then, though greener than before, it would lack the nourishment it had had, and because the moisture-retaining mulch would be gone it would not be as hardy.

This move must be made quickly; and so these were the worst drives of all. The cattle would scuffle through mile upon mile of ashes, their hooves bringing up great clouds of sooty, weightless dust until the air was like hot smoke and the world was blotted out. Their hides and the skin of the cursing riders would turn black; flesh would crack and burn with the dryness, despite the scarf flung up to protect the face. Eyes ached from the grayness and the baking heat, and tears which dried before they could be shed gummed eyelids with mud.

Soon the cattle would bawl for water, and there would be none. The rider would curse a little louder, lest the heat and his wretchedness put him to sleep: for now he must be watchful. Many miles away, perhaps in the direction whence they had come, there might be a little stream—too small to water this herd. But a sudden wind might carry the scent of that water to the cattle; if it did, the herd would swing instantly and be gone on a run. It might be impossible, under these conditions, to head them, and they would die—every last cow—of exhaustion, starvation, and thirst.

So the rider tried to straighten his aching back and open his aching eyes and watch the herd for the first sign of madness. He had to watch his horse, too, sometimes; and he caught himself musing over strange fancies which left him even unsure of himself. But above all he must see that the herd, if it were going to stampede, stampeded in the right direction; then the boys were in position to handle it. . . . If they were still there; if he were not riding alone in a dead and desolate world, alone with thousands of filthy, half-mad cows. He pulled the bandanna down from his nose and sang out to his partner, riding "point" on the other side of the herd. His voice was cracked; so was the reply, when it came back. But, anyway, **it came.**

Such were the drives from burned-out range. It is little wonder that cattlemen would spend prodigally, that they and their cowboys would even risk their lives, to forestall such disasters. Owners would not hesitate to have their men slaughter $50 steers and drag their expensive carcasses—drawn by ropes from saddlehorns—over the burning prairie. Sam Remington, who ran a few head of cattle, was told by his neighbor, a big operator: "If a fire starts, strip the hide off one or two of my cows; I can spare a few head." But whether they could "spare" them, like this operator, Sam Spencer, or couldn't— it was better to take this loss than take a chance on losing the whole herd. When there was no time to skin the animal, the carcass was dragged between two horses, one on the burned-over side of the flames, the other in the unburned grass, both riders going hell-for-leather in an attempt to smother the fire with their "drag." It was a sickening ride, but sometimes it worked. In later years a chain "drag" with an asbestos blanket was devised but few had come into use before the open-range period ended.

It took an empire of grass to feed such fires, and they will never be seen again. One of the last, as well as one of the worst, occurred in the '90's. It crossed an international border, leaped a large river and numerous creeks, and was stopped only after it had started a forest fire, too.

This blaze, started by lightning, broke out in the Cypress Hills of southern Saskatchewan, approximately forty miles north of the boundary. Pushed by a screaming northwest gale, it swept straight south to the Milk River in Montana, which is forty miles south of the boundary, fired a cottonwood tree, and rode across the river on a wind-borne blazing branch. Swiftly it caught in the grass south of the river and flew on as desperate riders of two of Montana's most famous outfits—Stuart's D H S and the Coburns' Circle C—tried to beat it out. Thirty miles farther south the flames entered the pine forests of the Little Rocky Mountains, where the weary cowboys, one outfit working from the east and the other from the west, finally "pinched" the fire out. It had destroyed all the grass in an area more than one hundred miles long and from five to thirty miles wide.

Lightning started most of these fires, but there were other, less innocent agents. Indians resentful of being driven off their buffalo range were responsible for many of the earlier ones; a cattleman coming onto range which had never been used before for domestic stock had to watch constantly for this. Indian hunters occasionally started a fire to stampede a herd of cattle deliberately in order that they might cut out some and get away with them; these hunting parties also set fires to drive game. White rustlers set a few. Some were the result of carelessness—a cigarette (though the cowboy's hand-rolled smoke, which goes out when dropped, is not such a hazard as the tight "tailor-made") or a spark from the chuck-wagon stove. Such a spark started the disastrous fire on the X I T ranch in Texas in the fall of 1885, and the cook who started it lit out in a hurry, fearful he would be lynched.

These fires, in addition to destroying the grass, wiped out cattle herds, ranch houses, and sometimes humans. Several men died in a blaze which swept eastward from the Sweet Grass Hills following the drouth of 1884, blackening the tinder-dry grass for seventy miles in a strip thirty miles wide. Indians set it.

But it was the winters—when icy gales shrilled across the crusted prairies and sliced through the sturdy logs of the ranch houses, when the deadly "white cold" crept slowly down from the Height of Land in Canada's Northwest Territories, when snow fell interminably, burying range, stock, and ranch house—it was the winters which finished the cattlemen.

Even as the first big herds moved onto the plains of central and eastern Montana, the first in a series of bad winters which was to dog the industry was wiping out the herds in the west and on the Sun River-Rockies slope. This was the winter of 1880–81, when blizzards began in December and continued with hardly a break until May: temperatures were seldom less than 20 below and for weeks at a time stayed at 40.

Most of the cattle on the Sun River range had been brought in a few months before the blizzards struck; still unfamiliar with the country, they drifted desperately with the incessant wind and died finally of exhaustion as much as of hunger. Losses on that range were 90 to 98 per cent; thousands of cattle lay dead in the water courses and their ruined owners said, "you can walk from Sheep Creek in the Belts to the

Dearborn in the Rockies and never take your foot off a dead cow." Some of the stockmen made frantic efforts to get feed to their animals, but hay was scarce. Ten strawstacks sold for $1,000 at Cascade, though straw was "stuffing," not nutritious feed.

Central and eastern Montana did not suffer so badly that winter because there were as yet few herds on that range, grass was plentiful and the wind kept it freer of snow, and there was still tall brush in the coulees to afford shelter. Nevertheless there were catastrophic instances: an English company which had driven in 5,000 head the previous fall (the cattle thus were thin and weak) had 135 head left in the spring and went bankrupt. Granville Stuart's loss, however, was but 13 per cent and wolves and rustlers accounted for all but 3 per cent of that. He had carefully selected his range, not so much for grass as for shelter, and an early "freak" chinook which apparently blew nowhere else also contributed to his good fortune.

The wolves' toll increased sharply in such winters, as the herds were driven to unfamiliar country. One outfit which had been running 10,000 head of cattle including 3,000 cows found, at the spring roundup, not one calf. Another counted 700 calves lost to wolves and found its cows bitten in the hams, their tails chewed off, and otherwise bearing the marks of battle with the wolves: the range cow, especially the wild longhorn, would fight fiercely to save her calf from the shrewd gray killers which surrounded her in packs of 15 or 20.

Sometimes it was a race between the wolves and the "grubbers." These latter were skinners who took to the range in the winter and early spring to strip the hides from the dead stock. The first on the field got as much as $5 or $6 a hide, but the market was soon glutted after disastrous blizzards, and it became known as a "grubstake" job—just sufficiently lucrative to keep the skinner alive.

Most adept at this industry were the wolfers and trappers, who posted themselves in coulees and waited grimly for the cattle to totter in to die, stripping the hides while the body was still warm. Frequently they did not wait until the cows were dead and while this was perhaps merciful during the winter (the wolves were waiting) it caused considerable complaint when the practice continued after spring had come and there was some chance of recovery for the feeble survivors.

The bad winter of 1880–81 started the overcrowding of the central Montana range and thus led directly to the climactic disaster of 1886; but there were signs and portents in the five intervening years for those who could read. There was, for instance, the Starvation Winter of the Pikuni.

A day or two after Christmas, 1883, a luminous and glittering mist formed over the northern and eastern Rockies slope —where Glacier Park is today. Frantically the Pikuni-Blackfeet prayed to Aisoyimstan, the Cold Maker, not to persecute their people; pleadingly they sought of their Indian agent a few extra rations. But rations were low: the agent had reported (seeking to make a record for himself) that the Blackfeet were now nearly self-supporting.

The mercury dropped to 40, 50 below zero, and stayed there for sun upon sun. All travel ceased and the hungry Blackfeet huddled in their lodges. Every day was as the day that had gone before; the sun was a faint light in a colorless void, and it set far to the south. There would come slightly warmer days, and it would snow, silently, thinly, hour after hour; tiny, icy crystalline particles which glittered in the gray light.

Now the hunters would go forth to seek game afoot, for their horses had long since died or been killed for food; and when there was no more game, they brought back the inner bark of the fir and pine trees, or tissue scraped from buffalo skulls, or the hooves of cattle, left by the wolves—or even rats hunted out of their homes in the rocks.

They were deserted by their agent, who was being replaced; his successor arrived in the midst of the worst suffering and did his best. Word of their plight reached Montana towns, and rescue expeditions were organized. George Bird Grinnell, famous naturalist and friend of the Blackfeet, stirred the government to action. Cursing freighters fought their way over drifted trails to the reservation with wagonloads of food. They found some of the survivors mad with hunger and grief among the bodies of their kin; they found coyotes and wolves fighting in the lodges of the unburied dead; they found six hundred Indians—one-quarter of the tribe—starved to death.

The next winter was nearly as severe, and the *Mineral Argus* remarked casually in January, 1885: "Many of the Piegan [Pikuni] Indians are reported frozen to death." The *Chicago Times* printed a special dispatch from Montana's cowboy capital, Miles City:

Since December 1st there has been no break in the cold . . . until it culminated last night in the dreadful temperature of 52 degrees below zero. The whole valley on all sides of Miles City is filled with cattle, seeking what protection the scant shrubbery affords. Even in the streets of the town great droves of cattle wander back and forth, but there is no food for them.

Losses were mounting annually, but still new herds were being crowded onto the Montana range, as the established cattlemen appealed for opening of the reservation. Market conditions also were worrying them. The average beef price per hundredweight on the Chicago market in 1882 had been $4.75; in 1883 it was $4.70, and in 1884, $4.40. The next year it dropped to $3.90, partially because of the distressed selling of some of the herds Cleveland had forced out of Indian Territory.

The bonanza days were gone, and some of the old-timers recognized the fact. "There was no way of preventing the overstocking of the ranges," Stuart admitted, "as they were free to all. . . . The range business was no longer a reasonably safe business; it was from this time on a gamble, with the trump cards in the hands of the elements."

It soon became apparent that the elements were not going to help the situation any. The summer of 1885 was dry; that of 1886 was parching. Great fires swept the range; those cattlemen who could find new grass began the move through a haze of smoke which hung over Montana for months. "There has hardly been an evening in the last week," said the *Rocky Mountain Husbandman* in August, "that the red glare of the fire demon has not lit up our mountain ridges, while our exchanges bring news of disastrous fires in all parts of the Territory."

The grass began to die in July and all but the largest streams and water holes dried up. Water in the creeks became so alkaline that cattle refused to drink it. Cinders, ashes, and hot alkali dust covered the range and even the furniture in the ranch houses.

That fall wild game moved early from its favored shelters in the Missouri badlands and hurried south and west. Birds which customarily remained all winter fled, too. The horses' winter coats appeared earlier than usual; "even the range cattle," said Stuart, "seemed to take on a heavier, shaggier coat of hair."

Nature had set her stage for the last act.

Kissin-ey-oo-way'-o, the Crees said; "it blows cold." The Crees were the northern people, from the Height of Land; they had many words for cold, degrees of coldness, the effects of cold—but none more literally translating into speech the condition it described: in *kissineyooway'o* the north wind sang, softly at first, then rising to a wail and a howl. . . . It blows cold.

It began November 16, though Montana seldom has severe cold or heavy snow until after Christmas. The gale was icy, and it had substance: it was filled with glassy particles of snow, like flakes of mica; it roared and rumbled. After the first day the tonal pitch rose: from a roar it became a moan, then a scream. The snow rode the wind, it thrust forward fiercely and slashed like a knife; no garment or hide could withstand it. The gale piled it into glacial drifts; when cow or horse stumbled into them the flesh on its legs was sheared to the bone.

Now suddenly there appeared white owls of the Arctic. The cattlemen had never seen them before; but the Indians and the métis knew them—and like the beasts and birds, they fled south.

Slowly the temperature moderated. The stockmen prayed for what the Indians called "the black wind" from the arch of black cloud on the western horizon from which it emerged; but it was too early in the season for the chinook. The drifts dwindled but did not disappear; they spread, crusting the range.

In December there were two more blizzards.

January is the Moon of Cold-Exploding-Trees. On the ninth day of that month it snowed without an instant's interruption for sixteen hours—an inch an hour; and the temperature fell to 22 below zero. Intermittent snow continued for another ten days, with temperatures ranging from 22 to 46 below in central Montana; in some other sections it was 40 below day in and day out for more than two weeks.

There was a respite of a little more than a week; then, on January 28, the great blizzard struck. For three days and three nights it was impossible to see fifty feet in any direction and ranch thermometers read 63 below zero. A sudden break in the cold and a wind shift gave promise of a chinook, but the storm set in again and lasted through February 3. A rider who dismounted dropped into snow to his waist on level ground.

Cattle which had been pushed over the Missouri in the fall to the better grass on the northern range drifted back, for there was little shelter on the steppes north of the river. Half dead from cold and hunger, their bodies covered with sores and frozen blood, bewildered and blind in a world of impenetrable white, they blundered into the barbed-wire fences, crumpled against them, and perished. They were trapped in drifts above their bellies and stood erect until their bodies froze. They slid into air holes in the rivers.

Cowboys donned two suits of heavy underwear, two pairs of wool socks, wool pants, two woolen shirts, overalls, leather chaps, wool gloves under leather mittens, blanket-lined overcoats, and fur caps. Before putting on the socks they walked in the snow in their bare feet, then rubbed them dry vigorously. After pulling on their riding boots they stood in water, then stood outdoors until an airtight sheath of ice had formed on the boots. Sometimes instead of the riding boots they wore moccasins and overshoes or sheepskin-lined "packs."

Thus prepared, they mounted and fought their way through the snow to extricate cattle stuck in drifts, tried to herd the dying beasts into sheltered ravines and head them off from treacherous rivers. They blacked their faces and eye sockets with lampblack or burnt matches to forestall snow blindness, or they cut holes in their black neckerchiefs and masked their faces, bandit-fashion. They strained and gasped as the icy air stabbed into their lungs and stomachs; they froze hands and feet, and many of them died. Their bodies, frozen stiff, were lashed on the backs of their horses and borne back to the ranch houses, to be thrust into a snowbank until a chinook came because the ground could not be broken for graves.

For all this they got no medals, nor expected any. A cowboy's job was to look after the herd; he was being paid for it —$40 a month. But hundreds of ranchers and riders underwent such hardships in that dreadful winter that they forsook the range forever, crippled in body and spirit.

As the storms and cold continued through February, the tragedy of the range was brought into the towns. Starving cattle staggered through village streets, collapsed and died in dooryards. Five thousand head invaded the outskirts of the newborn city of Great Falls, bawling for food. They snatched up the saplings the proud city had just planted, gorged themselves upon garbage.

Kaufman and Stadler, Helena cattlemen, wrote to their foreman in the Judith Basin to inquire about their herd. When the delayed stage delivered the letter, the foreman tossed it with a derisive grin to one of his riders, a young Missourian who had attained some bunkhouse fame for his pencil and water color sketches.

"Got a postcard?" asked the young artist, whose name was Charley Russell. On it he swiftly sketched in water color a gaunt steer, legs bowed and head down, standing in a drift with a coyote waiting near by. Below he printed a terse legend: "Last of Five Thousand." The card was mailed back to the Helena men without other comment. It was the first Russell work to attain wide circulation; under the title he had originally given it or the later one, "Waiting for a Chinook," it made the artist famous throughout the cow country. It is now owned by the Montana Stockgrowers' Association and hangs in its Helena office. Russell died in Great Falls in 1926; his last painting sold for $30,000.

The chinook did not come until March—a month later than it could have been expected. Before the spring roundups were held to determine the extent of the disaster, the Montana Stockgrowers' Association met in Miles City, scared but hopeful.

"We are not here to bury our industry, but to revive it,"

said Joseph Scott, association president, whistling bravely in the dark. Then he went on to admit: "Had the winter continued twenty days longer, there would not have been much necessity for this association."

Sadly the stockmen went home for the May roundup. They were in no great hurry to learn the truth; most of them, in short rides near their homes, had seen thousands of rotting carcasses on the plains. There were coulees and sheltered valleys which they could not enter because of the stench of decomposing beef.

The popular estimate of the cattlemen after the roundups had been completed was a 60 per cent loss for the state, or about 362,000 head of cattle.

More conservative were official figures, showing a 40 to 50 per cent loss. The drop in cattle on assessment rolls was 200,000, but this did not account for all the loss by any means, since thousands of cattle, including all the fall calf crop, had not been assessed.

Officially, it was reported cattle worth $5,000,000 had perished; actually the cattlemen estimated the loss amounted to $20,000,000. They had to figure in the deterioration in their potential assets, including unborn calves, the cost of restocking, and other more indirect results of the disaster.

Nelson Story of Bozeman, who twenty years before had brought the first trail herd from Texas, lost more than 66 per cent of his stock. On the Yellowstone range losses reached 95 per cent. The Home Land & Cattle Co. had put 6,000 head across the Canadian border; 2,000 survived. James Fergus sold 1,500 hides from his dead stock for $2,000.

The great Swan Cattle Co. of Wyoming, Scotch financed, which had large Montana holdings, went bankrupt. The Niobrara Cattle Co., founded in Texas, collapsed; it had 9,000 head left out of 39,000 and it was $350,000 in debt. Gibb Brothers, typical of the smaller operators, counted 320 head left out of their 2,500. They sold the 320 and quit. Theodore Roosevelt decided the cattle business was not for him and sold his ranch just east of the Montana line in North Dakota. The French Marquis de Mores closed up shop in his ill-fated packing plant at Medora, N. D., and went off to India to hunt tigers.

Nevertheless, the *Yellowstone Journal* in Miles City commented sarcastically on the disaster: "It is comforting to reflect on the number of reputations that were saved by the 'hard winter.' It never killed half the cattle that were charged up to it. . . . The story was told of one manager who reported 125 per cent loss."

The newspaper's reference was to the strange bookkeeping practices of the range industry, which also accounted for the wide variation in estimates of the loss. There were two ways of totaling one's herds: the "book count" and the "tally." The latter—actual count of every cow, calf, and beef steer on the range—was the only way to determine one's true assets. The "book count" was easier and much more popular, especially among managers for absentee owners. It was based upon the number of cattle originally placed on the range, to which was added, annually, the normal expectancy of increase, and from which was subtracted, ostensibly, "normal" losses to rustlers, wolves, disease, and "winter kill." This paper computation bore little relation to the actual number of cattle on the range. It speeded the collapse of some of the large speculative companies.

But regardless of whether the losses were all valid or partially "paper," a panic had gripped the industry. Ranchers who intended to stick it out but who needed cash found that the forced liquidation of livestock assets had smashed the already tottering Chicago market. Prices slid until the going figure was $3.15 a hundred pounds—less than $38 for a 1,200-pound steer, of which there were few left. Then, on October 8, 1887, came word that a shipment of Montana cattle had been sold in Chicago for $2.50 a hundred—not much more than $25 a head, and with a freight charge of $6 a head to be deducted.

Eastern and foreign investors had lost interest and thrust their companies into bankruptcy; the big herds had nearly vanished. Hundreds of Montanans now became disgusted. "A business that had been fascinating," said Stuart, "suddenly became distasteful. I never wanted to own again an animal that I could not feed and shelter."

The range cattlemen had been fretting for some time under the criticism of eastern humanitarians stirred by highly colored accounts of the "brutal" range industry, gratefully promoted by eastern stock raisers who bought and paid taxes on their pastures and, not unreasonably, saw the free western grass as unfair competition. After the disaster of 1886–87 there was a new burst of condemnatory propaganda and tears were shed in Back Bay drawing rooms.

One of the Montana industry's severest critics was Julian Ralph, who wrote a piece in *Harper's New Monthly* for June, 1891, reporting that the era of large herds on the open range was ended, and continuing:

It is cause for jubilation that this is the case. It seems strange that cruelty should distinguish this branch of food-raising wherever it is seen . . . From the bloody fields of Texas, where the ingenious fiends in the cattle business snip off the horns of the animals below the quick, to the stockyards in Chicago, where men are found who will prod the beeves into pens, there to crush their skulls with hammers, it is everywhere the same—everywhere the cattle business has its concomitants of cruelty and savagery.

(Cattle had been dehorned and slaughtered for a long time in New York state, without much fuss in the quality journals!) Mr. Ralph went on:

The reader would not suppose that there was cruelty in the mere feeding of cattle on the plains, but let him go to Montana, and talk with the people there, and he will shudder at what he hears. The cattle owners or cow men are in Wall street or in the south of France, or in Florida, in the winter; but their cattle are on the wintry fields, where every now and then, say once in four years, half of them, or eighty per cent, or one in three (as it happens) starve to death because of their inability to get at the grass under the snow. The poor beasts die by the thousands—totter along until they fall down, the living always trying to reach the body of a dead one to fall upon.

Montana cowmen could be raucously scornful of the eastern writer's picture of a tottering steer hunting for the body of a dead comrade to cushion his expiring fall; but they could not take it so lightly when their own kind turned on them. They were shocked when the *Cheyenne Sun,* cowtown paper, had this to say about them: "A man who turns out a lot of cattle on a barren plain without making provision for feeding them will not only suffer a financial loss but also the loss of the respect of the community in which he lives."

From the *Rocky Mountain Husbandman* in Montana came another stab in the back: "The range of the past is gone; that of the present is of little worth and cannot be relied on in the future. Range husbandry is over, is ruined, is destroyed— it may have been by the insatiable greed of its followers."

The cattlemen retorted angrily. What could they have done? There was not enough hay in the United States to feed the immense herds on the Great Plains. Their operations had cheapened beef for the eastern consumer. They had improved the dehorning process: it was less painful than formerly. Branding, they insisted, does not hurt the animal much; he will get up and eat immediately, apparently none the worse for his experience.

In September, 1886, before the disaster had struck, the *Husbandman* had been worried but hopeful:

If we could close our eyes to the fact that there are more stock on the range than ever before and that grass in many localities has been very closely grazed, the outlook would indeed be flatter- ing. But these are stubborn facts that cannot be regarded lightly, although all may yet be well . . . We shall continue to have faith in a light winter and small losses until forced by polar waves and worlds of snow to change our minds.

The *Husbandman's* mind was changed in the spring of 1887, and so were those of most of the cattlemen. The over- lords of the range—those who were left—turned not without relief to a new livestock economy. After all, it had been the stockmen themselves who had heard most keenly the pitiful bawl of famished cows creeping into the creek bed near the home place to die. They began to raise hay: the acreage of this crop increased from 56,000 in 1880 to 300,000 in 1890 and 712,000 in 1900.

Cowboys who had been "line riders" in the first days of the open range, patrolling an unmarked boundary based on creeks or imaginary lines drawn from distant buttes, became fence riders, with wire cutters and pliers replacing the six- shooters in belt scabbards; finally they degenerated into hay-ing hands—or they quit. Most of them, traditionally hostile to any form of labor which could not be performed from a horse's back, quit.

But the snow which had brought ruin in the winter brought rich new grass in the spring and helped the transition to a new type of operation—fewer cattle, more limited but better range, supplemental feeding. Ranchers could restock in 1887 for less than $20 a head; more than 100,000 came in by trail from the south that year. By 1893 Montana had 100,-000 more cattle than it had had before the great storm—but individual herds were smaller so that they could be maintained on owned range, fed and sheltered.

Montana old-timers recall that one of the biggest roundups of all time occurred in the middle '90's, along the Canadian border from the Sweet Grass Hills to North Dakota—three hundred miles. It is significant that nearly one thousand riders representing nearly a score of ranches participated; a decade earlier there would have been a few hundred, representing half a dozen companies.

Most of the ranches in this big roundup now owned or leased at least a part of their range. One of these outfits was the famous Circle Diamond of Colorado, which had begun as Thatcher Brothers of Pueblo and became the Bloom Cattle Co. At this writing their foreman, John Survant, is still a prominent citizen of Montana. The Circle Diamond was destined to be the last big outfit on the northern range.

This company's shipments in the '90's had reached an annual total of 9,000 to 12,000 head. In 1902 the firm acquired, by lease, a dozen linked townships along watercourses in Saskatchewan. In the fall of 1906 on this range and in Montana the Circle Diamond had 12,000 head; that winter 9,000 of them perished. The company survived, but within two years it closed out its Montana and Canada cattle operations, and the big herds had disappeared forever from the open range.

In that winter of 1906–07 railroad tracks snapped in the cold and for two months freight shipments were tied up as wreck crews struggled to keep the trains moving. Again starving cattle invaded the towns; one old steer, little more than a scurfy skeleton, stood in the yard of a Chinook newspaper plant until he died. There was nothing to feed him.

Losses would have been as severe as twenty years before were it not for the fact that livestock practice had changed. The story of human heroism in a futile effort to save the stock was repeated: sheepmen and cattlemen rigged up flatboard scrapers to clean the snow off the range in long strips so their animals could get at the grass; again the herders underwent great hardships in efforts to save their charges from accident or starvation.

In April, 1907, the state sadly tabulated the winter's cost: 727,136 head of sheep, 110,628 head of cattle, 6,423 head of horses. It was the worst loss in all America, though it had been a bad winter nearly everywhere. The national average winter kill was 3.49 per cent for cattle, 6 per cent for sheep; Montana's was 12 and 13 per cent. The last open-range roundup had been held in the fall of 1906; little interest had been shown in it and it had been hard to organize because there were so few outfits left using unfenced grass. In the spring of 1907 it was apparent that there never would be need for another.

John Survant and his riders, snowbound that winter in their Canadian quarters, fought desperately to save the Circle Diamond's stock. They saw the winter as a challenge to the "last big outfit." As long as their hay lasted or more could be bought, they fed the cows—foundation of next year's herd. Finally there was no more hay. Survant sent his men onto the thatched grass roof of an old shed and had them fork the years-old grass and hay down to the cattle. Still there was no chinook and the snow piled deeper.

Now there was no chance of saving the herd; but if he could save something, anything, by his own efforts, Survant felt he would have answered the challenge of the northwest's ancient, inimical gods. The ranch boasted an old milk cow, he explained. . . .

I told the boys I hadn't done much good around there that winter, but by God I was going to save that old milk cow; I was going to save something from that winter. So we kept her in and I carefully fed her the kitchen slops—she would eat anything.

Well, one day the cook boiled up some beans but found they were sour, so he set 'em at the back of the stove until he got around to throwing 'em out. I came along when he wasn't there, and not knowing the beans were bad I swiped 'em and fed 'em to that cow; I figured she needed beans worse than we did.

You should have seen the yard next morning. . . . And the cow was dead, of course. I felt bad about it, wondering what she thought I'd done to her. But I was licked; guess I was foolish, thinking I could save even one old cow!

Plow;

XVI. THE DREAM OF JIM HILL

IT is said that the town of Ekalaka, on the baked prairie of eastern Montana, was founded when a trader who was having trouble with a balky team and a muddy trail unloaded his stock of whisky and some building logs there and set about to erect a cabin. "Hell," he said, "any place in Montana is a good place for a saloon!" The establishment flourished and a town grew up about it and was named for the Indian wife of the first white settler, a buffalo hunter.

It was by such accidents that the precipitate course of frontier history was directed, or perhaps diverted. There was, for instance, the casual remark to Jim Hill, empire builder, deriding Hill's Great Northern Railway, then pushing from St. Paul across the top tier of plains states to the Pacific coast: "You'll never bring anything out of that country but buffalo bones!" Time after time that gibe was repeated. And rage and a mighty resolve grew in the soul of Jim Hill.

Hill County, Montana, was named for the Great Northern's little giant. He had a big crowd that day in 1912 when he climbed to the seat of a buckboard in front of his railroad's depot to speak his farewell to Havre (in Montana, "Hav-er"), the county seat, after a visit to its annual fair.

Jim Hill had a vision. As he stood in the carriage in which he had driven about the little cowtown's streets, the railroad man explained that vision to Havre.

There were men in his audience, even then, who knew Hill's vision was a mirage; but not their opinion, nor those of others who had argued with him for twenty years, could impair Hill's conviction of the validity of his dream. He was driven now by that moral compulsion known only to those whose illusion, born of emotional need, has met instant ridicule from the "practical." In all but this Jim Hill was supremely "practical." He had determinedly built a railroad, without benefit of government land grants, through a country which was quite widely regarded in financial and political capitals as wasteland, useless as the Sahara. He had ruthlessly shaken down communities on his route for rights-of-way and other concessions. His financial maneuvers were deft and his intrigues with legislators shrewd; he got his railroad built.

So it behooved one, when Jim Hill moved, to act swiftly to protect one's own interest—even if one were certain that his premises were false; even if some of his hearers that day in Havre said "Jim's crazy." There were few who would contemptuously dismiss any mirage seen by Jim Hill, who finished what he started.

Jim Hill told startled Havre that day that the time had come for settlement of a farm family upon every 160 or 320-acre tract within Montana's millions of acres of public domain. That was his vision; and Havre looked at the powerful, stocky little man with the huge head and admitted that if it could be done Hill would do it.

He had been expounding his vision for two years now; and to make it live, thousands of newcomers had been pouring into Montana over the Northern Pacific road, a Hill-controlled carrier. In 1909 homesteaders had taken up more than a million acres of Montana land; in 1910, the rush under way, they had filed on 4,750,000 acres. But Hill had just started: the great trek of homeseekers and land speculators into the northern counties over his Great Northern road had not yet begun. How effectively Jim Hill set out to realize his vision may be judged from the fact that in the dozen years from 1910 to 1922 the homesteaders took up 42 per cent of the entire area of the state—93,000,000 acres—although more than 80 per cent of that area was unfit for crop agriculture, and increased Montana's wheat acreage from 258,000 in 1909 to 3,417,000 in 1919!

Many old-time Montanans lay much of the blame for their state's ruin upon Jim Hill and his tremendous campaign to encourage homesteading on the northern plains. Few hold any grudge. It was just one of those things that happened to Montana; but they argue that even if the homestead rush were inevitable—as it probably was—without the costly campaign made possible by Hill's great resources it would have been slowed down and thus its equally inevitable collapse would not have been so disastrous to the state and to the nation.

It does not matter now, except in so far as it illustrates again the history-making possibilities of accident and of the strong individual in the economic life of the frontier; and it could not matter then, for Montana was after all Jim Hill's state. Without his railroad, even the stockmen were helpless. Barbed-wire fences straddled their trails to the east. The towns—even stubborn Fort Benton—had seen Jim build his railroad completely around the community which rejected his demands, and set its station a mile or so away. Great Falls gave him a strip through the middle of its finest park (and parks were valuable on the prairie) ; but Great Falls owed its existence to Jim Hill, who had financed its founder, Paris Gibson.

The empire builder died four years after this Havre speech, believing that through his efforts the great wastelands of the northern plains would bloom forever, that the thousands of people then pouring into Montana would continue to do so until every available acre was under cultivation, that the hundreds of mushroom dryland towns would become flourishing cities—and that his railroad would earn from all this the deserved fruit of his foresight.

One year after his Havre speech a line of homesteaders stood for two days and two nights in front of that town's United States land office, waiting for it to open so that they might obtain free Montana land. Their wives or children "spelled" them in the line so they might eat or snatch a few hours' sleep. When the office finally opened, they were herded inside in groups of twenty-five. Two hundred and fifty homestead entries were made that first day. That month—March, 1913—brought sixteen hundred entries to that one office.

The Homestead Act, of course, was not of Jim Hill's making. It was in line with American tradition that the land belonged to the people and should be distributed for individual settlement. Also, it relieved industrial unrest in the east. Early homestead legislation (1862) had little effect upon the northern plains: its 160-acre limitation and requirement of five years' residence gave pause to the most optimistic. There were good lands "closer home," minus Indians. Grain had been grown in Montana, however, nearly twenty years before by Jesuit Father DeSmet, to supply his mission and to teach agriculture to the Indians. Montana's first homestead entry was made in 1868 on the outskirts of the present state capital, Helena. The second entry, soon thereafter, was made by a woman. She lived on her claim and proved up on it, which is more than a good many of her successors accomplished.

The Desert Land Act, a few years later, interested the Montana stockman. It opened 640 acres to anyone who would agree to irrigate it within three years. The initial cost was only 25¢ an acre; at the end of the three-year period the homesteader was to prove that he had done the required irrigating, pay an additional $1 an acre—and the land was his. The stockman, who began to worry in the '80's about restricted range, found it simpler just to pay the initial 25¢ an acre, which permitted him to use the public domain for three years. At the end of that time he turned the land back, overgrazed and still unirrigated. So under the Desert Land Act the homestead business picked up in Montana, though the land, as usual, suffered.

Some of the stockmen, however, lived up to their bargain with the government. They obtained broad stretches of rich, flat bottomland for hayfields and gardens, lying near a stream with sufficient flow for irrigation, the whole surrounded by good open range with water courses and brush for shelter, and near a forest from which they could haul wood for buildings and fire. Had not a horde of avid newcomers who had heard of the cattle bonanza descended upon these families, they probably could have established a permanently prosperous economy for the state: theirs was the ideal agricultural system for the plains.

They lived in log cabins, usually of one story, with roofs of packed sod sandwiched between two layers of boards. Fireplaces furnished their heat. The little "farms" surrounding the house often boasted orchards and chickens but seldom had dairy cattle. "It was and still is," a pioneer comments, "one of the peculiar contradictions of the cattle ranch that only condensed milk was served at the table, and butter infrequently."

They watched uneasily as Jim Hill's "horseback surveyors" rode over their range and sent him back reports on its potential population capacity—at 160 acres per family. They cursed the first "Dry Farming Congress" (Billings, 1890) out of which grew the Hill campaign. But it took further legislation —the Enlarged Homestead Act of 1909 and the "three-year" Homestead Law of 1912—to bring Jim Hill into his own. The first expanded the free land unit to 320 acres. Hill's "agricultural experts" decided this was enough, because the settler could crop half of it and leave the other half in summer fallow. The fact that this summer fallowing of virgin land, without safeguards later to be developed, would promote soil blowing was not foreseen by Hill nor by Thomas Shaw of Ontario, his principal "expert," whose name in Great Northern promotional literature was invariably preceded by "Prof."—a title to which he had a perfect right but which was earned in eastern Canada and not on the northern plains.

The 1912 legislation reduced from five years to three the time required to prove up on a homestead, and permitted five months' absence from the claim each year, thus requiring but twenty-one months' actual residence. This law, on the face of it, was an admission that the settler might not hold out for five years. "The government bets title to 320 acres against your filing fee that you'll starve before proving up—and the government usually wins." Even if the homesteader were to stick it out for three years, the law seemed to say, he would need five months each year to rustle some grub somewhere else. Strangely, this official admission of the hazards of the undertaking did not discourage many homesteaders. Naturally, it did not discourage at all the thousands who were to

fasten upon him like ticks and suck his blood—the land locators, the small-town boosters, the railroads, the politicians,
and those who took his filing fees.

Thus was the stage set for Jim Hill, tough man who loved
a tough land. There was in him something of the bravura of
northwestern plainsmen who had been known to walk deliberately and unnecessarily into a blizzard or into murderous
hail, mocking the gods of storm, testing their own stamina.
Jim Hill would show the scoffers back east. He would force
this "wasted" empire into the frame of his vision: his pretty
picture of little green fields and little white houses and big
red barns, with lightning rods to deflect the shafts of the
northwest's primeval gods.

He loved the northwest. Since the turn of the century he
had been promoting experimental farming, had set up laboratories of his own for plant study, had provided exhibition
and demonstration trains. In the brief intervals between
financial battles for control of other roads—or to keep control
of his own—he had made a sincere effort to reason out for
himself some adjustment for what he considered the wasteful
economy of the plains, some method of bringing its potential
productiveness into harmony with the new industrialization
of the east, and the east's new markets.

Then, too, there was the matter of business for his railroad.
Jim Hill hated an empty box car worse than anything in life.
He hated to send empties to the west to bring back the stockman's cattle; and as long as the open range, or even the restricted range, could last, those cars would be empty on the
westward trip. The sparsely populated cowtowns made small
demands upon the east; the notoriously parsimonious stockman got along very well without Grand Rapids furniture.
. . . To this day even prosperous cattlemen frequently live
in homes which would be scorned by an industrial laborer.

Jim Hill offered $1,000 in prizes for the best exhibits of
grain grown on dry land within twenty-five miles of his railroad and exhibited at the Billings Dry Farming Congress,
which had become an annual affair, with his encouragement.
At one of these sessions he had pleaded for a new, less-
disheartening name for the Montana agricultural process,
suggesting "scientific farming" rather than "dry farming."

This was challenged by F. B. Linfield, director of the Montana Experiment Station and professor of agriculture at the State College, who suggested that the newcomers be given at least that much idea of what they were up against. After the meeting an acquaintance earnestly urged Linfield "not to contradict Mr. Hill."

Delegates from the cowtown of Malta to the 1909 Dry Farming Congress were borne to the Billings meeting by Jim Hill's son, Louis, in a special train which picked up others along the Great Northern line. Some Minnesota men had been induced by Hill to come along too; and en route to Billings the party stopped off in Culbertson and took a trip over some lands which had been set aside for an Indian tribe. They then telegraphed Secretary of the Interior Ballinger urging that he open these lands to homestead entry. He obliged, within three months. What the Indians thought of the deal is not on record.

After the Dry Farming Congress, Great Northern exhibit trains toured middle western states. Incredulous farmers were shown proof that the remote west's waterless acres could produce yields double their own; and land in this fabled Eden was free! Little glass display cases popped up on Montana station platforms, and travelers strolled about and admired thick sheaves of golden heavy-headed wheat. Billboards appeared along the Great Northern's right-of-way proclaiming the rich future of Montana, the Treasure State.

The fever had infected the state itself. The legislature considered a $25,000 appropriation to advertise Montana's homestead possibilities. Dr. Linfield protested, suggesting that the money be given instead to establish more experiment stations. The state then (1905) had but one, at Bozeman; the first demonstration farm had been established two years earlier near Great Falls. Both the advertising proposal and the Linfield plea for research funds failed. Dr. Linfield, who was not only director of the experiment station and professor of agriculture but also superintendent of farm institutes, in charge of the college's 160-acre farm, and assigned to prepare a Montana exhibit for the San Francisco World's Fair, had neither time nor money for the research necessary to aid the newcomers.

The earlier homesteads, however, combined irrigation and

dryland farming—a system recommended by the experiment station and practiced on the demonstration farm near Great Falls. Lands suitable for this type of farming were soon taken up, and still the flood of settlers came. As they spread out onto unproven dry benches, the experiment station protested to railroad men; it was told that this was Jim Hill's show, there was nothing to be done about it.

Hill's motives for this promotion are worthy of sympathetic study, though analysis of them is not easy. There was, first, the challenge to his empire building, implicit in what he saw as the "waste" of the upland prairies—this we have already discussed, and there was more than this. An adulatory biographer has given another clue in a quotation from the Great Northern's 1902 report:

The large movement in the Northwest in the last few years, which still continues without abatement, has resulted in the settlement of a vast area of vacant lands adjacent to the Company's lines. During this period more than 5,000,000 acres of Government land in the northern part of the country have been taken under the homestead act. It has also been satisfactory to note that many of the large farms are being cut up into smaller ones.

That last sentence sounds odd today, when a score of governmental agencies direct their efforts to consolidation of the small units, or their abandonment; but there was justification for the railroad's position. Hill's biographer continues:

Up to this time what was called "bonanza farming" had caused curious and often gloomy inquiry among students of agricultural economics. Thousands of acres of farm land in single tracts were taken up or purchased by men with capital, who made use of the latest machinery, were able to buy, sell and ship on the wholesale system, and realized large profits. It was feared in many quarters that this competition might crowd the small farmer to the wall . . .

Hill was disturbed by this development, then gaining ground in Minnesota and eastern North Dakota. We can dismiss his biographer's claim that self-interest should have led him to prefer large operations to small ones; on the contrary, it is obvious that, from a business standpoint, he would have the same objection to large farming operations that he already had to the large stock ranches. A railroader could not look kindly upon an agricultural economy made up of men who were able to "ship on the wholesale system."

As a matter of fact, up to this time the few "bonanza" farms in Montana were primarily livestock operations, or combined stock-and-crop properties, with some irrigation; they were much better suited to the soil economy than Hill's dream homesteads. It is true, nevertheless, that the "bonanza" crop operation which Hill feared was attempted in later years, fortunately under the handicap of market conditions which ensured its speedy collapse.

All this made a good talking point for Jim Hill, for just at this period of his career, involved in a war over control of the Northern Pacific, he was being damned as a "monopolist." Now he came forward as a spokesman for the little man on the frontier, a bitter foe of the large-scale farm operators, whom he saw threatening to become "veritable patroons of the manor who would lord it over the multitude of hard-pressed farmers, reduced by the system to the status of tenants and sinking gradually almost to the level of serfs." They were to sink, through a promotion engineered by Hill, to a level of hopelessness probably worse than that of serfs within the next two decades, but Hill could not have known that. . . .

Incredibly enough, Hill's most intricately reasoned excuse for the homestead promotion grew out of his genuine, even if much publicized, concern for "resource conservation." It is grimly ironic that a movement which brought about the most rapid and wasteful exploitation of soil resources in American history should have been actively encouraged by a man who was honestly distressed by the nation's rapid depletion of its natural wealth. It was Hill's plea for reforestation which was at least partially responsible for President Theodore Roosevelt's initial conferences leading to that national program; and Hill's long experimentation with plant life in his own laboratories was more than a hobby. Yet he could and did advance an amazingly ingenuous theory of soil conservation, and by personal force backed with millions of dollars could sell that theory to thousands of people who should have known better, could sell it in the face of expert contemporary opinion and expert testimony reaching back to Powell's 1878 report which refuted his principal conclusions.

Hill insisted the land of the northern plains was very rich indeed, simply because it produced luxuriant crops of native grasses. He believed—or said he did—that eastern and middle western farm lands were threatened with exhaustion. There was, he said, an imminent shortage of foodstuffs for America's growing population, and the only solution would be to increase the productivity of the land without further exploitation of the "worn-out" areas of the east. It was as simple as that: merely dig up the virgin soil of the prairies. To bring this about, Hill offered four agricultural practices for the northern plains: deeper plowing, repeated cultivation of the soil, rotation of crops, and raising of livestock. With the last two few could quarrel today (except on the ground of oversimplification); but it was on the first two that his dream of empire was based, and it was the first two which brought disaster. They were intended to "conserve" the meager moisture of the high country, although Hill, looking at the bright side, was careful not to stress its meagerness. However, these practices not only could not conserve the moisture very long when it did rain and could do no good at all in dry years but, more importantly, could and did tremendously speed up soil erosion through blowing.

A newspaper in Malta, Montana, reported wheat yields of thirty-seven bushels to the acre on dry land in the Judith Basin during the 1909 season. But the principal position on page 1 of that paper was still reserved for market quotations on livestock. . . .

March 10, 1913, cowboy artist Charles Russell of Great Falls wrote to a friend.

Bob you wouldent know the town or the country either it's all grass side down now. Wher once you rode circle and I night wrangled, a gopher couldn't graze now. The boosters say its a better country than it ever was but it looks like hell to me I liked it better when it belonged to God it was sure his country when we knew it.

That was the month of the 1,600 homestead entries at Havre. In 1912 there had been 12,597 in Montana; by 1914 the total was to soar to 20,662, nearly seven times the annual average of the first decade of the century.

Another of the mass migrations of the American people had begun.

XVII. HURRY, HONYOCKER!

Honyocker, scissorbill, nester. . . . He was the Joad of a quarter century ago, swarming into a hostile land: duped when he started, robbed when he arrived; hopeful, courageous, ambitious: he sought independence or adventure, comfort and security. Or perhaps he sought wealth; for there were some who did not share the Joads' love of the soil, whose interest was speculative. . . .

The honyocker was farmer, spinster, deep-sea diver; fiddler, physician, bartender, cook. He lived in Minnesota or Wisconsin, Massachusetts or Maine. There the news sought him out—Jim Hill's news of free land in the Treasure State:

"More Free Homesteads; Another Big Land Opening; 1,400,000 Acres Comprising Rocky Boy Indian Lands Open to Settlers; MONTANA. . . .

"By order of the secretary of the interior, the lands shown on the map herein will be opened to homestead settlement March 1, 1910, and to entry at the Glasgow, Montana, land office.

"Professor Thomas Shaw, the well-known agricultural expert, after making a thorough examination of the soil and crop conditions of this land, writes as follows:

" 'The soil of this entire area is essentially a clay loam, very rich in mineral matter . . . has great staying power. The native grasses are more than ordinarily abundant and in this fact is evidence of producing power that can be relied on. The water supply is relatively good. In much of this area it is possible to secure a quarter section without a single foot of broken land on it. . . . A portion of this region has been homesteaded for the past *two or three years* by persons who have prospered since they came.' "

The italics are this writer's, not Professor Shaw's!

The honyocker read on:

"The winter climate . . . is less cold than that of eastern Dakota. The snowfall is also usually considerably less than that of the Red River valley. [Was this supposed to be advantageous?] There have been no records kept of the rainfall for any lengthened period, but it is safe to conclude that it is not far different from the rainfall of Williston in North Dakota. This would mean the average rainfall is about 15 to 16 inches in a year, sometimes running higher than 18, sometimes, but rarely, as low as 11 to 12. This is not high rainfall . . . but is sufficient to grow crops fair to excellent on summer fallow land *any season.* . . ."

Again the italics are mine.

"The statements made above are not mere guesses. They are based upon observation and experience. North from Culbertson 20 miles, and not so very far from the heart of this area, is a postoffice named Homestead. The farmers around have tilled their lands for two to three years. They have grown nearly all the crops enumerated in this circular and with gratifying success."

Hurry, honyocker, hurry!

"As stated previously, these lands comprise 1,400,000 acres. Giving each man who files 160 acres, this area will furnish 8,750 farms. At first thought it might seem to be many months before all these farms would be taken. If any cherish such a view they will be greatly disappointed. It is questionable if a single farm will be left unfiled upon one month after the opening of the lands for entry."

Hurry, honyocker!

"One-way settlers' fares, $12.50 from St. Paul and Minneapolis to Bainville, Culbertson, and other points in eastern Montana."

Hurry, honyocker, and do not investigate too closely!

To be sure, no records of rainfall had been kept "for any lengthened period" at Culbertson: once a cowtown, careless of statistics, it was just being reborn. But in Glasgow, a hundred miles west, the records had been kept since 1894. There the 15–16 inches which you were told were "average" had only been recorded three times in fifteen years; precipitation had been 12 inches or less ("rarely," said the brochure) seven times in fifteen years. Williston was less than half Glasgow's distance from Culbertson, and Williston, though no Garden of Eden, had a better record; but you could not go by that, honyocker. Bozeman, Montana, has an average annual precipitation of about 19 inches. Sixty miles west as the crow flies the average is 11. That is Montana.

And how could you have been expected to know, hon-yocker, that even a "normal" 15-inch rainfall would have given you no guarantee of success, for "normal" means nothing on the arid high plains? It is not the "normal" (which, anyway, can only be determined by study of precipitation over a score of years) but the frequency and extent of *variation from the normal* which indicates the crop potentialities of the soil. On the dry Montana prairie the "normal" is always so close to the minimum for crop production that any variation extended in degree or in time must mean failure.

You could not know; but Jim Hill didn't know either. . . . Though had he listened to the old-timers and the experts, he could have guessed. It was fifteen years, however, before a Montana scientist, after thorough study of the state's young weather records, was able to report:

From the crop standpoint [as differentiated from the meteorological] the term drought must include not only lack of rainfall, but a consideration of temperature, relative humidity, winds, soil moisture content, weather and precipitation preceding the rainless period, and the stage of the plant's growth. A year of abundant rainfall may be followed by one of great deficiency, or the reverse, and with no apparent order. All such plans [agricultural programs] should be developed in the light of the erratic nature of the rainfall, and the number of years with the different extremes should be known.

And what would you know, honyocker, of humidity? It was fifteen years before this admission came: "During the major growing season the relative humidity [ratio of actual moisture in the air to the total amount it could hold] in this region is low. Extremes as low as 4 per cent have been recorded."

You did not know these things, honyocker, and so you were coming. On one day—May 3, 1913—one Great Northern railroad conductor took up 503 railroad tickets from you folks who were bound for Montana!

The origin of your name, "honyocker," is obscure. In Minnesota, the Dakotas, Canada, Slav immigrants were "hunyaks." There were Slavs among you, though most of you were native-born, hailing from middle western states. Your advance guard was greeted with hostility in Montana, and it may be that the contemptuous term "hunyak" had been expanded by custom to cover all "foreigners" or outlanders. The Montana cowboy's original term for the tenderfoot arrival was "pilgrim"; but that was an honorable, if slightly derisive word, and too good for the likes of you!

The honyockers came in tourist sleepers which reeked with the greasy odor of heavy food cooking. These cars were equipped with stoves upon which the wives took turns preparing the family's meals.

They came in model T Fords—and model T Fords, with their high, slim wheels, are still good cars for a muddy farm road. They came in rattling little Maxwells, and broke their axles on rutted trails.

And they came on immigrant trains. The honyocker rented a freight car (St. Paul to eastern Montana, $50) and in it he was permitted to place "all second hand articles such as household goods, machinery, agricultural implements, vehicles, wagons, tools, etc.," and the following: "Fifty bushels of grain, a sufficient amount of feed grain for animals in transit, 2,500 feet of lumber, 500 fence posts, a small portable house, trees and shrubbery, small stock including hogs and sheep not to exceed 20 head, or horses, mules and cattle not to exceed 10 head," or equivalent numbers of both. Some of the immigrant cars were a bit crowded.

When a car contained livestock the owner could ride in it free, to care for his animals. Frequently his son was smuggled into the car to help his Dad with the stock—and to save payment of another fare. Occasionally other wanderers sneaked in, too—ambitious adventurers looking for homes in the west, or just plain bums. When trainmen spotted these extra passengers at division points, the farmer who had engaged the car was called upon to pay their passage. If he refused, the stowaways were thrown off the train. There were instances, however, when the glib-tongued vagrant had become so popular with his host that the latter paid enough out of his meager store of cash to retain his new friend's company.

The trip from St. Paul to Malta, Montana, in an immigrant car took from Sunday night to Thursday morning. Then the freight car door was rolled back and the honyocker climbed stiffly out—into a den of wolves.

"Almost every man, woman and child," wrote a pioneer Montanan of the scene when the immigrant trains came in, "had become obsessed with a wish to help locate the 'scissor-bills' and secure a little of the money they were bringing into the country—get it while they could, as too many of them had no hope that these people would succeed in making a permanent home for themselves."

The land was free to the homesteader (save for his nominal filing fee) but first he had to find it. Standing bewildered in the railroad yard, back to his loaded car, he gazed across thousands of acres of grassland and wondered what to do next. He was not long left in doubt, for here came the locators. Some were Montanans, but many came in from "outside" with the homesteaders.

Locating homesteads was just about the juiciest racket Montana ever had. It got so good that before the vein had run out locators were traveling east on the cushions to round up their own suckers and bring them to the promised land, thus making sure that no other locator would get to them first in that confused moment when the Great Northern train slid to a stop in front of a prairie depot.

The locator's standard fee for finding the homesteader his place and helping him to file upon it was $20. Not infrequently, however, the fee was $50—if the honyocker had it, if competition were not too tough, and if the prospective settler seemed to be in enough of a hurry. The $20 fee perhaps would not have been excessive had each honyocker been escorted singly about the country until a site could be found for his home. . . . But the locators took several in their democrat wagons on a single trip. Frequently the men arriving on one immigrant train were from the same, or neighboring, districts "back east"; usually they were eager to locate near each other. The fortunate locator who got to them first could take the whole bunch and collect $20 from each. During the peak of the boom, some locators carted five to ten newcomers in a day's trip over the prairie. In a few months they were rich.

Sometimes they earned their money; sometimes their clients were fussy. And there were honest locators. There was one who tried earnestly to talk a woman settler out of the tract she had chosen: it contained a lake and she wanted her home to front a lake. The locator's arguments (he could not

bring himself, however, to tell the whole truth) proving fruitless, he bore the woman back to town to file on the place and
gather her belongings. When she returned to her farm a day
or so later, her "lake," one of the type frequently formed by
"flash floods" in the spring, was gone—dried up. That was
twenty-six years ago; the woman is still there but her lake has
never come back.

This first well-paid service did not end the locator's rela-
tionship with the homesteader. Most of the locators were real
estate men or had ranches of their own. A few were ex-
stockmen, bitter and cynical, hating the newcomers and convinced they were doomed, getting their revenge in advance.
Most of them had land to sell; and the homesteaders often
were infected on their first day in Montana with the germ of
greed for land which later was to step up the pace of disaster.

Of course, the honyocker was told, his homestead was all
right, the soil and weather were perfect, and he would make
a good living; but to *get rich*—then he would need more land.

It was a clever argument, so good that some of the locators
believed it themselves. And it did more to wreck the state
than even the initial homestead rush had done. . . . It held
out hope to those for whom there was none now, and never
would be; it extended the life of a futile experiment entailing
criminally wasteful exploitation of unfit soil, and it created
a credit boom based upon inflated crop values which was to
end in financial collapse.

The years 1910–18 were "good" years on the northern
plains. It rained, and the war sent wheat to above $2 a bushel.
The price doubled between 1914 and 1918, and in that final
year of war Montana expected the greatest wheat crop in its
history—50,000,000 bushels. City men, said the newspapers
in May, were going to be needed to help with the harvest.
They were not needed, for drouth brought crop failure that
fall, and the next, and the next; but in the meantime the
honyocker, egged on by virtually every public and private influence, had bought more land, more machinery. From 1910
to 1920 the number of farms more than doubled, the crop
land acreage was trebled. The inflation in land "values" was
even more startling: from less than $250,000,000 in 1910 to
nearly $700,000,000 in 1920.

Montana newspapers in May of the disastrous year 1918

carried advertisements signed by Alfred Atkinson, United States food administrator for the state, which said: "The government of the United States, as well as its war associates, is in great need of wheat. Every available pound is needed if the German flood is to be stemmed." Newspapers in dryland towns began calling upon the honyockers to increase their purchases of mechanized equipment. (The machinery companies were good advertisers throughout this period.) Montana had sent its young men to war—too many of them, as we shall see later—and farm labor scarcity was becoming serious. Machinery might be the answer, the homesteader thought. True, its cost was high—even the newspapers admitted it; but on the other hand wheat had doubled in value in four years. There were some who said that in 1920 it would bring $4 a bushel. With machinery the farmer could handle more land, grow more wheat, stop the Germans, and grow rich.

The homesteaders began to buy the new combine harvester-thresher, paying $1,500 to $2,000 or more for it. They bought tractors, and Ford trucks. From 15 men and 14 horses for harvesting and threshing 25 acres with the header system, they reduced the labor and power factors to 2 men, no horses, a tractor-drawn combine and 2 trucks. . . . But there was nothing to harvest.

During the good years it had been possible for some homesteaders to pay off their initial indebtedness and find themselves square with the world after one or two years, perhaps even make a few hundred dollars. Now, even as bad year followed incredibly upon bad year, their credit was still good. They were improving their farming practices; surely, in the long run, it must rain.

Their credit was good, too, for land. If, in those few good years, they were able to make money on 320 or 640 acres, simple arithmetic (too simple) indicated that they could double it on 640 or 1,000. But most of the homestead land had been taken up, or that which was still available was too distant from the homesteader's place to make it practicable. There was plenty of land to be bought, and according to middle western standards it was still cheap. The locator who had helped the honyocker select his farm had some land for sale; he had quoted a price of $5 an acre.

But that had been some years ago, the locator now explained. The price had gone up and 160 acres were now worth $1,000. He urged the farmer to make up his mind, for values were rising rapidly. Before the boom collapsed there would be instances when 160 acres of virtually worthless land would sell for $4,000.

Nevertheless, $1,000 was a lot of money, and the honyocker went home to think it over.

That night the banker came. The honyocker had met him before, several times. This same banker sent his clerk to copy the names of homesteaders as they were posted at the land office; on follow-up visits he offered the facilities of his institution for loans to purchase machinery or land. He kept in touch with the real estate men, too; and tonight he found the honyocker in receptive mood. A thousand dollars? It was chicken feed in Montana!

The banker had plenty of money. Eastern capital was coming into the state now; the banker paid 6 per cent for it, charged 10. With wheat at $2 a bushel, he told the homesteader, and with some of the land producing 50 bushels to the acre (when it produced at all) how could he lose, if he had any crop? The deal was closed.

But that year the homesteader's crop was insufficient to pay the cost of harvesting. . . .

Well, he hadn't had enough land. His neighbor had a crop; not very good, but still a crop. If you had land enough you were sure to get crop on some of it; and he had always suspected that the first 320 had been poor soil. Now he had 480, but a man needed 640 in this country. . . . He went back to see locator and banker. Sure, his credit was still good!

Strange tales have come down in Montana from the days of the land boom which accompanied the homestead rush.

There was the rancher who entertained all the young, single women of a whole town—teachers, stenographers, salesgirls—at dinner and a dance on his place. Before they left he had the signature of each on a homestead claim.

There were other ranchers who took up homesteads in the names of their cowpunchers, built shacks for them, and had them live there to establish residence. When the punchers had proved up, they were to turn the places over to the rancher and receive their reward—$100 each; but frequently these well-laid plans went awry. The cowpoke might have caught the fever himself, and then he would announce calmly that he was staying on his place; in that case the boss sometimes sent other cowpunchers to make things uncomfortable for the treacherous nester. Or the cowhand might calmly repudiate his earlier, verbal agreement and demand $1,000 or more. Then the boss would curse, but sometimes he would pay: the homestead frequently was so situated that the rancher had to have it to preserve his range.

The epic double-cross of the Montana homestead era involved a banker and his loving son. The banker had lent $1,400 on a homestead which had not yet been proved up—a fantastic piece of financial recklessness, as the borrower had as yet no equity in the land he offered for security. Discovering that the debtor was about to abandon the place, the banker secured a "relinquishment" in his son's name and put him on the land to serve out the residence requirement, prove up, and enable the father to sell the place and get his money back. The son stayed a few weeks; someone then appeared and offered him $500 to relinquish the homestead. He took the $500 and skipped the country.

Few of the homesteaders were smart enough to sell when land and crop values were up. The immigrants were still coming, still clamoring for farms. United States commissioners, in towns which had no land offices, received entries for a fee of $2, and at the rate of a hundred a day soon became tolerably prosperous. Homestead land gone, the "scissorbills" bought from land companies and ranchers. The big cattle and sheep spreads were being broken up.

We feel [one brochure asserted] that there is not a place offered by the Montana Ranches Co. which will not pay at least 10 per cent interest yearly on the investment if properly handled. Most of our properties are priced so that they should yield from 20 to 25 per cent as an operating return, and in addition to these returns there is bound to be an enormous increase in value with the great influx of immigration that is now being brought to this state . . .

Thus Montana pulled land values up by their bootstraps. "There is bound to be an enormous increase in value . . ." The refrain echoed in the land dealers' circulars, in the press, in the railroads' advertising; especially in the railroads' advertising. There was no audible questioning of the state's ability to support this influx; it was taken for granted that where there were so many people the formula for their support would develop automatically. It was a naïve theory of economic perpetual motion which had caused trouble for older empires than this.

The homesteaders, however, were convinced. They responded eagerly to the railroads' request for testimonial letters. H. W. Lebeck wrote the Great Northern in 1912 that he had been a store clerk six years before, in Iowa, that now his land in Montana was worth $100 an acre "due to the increase in value of real estate, also the prospects of the Great Northern building through this section." Ola L. Grice of Dawson County started with $500; he wrote that he wouldn't take $5,000 for his place, "with the railroad coming so close to me." William C. Moores, also of that county, had only 88 acres under cultivation, but "I consider my place worth $8,000; land is increasing in value with the prospects of the new railroad."

The railroad never got to their town; a spur did, however, finally reach a town fifteen miles from them. From 1920 to 1930 their county lost 7 per cent of its population; in the succeeding ten years it lost another 15 per cent. In 1939, two hundred of its farm families—20 per cent of the total— were "stranded or migratory," destitute and unable to make a living. The Montana planning board, surveying rehabilitation possibilities, found that even with expensive irrigation development only about half of these families could subsist in that county. The rest, said the planning board, are "surplus."

And what of the Lebecks, the Grices, and the Moores— those hopeful Dawson County Joads of three decades ago?

Some of their neighbors are included in that "surplus"; of these particular individuals, however, there remains no trace. The Grices stuck it out until a few years ago, then moved away; friends reported they had gone back to the Ozarks.

Moores, who valued his dryland farm of 88 cultivated acres at $8,000, abandoned it in the cropless '20's and moved to California. Good farm land, better than his, today is worth in that district about $10 an acre—a little more than a tenth of what Moores thought his place was worth.

XVIII. THEY BOUGHT SATIN PAJAMAS...

But it was a great frontier while it lasted.

There had been bonanzas before in America, and there had been more picturesque land rushes than this—to Iowa, to Kansas, to Oklahoma. The Model T and the Studebaker wagon had replaced the prairie schooner. There were no Indians to fight. Yet there never had been anything like the homestead rush in Montana in the second decade of this century, and there never had been anything like the collapse which ensued.

Overnight, homestead shacks sprang up on lonely prairies over which a few vicious gray wolves still prowled. The shacks usually were of one room, about twelve by fourteen feet, with a gable roof, a window in each end, and a door in the middle of the long side. They were set flat on the ground without foundation, but often had a tiny "cellar" under a trap door in the floor, to serve as a refrigerating compartment. The better houses were clapboarded, but thousands of them merely had tar-paper tacked over the exterior siding; the first strong wind ripped much of it off.

Old newspapers, especially rotogravure sections, were pasted up for wall covering. A sagging bed, stools, a table made of boxes, and curtained shelves for cupboards made up the furniture. There was a cast-iron cookstove. Outside the door a washpan sat on an up-ended box; a dispirited cake of soap rested on two nails driven into the wall, and a ragged, grimy crash towel or strip of grain sack hung above.

Usually the doors and windows did not "hang." Few of the honyockers were experienced builders. Their materials were the cheapest available, and the extremes of Montana's climate quickly warped the window frames and lintels. Rags had to be stuffed into widening cracks. Even then the prairie wind in winter, whipping the shack in fury, sliced through the thin walls: tiny drifts of snow blew in under the door and twisted and ran about the splintered, untreated floor. The honyocker and his family then huddled about the cookstove or the heater, which was sometimes a cheap commercially produced "airtight," sometimes just an old oil barrel resting on a cradle of strap iron.

Starvation threatened thousands of the newcomers in their first winter. Then the honyocker would trudge off through the snow to find a job and feed his family, leaving behind a frightened but courageous wife.

"When he went away," said one of these wives, "I was left once more on the homestead without a man, and this time with nine children, the youngest a baby three weeks old. He sent every dollar of his wages home as fast as it was earned, yet with me the winter was one long struggle to keep my family warmed and fed, and to save our horses from starvation. Upon the horses depended our ability to put in one more crop."

Three of their horses froze to death that winter. When feed for the pigs was exhausted, the woman butchered the eight of them with the help of her son and two neighbor boys. Hung in a shed, the carcasses froze, and the job had to be finished in the living room, the only place they could be kept warm. It was then 30 below zero.

Her husband wrote her: "If your fuel gives out, burn the fence posts, tear boards from the barn and burn them, burn anything about the place—don't take any chance of freezing!"

That was the ever-present danger, the nightly horror for the honyocker's wife after her family was asleep. Coal had to be brought from town, and recurring blizzards closed the road and isolated the family. Even water had to be hauled a considerable distance. The crusted snow gashed through the flesh on the horses' legs, and the horses were weak from hunger. Water had to be rationed, finally; and so did food and fuel. The children's faces whitened and the flesh was drawn tautly over cheekbones and jaws. Each day the relentless cold which walled them in pressed a little farther into the room. The chilled wood which had been gathered to augment the dwindling stock of coal would char but would not burn. . . .

This woman and her family came through that winter; ultimately they prospered. Many others did not come through. Those who did put in "one more crop." And in the spring it rained.

"The mushroom towns bustled with activity," said a veteran of those few good years. "It was no uncommon sight to see long strings of wagons full of sacked wheat . . . all drawn by a tractor, moving along the country road bound for the shipping point. The little stores were packed and clerks worked overtime putting up huge orders which included everything from harness to satin pajamas. Optimism ran high. Real estate dealers talked largely of future values and began laying out new additions; but a series of dry years followed."

A little Montana town, Scobey, with a population of less than fifteen hundred, once was the largest single primary wheat loading center in North America. In the "good year" of 1924 which followed the long period of drouth, more than 2,750,000 bushels of wheat were shipped from that village.

Some of the grain had been hauled by horse-drawn wagons for forty-five miles over rutted and muddy trails. Hundreds of wagons stood for days in Scobey waiting to be unloaded. Jim Hill's railroad ran out of cars. Elevator men handling the grain passed out tickets to the waiting outfits to record the order in which they had arrived. Loading the cars was a twenty-four-hour job, and farmers went off to the hotels to snatch a little sleep as they awaited a call that a trainload of empties had come in.

Strikes of railroad workers in two successive years complicated the Great Northern's problem of supplying cars. Angry farmers and elevator men, watching an uncertain market, cursed Jim Hill, his railroad, and the unions.

The usual "grain box" wagon held 125 bushels. Most of the honyockers could load four to seven of these; but sometimes by the time they had reached the elevator the market had fallen and the value of their grain was less than the cost of the haul. Sometimes double-decked sheep wagons were used. There were a few mechanical rigs, tractors usually of 30 horsepower hauling seven 125-bushel wagons, but the cost of this form of transport was high and horses still were favored.

Although the rush came immediately after harvest—from September through November—the hauling continued until snow had made the roads impassable, and sometimes in bumper crop periods it was resumed in the spring.

Frequently the haul was too long for one day. "Halfway houses" appeared and flourished on the trade of temporarily prosperous homesteaders. A few of these grew and became towns as the railroads built spur lines and they acquired elevators of their own.

The log cabin, tent, and tepee town of the open range, with its Indians, dogs, horses, and saloons, was displaced by the hideous "shack town" of the honyocker: a one-street, one-side-of-the-street "business section," stores with dirty showcases and third-rate goods with unfamiliar brands, soda fountain without charged water, firetrap movie theater. By day the angry sun blazed upon the treeless, dusty street; by night the town lay dead and cold and insignificant under the great sky while howling coyotes circled it and sometimes slunk into its alleys to fight the dogs nosing its garbage. Perhaps no one has ever pictured better the loneliness of such towns, their cheap and alien tawdriness in the grandeur of the prairie scene, than did Burchfield in a great painting he called "November Evening."

The sterility of their community life was the most serious shortcoming of these homestead towns, the one which was most damaging in the long run to the whole social structure of the state. In the rural east and middle west and in the better-settled Pacific coast states, there exist hundreds of "cultural communities"—groups of neighborhoods about a central medium-sized city. These fulfill the cultural needs of the residents of that section, and through education, entertainment, and the building up through generations of an intangible but stalwart community loyalty, they tend to hold people within their borders.

Such communities have no counterparts in Montana. The few cities are scores of miles apart, and none of them has a surrounding group of rural communities. The rural towns, with some exceptions, have a deadly sameness and frequently consist of nothing but a grain elevator or two, a general store, a saloon, a church, and a handful of nondescript houses.

The worst of these starved towns (and many others have vanished in the last twenty years) were the creation of the honyocker. They were grimly utilitarian, uncompromisingly ugly; and when the economic excuse for them passed, those which did not perish at once lingered on year after year to become grayer, dirtier, more shrunken, as if they were being dehydrated.

Most of these towns grew out of a largely speculative move-

ment. Their founders and some of their customers were in the
state primarily to "clean up" and get out. Thousands of the
newcomers (though not all, by any means) had no intention
of permanently occupying their homesteads—but it was not
from such as these that the railroads obtained testimonial letters! They took up their lands as a miner would stake out a
placer claim. Others, sincere homeseekers, were either too
young to have felt the need for a community culture, or too
old and too burdened to bother about it. When the time came
for that need to be realized, the towns were dying and the
people had been broken by economic disaster.

In the absence of a cultural community there was nothing
to hold even successful homesteaders in the state except continued profit. When the cash returns began to dwindle, they
sold out and moved on.

Many Montana towns missed the opportunity to become
such cultural communities. Out of the rowdy pioneer tradition grew the belief that "bigness" and "toughness" were
synonymous. Several of the larger towns, when they set out
to attract visitors or even settlers, did so frankly on the promise that within their borders "anything (within reason)
goes." Butte still advertises its attractions thus, but Butte is a
special case and outside this particular phase of our study;
it has never been the center of a rural region. The scheme
works for the metropolitan mining city, Montana's biggest;
it failed for others.

There were attempts, during the homestead days, to make
the shack towns more livable and to give them character.
Many of the honyockers were well educated and reasonably
cultured: hundreds had been teachers. But homestead life
was harder than they had expected, and for the first few years
they had neither time nor strength for much community activity. They started a few feeble clubs, financed a few Chau-
tauquas; then, suddenly broke and disheartened, they gave
up.

A few of the newcomers brought their culture with them,
refused to modify it to fit the land, and died or fled with it.
Among these were the tragic Mennonites, many of them
foreign-born; some of their communities were established by
children of Mennonites whose colonies had prospered in Minnesota or Canada. The young people pushed out for them-

selves, to the new promised land; they knew nothing of dry-land farming, and such was the stubborn isolation forced upon them by their faith that they could not learn. In addition, many of them feared and distrusted government in any form, even that of relief. They were splendid farmers—somewhere else. They loved the soil, they worked with single-minded intensity; they lived cleanly and thriftily—and they failed. They failed, and starved; they built rude coffins for their dead and came to town to buy from the undertaker a few gewgaws for the pine boxes, some handles or crape. One bereaved family put the corpse under the house and surrounded it with ice because there was no time for burial until after the harvest. They took their farming that seriously, and still they failed. . . . And in the end they could only look at their parched fields, at the gray, flaked soil underfoot, and pray humbly for the strength to go back whence they had come.

The honyocker destroyed the roistering cattleman's town. Its character may not have been of the best, but it had character of a sort, nevertheless: there was more friendship and less commercialism, and the town was loved and remembered. Its resources were slight, for the cattle industry only needed its towns occasionally; besides, towns cluttered up the range, and the fewer of them the better.

Principal establishments of the homestead town, in order of importance, were the grain elevator, the bank, the general store, restaurant, and hotel. None resembled cowtown Glasgow, which a year after it was founded consisted of eight saloons, three restaurants, and one store—all but two of the enterprises housed in tents.

There was some boisterousness in the honyockers' towns, but there was none of the cavalier spirit of the cowtowns, none of their jaunty rowdiness which survives to this day, though sadly watered down, in a few remote Montana villages which subsist precariously upon the periodic visits of the free-spending puncher.

The latter part of the homestead era coincided with prohibition, during which, according to the Federal Writers' Project Montana almanac, "baffled federal blotters ranged this huge state in a vain effort to dry up millions of gallons of 'mountain dew' made for 537,606 prospective drinkers who had 94,078,080 acres to hide it in." Significantly, prohibition made little difference to the honyockers, and in fact was supported by many of them, while it was bitterly opposed by most of the stockmen, and numerous cowpunchers found in border rum-running a new and profitable adventure.

The honyocker drank sparingly, usually beer. He gambled hardly at all. He could not afford either indulgence, and usually he was thinking of the folks at home. The puncher's home was wherever he dropped his war bag and his bedroll, and he seldom had any "folks" dependent upon him. Without liquor, cards, and women occasionally, his life would hardly have been worth living.

Sometimes the antagonistic cultures of cowman and honyocker fought for supremacy in the same town. Such a struggle was waged over dying Ubet, once the most famous stage station of Montana Territory. Ubet, born in 1880, had a two-story log-cabin hotel, a barn for the stage teams, a livery stable, blacksmith shop, ice house, saloon, and post office. It survived until 1903 when a railroad passed it by to put its station three miles away. The railroad named the station Ubet, however, and the old town was moved over there. But that happened to be the site of a new trading post named Garneill in honor of Garnet Neill, wife of a prominent cattleman, and Garneill determinedly maintained its identity, much to the bewilderment of train passengers.

Homesteaders arrived, and the sadly divided community of Ubet-Garneill was still further rent. The newcomers frowned upon the free-and-easy ways of traders' and drummers' Ubet, clustered about the depot, and of cattlemen's Garneill, which by this time boasted a pretentious hotel, a saloon, blacksmith shop, and several stores. So the honyockers built their own Garneill, just north of the other two communities. Thereafter, for a few years, there existed in uneasy neighborhood, North Garneill (of high moral tone), South Garneill (not so particular), and Ubet (fast becoming only a memory). The railroad, despairing, finally dropped Ubet, changing the depot's name to Garneill. Perhaps it was the wages of sin, but probably it was the collapse of the livestock

industry and a fire, which killed South Garneill. North Garneill, the honyockers' town, survives; but it is a flag stop
filled with abandoned buildings.

In 1878 Powell envisioned communities in his "colony"
system which would have grown, not out of speculative hopes,
but out of the common needs and aims of the settlers in a
well-balanced agricultural economy. These communities
would have been small and their institutional and cultural
services limited, but they would have been integrated with
the economic lives of their people far better than were the
dryland towns, including those which have survived to this
day. In a few instances this integration is now being sought
in Montana planned communities. Until such planning is extended and its ends achieved, however, much of rural Montana must be served by the shack towns, shabby residue of the
homestead jamboree.

The dreams of great men often live a long time, as dreams.
That of Jim Hill, which he sought to bring to life in fact, became a witless nightmare. His trains rattled empty through
dying towns. His neat little green fields were transformed as
if an evil spirit had sped overhead, laying a curse upon them:
suddenly they were fenced deserts in which the trapped
tumbleweed spun and raced nowhere all day. The little
houses stood slack-jawed and mute, obscenely violated by
coyotes, rats, and bats, and finally faded into the lifeless fields.

Panic. . .

XIX. RAIN IS ALL HELL NEEDS

IN the first sixteen years of the twentieth century Montana's grasslands yielded an annual average of more than 25 bushels of wheat to the plowed acre. In 1919 the yield was 2.4 bushels.

June, 1919, was the driest month in the recorded history of the state. Precipitation at the State College in usually fertile Gallatin Valley was .09 inches, about one thirtieth of "normal." In Hill County, Jim Hill's own, this month of crop-producing rains yielded but 1.5 inches of moisture; for the entire growing season, precipitation in that county was 4 inches under "normal." It was the third straight year of drouth.

The 2-bushel yield that fall even at the war-inflated price represented a return of less than $5 an acre. A month before harvest the crop loss was estimated at 23,000,000 bushels; that meant, with wheat at $2.23 a bushel, that the drouth had cost Montanans in 1919 alone some $50,000,000. An important sum, $50,000,000; loss of that much money would constitute a spectacular financial disaster even in New York.

Day after day in that terrible summer the homesteaders watched the sky, saw "thunderheads" form behind the blue-shadowed peaks on the horizon, spill over the mountain crests, roll out above their fields—and race past, unbroken. Or, if the black cloud broke, they saw the few drops of rain it released dispersed before they touched the ground, borne off by a howling wind.

In July, 1919, farm agency representatives met at Havre to consider the plight of the homesteaders. They accomplished nothing save to issue a statement expressing their confidence in Montana agriculture and attributing the farmers' distress, now in its third year, "solely to unusual climatic conditions."

Down from Havre to Great Falls came District Judge W. B. Rhoades, with a chip on his shoulder. For some time, he told a newspaper interviewer, solicitors had been demanding funds of Montanans to feed Europe's starving victims of war. But . . .

The other night there was a meeting at Chester [Hill County] of people in need of help. The general expression on the faces of these people was tragic . . . Several gentlemen undertook to talk about organizing farm bureaus, government irrigation and road work. Many an inhabitant of that region will be an expert harpist before the Milk river reclamation project is complete. That audience was not interested in such subjects—they wanted to know what they were going to have for breakfast!

Hundreds of people in Hill County had been living for weeks on potatoes and eggs—the only food they had left. The judge demanded that the Red Cross provide relief at once; but the Red Cross, which was pouring millions of American dollars into Europe, said at first that Montana drouth was "not a calamity" in its definition and it could not help. Later, however, it did.

Newspapers in front page editorials clamored for work for the farmers "lest they beg, borrow, or starve," and urged federal appropriations to complete Montana irrigation projects. The manager of one project appealed to the government for $2,000,000 and finally received $141,000.

Forest and grass fires swept Montana and the whole Pacific

northwest. By July the fire damage had reached $20,000,000; a month later the fight against the hundreds of blazes was declared hopeless, and abandoned.

Workers on a dam project near the Yellowstone River found scorpions in the gravel, the first ever seen in Montana. At Rocky Point, which had dreamed of becoming a Missouri River port for steamers, you could walk across the stream without wetting your knees. The owner of a great livestock company appealed in the press for leased range: for the first time since he organized his firm in the '90's, his twenty-five thousand acres would not support his herds.

Desperate stockmen demanded emergency freight rates to enable them to bring in hay from other states or to ship their cattle and sheep out for feeding. The railroads acceded, but speculators' interest was thereby attracted to hay, and it rose to $21 a ton in Minneapolis, with $4 added for freight to Montana. This was about double the normal price, and the rate of tribute increased steadily until in midwinter Montanans were paying $50 or even $60 a ton for inferior midwestern forage grasses. Word got around that the harassed Montana ranchers would buy anything: grass arrived frozen solid in cakes of mud so that it had to be cut out of the cars with pick and ax.

The increased price of feed nullified the advantage of the emergency rates, and meanwhile other rates went up. In 1920 western carrier tariffs were generally advanced 25 per cent. There were storms of protest, and hearings, and political campaigns, and finally there were some reductions; but when it was all over the rates were still up 17 per cent. The effect had been to move Montana's producers four hundred miles farther away from their already distant markets.

By August, 1919, Hill County alone had three thousand destitute. The despairing trek of the bankrupt and destitute began, all over Montana. The Salvation Army threw open its citadels to a new type of wanderer—the stunned and helpless honyocker—and provided free meals and beds. Upon the amazed merchants of the dryland towns there descended first one or two families, then dozens, with their belongings packed into rickety farm wagons; they asked the storekeepers for food or feed or gasoline to carry them east or west. They were hungry, bitter, and bewildered; few could admit, even now, their personal failure as farmers or the insufficiency of the land: it was the incomprehensible drouth which had beaten them, a malignant act of God which either destroyed their faith altogether or confirmed them in some graceless creed of inexorable doom.

There were few to cheer them on their way. The state commissioner of agriculture, complaining about "wild reports back east" of catastrophe in Montana, had admitted "less favorable conditions"; but he had added this: "It must be remembered that in settlement of non-irrigated [not "dryland," note!] sections, there were men induced to enter farming who had no previous experience, such as clerks, barbers, factory hands and others." The statement was true, of course; it was also very significant, coming at this time. The campaign had begun to blame the inevitable disaster upon the duped victims themselves, just as in a later, more widespread panic millions of Americans allowed themselves to be convinced that "any man who wants to work can get a job." This frontier-born American fallacy was to prove particularly damaging to Montana, where it goaded desperate farmers into carrying on, year after year, trying to drag subsistence out of soil of whose needs they were completely unaware, soil unadaptable to the only farming practice they knew.

Thus the comfortable conviction took root that the honyockers, a stupid lot, had only themselves to blame. Besides, the dryland towns had begun to wither and their businessmen were worrying about their own fate. There was no organized relief for the refugees. After a year or so the federal government and the counties decided to assist, with seed loans, those who chose to continue the futile experiment; but they had nothing for those who had been forced to quit. The surviving stockmen were not moved to pity; those who still had money or credit went to the county seat and bought up as much of the tax-forfeited land as they considered worth restoring to range. Instead of being relieved, the hostility of the two cultures, cattlemen's and farmer's, was briefly intensified, for the homesteader, desperate now and frequently angry, was not always careful to see that all which went into his departing wagon was his own. And so Charley Russell wrote thus to a friend:

Henry Keeten still has his ranch but winters in town. His house
is near me and we often meet and talk over old times. About two
years ago he leased his ranch to an honest prohibition farmer, and
while Hank's in town shoveling coal in the furnace and sweeping
off the front porch, Mr. Prohibition is busy moving Hank's ranch.
He don't get the fences 'cause the posts are froze down, but everything that's loose, like stoves, harness, oats, tools, was his. He even
rounded up the china nest eggs that Henry had to fool the hens
with. All this goes to prove that this honest prohibitionist would
take anything but a drink. Keeten says he had a hard time identi-
fying his ranch; it looked like the day he filed on it. And now
when anybody speaks of the honest farmer, Hank gets ringy.

Governor S. V. Stewart summoned the Montana legislature
into special session in July, 1919, to consider the agricultural
emergency. Newspapers announcing his call carried brief
mention of an apparently unrelated fact reported that same
day by the United States Department of Labor: living costs in
the United States had risen 88 per cent since 1913. That
month, too, was chosen by a party of eastern industrialists as
the one during which they would look Montana over. An
embarrassed Great Falls businessman told them it was unfortunate that they had come at such a lean time; but, he said
loyally, "all Montana needs is rain." A Grand Rapids capitalist looked up Great Falls' blistered Central Avenue, closed
his aching eyes against the sun, and thought of the hundreds
of miles of parched prairie over which he had come in an
oven-hot train. "Yes," he said quietly; "and that's all hell
needs!"

But Mark Skinner, vice-president of the First National
Bank of St. Paul, arrived also in that awful month, and
brought the banker's practiced optimism. "There's no reason
to get excited or discouraged," he declared. "The banks of the
Twin Cities will do their part."

Wheat was high in the fall of 1919, but there was virtually
no wheat in Montana. It was still high next year when the
homesteader sought seed. He paid $3.50 a bushel for seed
wheat and more than $5 a bushel for flaxseed. To put three
hundred acres in wheat he had to invest $1,000; and because
three years of drouth had used up his reserves (if he had ever
had any), he was forced to borrow again.

In the spring of 1920, however, it rained; hope returned briefly to the honyocker. Then the rain stopped, and the wind came.

Those winds were the first "dusters" the northern plains farmer had ever seen. Day after day he watched, first incredulous, then despairing, as the gale whipped his fields into the sky. He saw his $1,000 worth of seed blown out of the ground in forty-eight hours, and still the relentless wind tore at his land. He saw the dust driven through the flimsy walls of the homestead shack while his wife put the children to bed and covered their faces with wet cloths which dried in a few moments. There was no day or night for nearly a week; and then, after a few days' respite, the wind began again. When it was over at last, dust was drifted against the doorway like snow and the seven-foot-high tractor was buried to the roof of its cab.

The ruined homesteaders gathered in little groups in the towns to compare notes, to talk it over with frightened merchants. The fourth dry year, and now the wind! Nothing like it had ever happened before. . . . But the stockmen grinned wryly, knowing it had happened before and would happen again; only the quantity of soil lost was new, and that was due to the "deep furrow" practice which had been urged upon the farmers by Jim Hill's experts. Plowing to the depth of eight or ten inches, without attention to contour or wind direction, wasted moisture instead of conserving it.

Wheat in August of 1920 sold for $2.40 a bushel, and those farmers who had escaped the "dusters" cashed in. Labor was short, however; threshing helpers demanded, and got, $6 a day and were paid day in, day out, even if rain (for some came, tardily, that fall) prevented field work. But two months later wheat had plunged to $1.25 a bushel and farm labor was plentiful at $1.50 a day. Ruined drylanders swarmed into the labor market, seeking jobs from their more fortunate fellow farmers at almost any price.

That brief labor shortage had called Montanans' attention to the fact that the boys who were marching home from World War I weren't marching as far as Montana. More of them had marched away, in proportion to population, than from any other state; and more than from any other state, proportionately, would never march anywhere again.

Before there was a draft law, 12,500 Montanans volunteered. That was 1,000 per cent above the national average for enlistments. When Selective Service was set up, draft quotas were based upon population estimates, and the estimate for Montana, God only knows why, was 952,478. The state adjutant general thought maybe the population estimate had been based upon the early enlistments, on the theory that these eager military-age recruits represented a certain proportion of the population; whatever the reason, the estimate was an incredible blunder. Montana's actual population was 496,131.

As a result of this error (the war was over before anybody got around to correcting it) Montana contributed more than 40,000 men to the armed forces of the United States in the first World War. This was 25 per cent more than any other state was called upon to give, in proportion to population; it meant that for every 10,000 people 796 were in the services, whereas Georgia, whose man-power contribution was the smallest, gave up but 296 per 10,000.

Of these 40,000 Montana soldiers, sailors, and marines, about 1,500 were killed in action or died of wounds or disease. This loss was 26 per cent above that of any other state in proportion to population and 2 per cent greater than any state's, regardless of population, in proportion to number of troops engaged. And in addition, 2,437 Montanans were wounded.

Economic factors as well as bureaucratic bungling contributed to the amazingly disproportionate role of Montana in that war. The rush to volunteer during the first few days of the hostilities reflected the unique composition of the Montana population at that time. Always predominantly a man's state, it was in 1917 also a *young* man's state. The eight-hour day, adopted earlier in Butte's mines than elsewhere in the country, and the homestead boom had attracted thousands of young, unmarried, and enterprising Americans to this new frontier of good wages and free land. There was, therefore, a tremendous overbalance of men of military age, eighteen to thirty-five.

Socialist Butte and a few remote farm communities in

which Nonpartisan League sentiment was strong grumbled when war came. The League, an agrarian political importation from North Dakota, had semisocialist aims and was hostile to American participation in the "imperialist" conflict. Troops broke up a brief antidraft demonstration in the mining city. But on the whole Montana made no complaint as the army and navy took nearly 10 per cent of its total population and war killed or maimed 10 per cent of these.

Nor was there much grumbling when thousands of Montana veterans didn't come home; as a matter of fact, the state's tottering economy would have found it hard, just then, to absorb them. The homestead boom had collapsed; Butte's mines and the copper processing plants in Anaconda and Great Falls were closing down or curtailing operations. Soldiers who had left their farms in the care of their neighbors learned that the neighbors were destitute and Russian thistles had taken their fields.

But the failure of the young men to return and raise families in Montana, coupled with the loss of thousands of young homestead families, changed the whole structure of the population. The census chart took on the appearance of a bull fiddle or an hour glass—wasp-waisted where it should have shown the "earning-age" group. Within a few years Montana was transformed from a young people's state to a state of young children and old men and women. The injury to the economic organism was permanent: nothing could ever reestablish population balance save a catastrophe which would wipe out the entire citizenry and leave a clean slate for a new start. Grave pension and relief problems could be anticipated: more and more unemployable and aged Montanans to be supported by fewer and fewer young workers.

Gallantry in action won distinguished service crosses for 53 of the 40,000 Montanans in service. There were no decorations for the homesteaders, the cattlemen, and sheepmen, the small town merchants they left behind; but some of these showed considerable gallantry too.

Some of the homesteaders who had watched their seed blown out of the ground in 1920 could still borrow money, and they set about determinedly to try it again. One of them, who had paid $3,000 in 1919 for an additional quarter section

(160 acres), was happy as harvest time approached in 1921; it had been another dry year, but he had a good crop. Shortly before threshing time, wheat stem maggots—creatures he had never seen before and has never seen since—destroyed every head of grain. In other sections it was grasshoppers, or Mormon crickets. Still those who could borrow, from the government's seed loan fund, from banks or other sources, held on. A few managed to pay their major debts, get jobs, and retain their farms. Others were not so lucky.

Most fortunate for a while were those who had found the capital to mechanize their operations, but the inflated prices of industrial products soon threatened them with disaster, too. A tractor part which in 1916 had cost them $10 rose to $39, the tractors themselves increased in price, and were virtually "custom-built" machines. Most of them were of the 30-60 horsepower type, too large, too slow, and too costly to operate for all but the largest wheat outfits. Another serious disadvantage was the deep and wide track these monsters cut in the fields, leaving large areas uncultivable.

Lighter tractors at first were unsuccessful. Models which would pull three moldboard plows in Minnesota soil could barely draw two in Montana. The heavy soil would not "scour" (fall cleanly away from the plow); the deep furrow practice was difficult and expensive because of this extra power factor. Gasoline for the tractors cost 35¢ a gallon, a price maintained by monopoly control of the state's petroleum marketing. One large-scale wheat operator found it cheaper to buy special barrels and ship the fuel to his Montana place from Spokane than it was to buy gasoline a few miles from his Montana ranch and pay the 27¢ to 28¢ a gallon wholesale price demanded.

Some of the tractor farmers reverted to horses and cast about desperately for some way to put in one more crop. Accidentally, they discovered a new tillage practice. With a four-horse team drawing a moldboard plow, they could handle but 3 or 4 acres a day; but with the same team drawing an 8-foot disk they could cover 20 acres a day. The disk broke the ground to a depth of only 4 to 5 inches against the plow's 8 to 10, but they had to chance it; to their surprise, in many sections of Montana, it worked. In some cases the shallower and cheaper cultivation brought just as good crops and Jim

Hill's deep furrow was abandoned; but the new practice was not generally successful and in later years Montanans compromised on a furrow depth of about 6 inches.

It was apparent that mechanization, at this stage, was no solution. Nothing had been done for the thousands of "little fellows" who had lost their places, and the bigger operators, harassed by debt, were going to join them unless some answer could be found for their mounting costs.

M. L. Wilson, then agricultural economist of the Montana Experiment Station and now director of extension of the United States Department of Agriculture, turned to the more stable farm economy of other sections for the answer, and thought he had found it in the "big hitch" and the "combination farm." Wilson, one of this country's outstanding agricultural planners, undoubtedly was proven by experience to have guessed wrong on the first of these projects and right on the second.

Montana farmers had used four-horse or at most eight-horse teams. Wilson, returning from Washington state and Alberta, sought to persuade them to adopt methods by which from a dozen to thirty or even more horses could be utilized in a single operation, handled by one driver and so hitched as to equalize the burden on all the animals. Horses were still available and, in theory, should have provided cheaper power than the unwieldy tractors.

The few wheat ranchers who were able to adopt the "big hitch" (it did save some from going under) participated thereby in what was probably the most romantic and personally satisfying experience ever enjoyed by a farmer; one may doubt if even piloting an airplane could provide the sense of power and skill given to him who, alone in a tossing seat high above the ground, drives thirty horses. The "big hitch" still functions on some Montana ranches, and on one in the western part of the state a girl is the driver. But for most Montanans it simply was not possible, considering the uncertainty of the then-current climatic cycle, to raise sufficient feed on their places, in addition to wheat, to provide the fuel for this animal power. Importation of feed, as previously pointed out, became prohibitively costly. So the "big hitch" failed, and in the next decade (to 1930) the number of horses declined 37 per cent.

The "combination farm," on which wheat is grown and a small livestock herd, usually beef cattle, also is maintained, was successful, and continues to be so.

The "big hitch" was doomed, anyway, as the new, smaller but adequately powered tractor appeared in the early '20's. Unquestionably Henry Ford sold the tractor idea by his advertising and his field demonstrations, although his own little Fordson machine was not sufficiently powerful for Montana use. New, tough, maneuverable little 15-30 horsepower models appeared. The potential purchasers were interested, because Ford had made them so; but they were so prejudiced against tractors because of earlier experiences that at first the machinery dealers would not unload one from the freight car in which it came until the buyer made a one-third down payment and contracted to pay another third in the first fall of use and the balance in the second fall. The new tractors cost $1,400 to $1,600, half as much as the old heavy machines— and they were twice as efficient. They were mass-produced. An era of cutthroat competition began in the farm machinery industry, and those farmers who still had money or credit benefited.

Out of the tragic homestead experiment one great discovery came: Montana, under proper conditions, can grow and still does grow the best wheat in the world. Its No. 1 Heavy Dark Hard Northern Spring and No. 1 Dark Hard Winter are the top premium cereals on all markets.

But it was an experiment with natural resources and human lives.

One out of every two Montana farmers lost his place by mortgage foreclosure between 1921 and 1925. Of the 34,000 foreclosures in the history of the state, 20,000 occurred in those five years and 10,000 more in the next five. In Jim Hill's county there were 120 foreclosures for every 100 farms—more than one mortgage per farm, or more foreclosures of parcels of land than there were farms—in 1920–25; and half of the county's farm land was seized by creditors. When the wave of liquidation finally ended in the '30's, 90 per cent of all the farm mortgages in Hill County had been foreclosed.

In the first half of the '20's 2,000,000 acres went out of production in the state. That was about a fifth of the total land area then in farms, and it was more than the total which had been farmed in 1900; in the twenty years 1900–20, farm acreage in Montana had increased 2,325 per cent.

Eleven thousand farms, a fifth of the total in Montana, disappeared. Farm mortgage indebtedness soared to $175,000,-000 and in the sixteen counties hardest hit nearly two fifths of all mortgages were foreclosed. The state's bankruptcy rate was the highest in the country.

A fourth of all mortgage foreclosures were made by nonresident individuals and another fifth by nonresident mortgage companies; in 1925 Montanans owned 33.5 per cent of the state's total acreage and today they own but 28.22 per cent. The loan basis of the foreclosed mortgages had averaged 1.33 times the productivity value of lands upon which the mortgages had been given; resident lenders were much more successful than nonresidents because they were more familiar with true value of the land.

The average acre value of farm lands was cut in half—from $22 to $11, between 1920 and 1930.

The number of farm tenants increased from 2,000 in 1910 to 10,000 in 1925, and continued to grow; today less than two fifths of Montana's farmers own the land they work, less than one acre in five is owned by the farmer-operator.

And sixty thousand people quit the state.

Even at that, not all the destitute honyockers left. Montana at last count (shortly before the United States entered World War II) still had a "stranded or migratory" farm population of nine thousand, which was nearly a fifth of the total farm census. In one county 77 per cent of the farmers were so classified.

Not all of the land they plowed has regained its natural grass cover. The range in the eastern two thirds of Montana, except for scattered sections, is rated "50 to 75 per cent depleted." Wind erosion is "severe" in a dozen counties, "moderate to severe" in two dozen.

The derelict privy, the boarded-up schoolhouse, the dust-drifted, weed-grown road, and the rotting, rusted fence were left to tell the story of the '20's, Montana's disastrous decade.

Montana, Powell had warned in 1878, "must not be homesteaded." Eleven years later North Dakota, celebrating statehood, recklessly asked him to make a speech. . . .

"You're going to need, each year, a little more water than you're going to get," Powell told North Dakota brutally.

North Dakota is considerably wetter than Montana. Nobody believed Powell then. They believe him now.

XX. THE ROLE OF THE FEDERAL RESERVE

During World War I it was a patriotic duty for Montanans to borrow money, buy more land, grow more wheat, produce more meat and wool. It was a patriotic duty for the state's 440-odd banks (about one to every 1,000 persons, against a national average of one to 3,500) to lend—even beyond the safe limit. This was war finance, to spur food production and the purchase of Liberty bonds.

Governor Stewart recalled all this in his message to that 1919 emergency legislative session. He recalled, too, the state's record of voluntary contribution to war charities, and suggested a state commission to receive and administer donated funds for the benefit of destitute farmers and ranchers. (Montana, like the rest of the country, still had a lot to learn about relief.)

As the special session convened, another ominous little item appeared in the newspapers. It was overlooked by almost everybody. A summary of the monthly report of the Ninth District Federal Reserve Bank in Minneapolis, it complained that commodity prices were still climbing and "there is a possibility that speculation may be carried too far."

How far is "too far" and what is "speculation"? Is it gambling in stocks and commodities on eastern markets—or is it staking home and future in a contest with Montana's sun and snow to fulfill the patriotic (yes, profitable too) duty of production?

That was when the Great American Headache began: in 1919, not on October 26, 1929. It can hardly be said to have started in Montana, though certainly Montana suffered most severely in the early stages, and continued to suffer throughout the course of the nation's sickness. Moreover, certain trends in financial policy—or certain tendencies toward vacillation and timidity in that policy—which were clearly observable in the Montana experience seem to have contributed to the national debacle a few years later.

Most of the country soon forgot the brief recession of the '20's, the delayed postwar deflation which some economists believe was finally precipitated by economic collapse in Japan. Industrial "recovery" began in 1923. Industry and finance—eastern branch—thereupon clambered back onto the spiral staircase of credit inflation; Montana, perhaps fortunately, never did get back up more than a step or two.

The financial practices of the '20's all served the same end, by accident or design: to concentrate productive capital in the east's financial centers, where it encouraged overexpansion of the industrial machine and speculation in foreign and domestic promises-to-pay. Throughout the war years the nation's producers had been pulling themselves up by their bootstraps, obligingly supplied by government. Suddenly the government cut the straps off the western farmer's boots, and soon thereafter sewed them on those of the industrialist and speculator.

President Hoover's Research Committee on Social Trends, reviewing the 1929 crash, found this basis for it:

As a result of the war, plant and equipment had expanded much faster than the production of goods bought by the ultimate consumer . . . While industry prospered and yielded high wages, fairly good employment and more than normal profits to business, agriculture languished and found it increasingly difficult to maintain the standards of well being achieved during the war . . . Price movements of the period contributed further to the disparities among various groups of prices—agricultural and industrial, raw material and manufactured goods, wholesale and retail, securities and commodities—and this intensified the strain already characteristic of the war and post-war price system.

"Agriculture languished . . . there was disparity between groups of prices . . . the price system was severely strained."

These conditions all but ruined Montana, whose contribution to the national economy was, and still is, wholly raw material. Montana did not appear to be concerned with premonitory rumblings in distant markets, nor by the fact that wholesale prices had risen 134 per cent since 1913, common stocks 84 per cent, and the public debt from $1,250,000,000 to $25,-500,000,000. But Montana was concerned, and disastrously involved, because:

The Federal Reserve System, a quasi-public agency, set out coldly and deliberately to smash prices, including the inflated agricultural values its wartime credit policy had helped establish; and despite its protestations to the contrary, it did this with brutal haste. After agricultural values had collapsed, the system swung back to a policy of liberal "accommodation" of business and industry—but not of agriculture.

The Federal Reserve System, deploring the banks' large holdings of Liberty bonds (which it had itself forced into these institutions), demanded that the banks get them out, and actually, by tightening up on credit, forced them out of country banks at 80¢ on the dollar. The objective was to curb further "inflationary borrowing," for which the bonds, while remaining in the banks, provided an essentially sound base; the effect was to strip Montana of its last liquid assets. Montanans, under the pressure of patriotic enthusiasm, a fictitious population quota, and wartime social sanctions, had invested $87,500,000 in these federal issues which went far below par, impairing the little man's confidence in his government's good faith.

Finally, the Federal Reserve System, by relentlessly squeezing agricultural paper out of the rural banks of the northwest, left them without adequate economic function in their communities. This undermined their customers' trust in them and in the whole financial structure; ultimately it helped to open the way for absorption of these home-owned institutions by the absentee-owned group bank, whose coming was perhaps the greatest disaster of all. The group bank brought a catastrophic credit drouth beside which all other drouths would have been puny indeed had not government financing entered the agricultural field. The group banks' money went into Swedish matches and utility holding companies; their semidetached bucket shops persuaded depositors to sink into common stocks whatever portions of their earnings they didn't deposit.

That is Montana's indictment of the Federal Reserve, dominated by the reactionary Treasury administrations of Carter Glass, David Houston, and Andrew Mellon. Those are a few of the reasons Montana and the northwest collapsed five to ten years before the rest of the country.

The east could not or would not pay war-inflated prices for the finished products of Montana's wheat fields and livestock ranges; packers, bakers, and jobbers said raw material costs had to come down. The government, speaking through the Federal Reserve System, parroted the demand. W. G. P. Harding, Governor of the System, said in his 1919 report that the Federal Reserve had met the requirements of war and readjustment by expanding credit and could expand further without endangering its reserves. "But," he said, . . .

the time has come for it to demonstrate its power to move in the opposite direction, and to prove its ability to do so without shock and with a minimum disturbance to business and industry. Fortunately the condition of the Treasury is now such that the Board can now feel free to inaugurate discount policies adjusted to peacetime conditions . . . [But] it must never be forgotten that productive industry is profoundly affected by credit conditions. Modern business is done on credit. The mood and temper of the business community . . . may easily be disturbed by ill-considered or precipitate action . . . Radical and drastic deflation is not, therefore, in contemplation.

So much for "productive industry, modern business, the business community." Perhaps it would be unfair to read special significance into the fact that nowhere in his discussion of the contemplated deflation does Mr. Harding mention what such a policy might mean to agriculture; but it certainly is significant that a couple of years later Congress felt called upon to amend the Federal Reserve Act and remedy a notable omission in the original law. The amendment increased the number of appointive members of the Reserve Board from five to six, and provided that in selecting these men the President "shall have due regard to a fair representation of the financial, *agricultural,* industrial, and commercial interests, and geographical divisions." The section originally had provided only for representation of "commercial, industrial, and geographical divisions."

The original Federal Reserve Act provided in Section 13 that Federal Reserve credit was to be supplied for *"agricultural,* industrial, or commercial purposes." And Senator Robert L. Owen, one of its sponsors, insisted the act's purpose was "to put behind the individual credit of the *farmer,* merchant, manufacturer, shipper, and businessman the credit of the United States, enabling him to meet his current obligations

without difficulty and providing an ever-present supply of
sound currency for business needs."

This purpose was not served.

Any critical study of the Federal Reserve System must take
into account the fact that the System was only a year old
when it was confronted by the gigantic financial problems
arising out of Europe's greatest war and the transition of the
United States from debtor to creditor status. The System was
only four years old when called upon to act as the government's agent in the greatest borrowing operation ever undertaken—the Liberty bond flotation. In its major wartime tasks
the system succeeded; in fact, according to John Skelton Williams, then Comptroller of the Currency, "this one act [Fed-
eral Reserve Act] won the war." It enabled United States
finances to weather every storm, Williams said, and gave this
country the power to help its allies instantly and generously.

The Reserve Board explained that credit had to be expanded in wartime unless private consumption were curtailed so drastically that the citizens could be forced to save
enough to meet fully the government's need of funds. To the
extent that this curtailment of consumption fell short of
federal requirements, there was a margin of bonds which
could not be paid for immediately out of the citizens' savings; these the banks had to carry, either by purchase themselves or through loans to private purchasers. These purchasers' notes were rediscounted with the Federal Reserve
Bank, and the member banks themselves borrowed from their
Federal Reserve Banks to buy bonds. It was obviously essential, therefore, that as long as the member banks were lending to bond purchasers and were themselves borrowing to
buy bonds, their interest rates and those of the Federal Reserve had to be low—related to the bonds' coupon rates.

But when this war financing had been successfully completed, the Federal Reserve began to "move in the opposite
direction," first by raising its rediscount rate from 4.5 to as
much as 7 per cent. Sentiment in favor of this drastic step,
reports S. E. Harris in *Twenty Years of Federal Reserve
Policy*, "was not by any means unanimous. For example, Mc-
Dowell of the Minnesota Reserve Bank feared that the 'little
fellow' would be penalized; Scott of the Dallas Bank contended that a 10 per cent rate would leave the situation un-

corrected; and McIntosh of the San Francisco Bank would not wield a club on friends and foes alike."

The "shock and disturbance" which the System ostensibly had wished to avoid were immediate; but the initial impact was confined largely to the ninth district, especially Montana, where credit conditions were already severely strained because of years of drouth which had made it impossible for bank borrowers to meet their obligations. The victims were the "little fellows" for whom McDowell of this Ninth District (Minnesota) Bank had feared—those doltish Joads who had come west with a nation's blessing to build an empire of wheat for victory; or they were the hardheaded conservative pioneers of the sheep and cattle industries who had outlived blizzard and fire and reduction of their range, but could not survive without credit.

The rise in rediscount rates, however, although it initiated the process by which bank earnings were to dwindle and disappear, was not sufficient to accomplish the principal objective—the smashing of commodity prices. Montana's banks, which insisted on carrying the desperate producers even if doing so had become a losing proposition, still had Liberties to pledge with the Federal Reserve for loans with which to tide some of the wheat growers and ranchers through another season; and many of their customers still had these unimpeachable government securities to put up, too. As long as they retained such assets, the producers would not sacrifice their grain and livestock on a depressed market, and they would continue to plant and to feed.

So early in 1920 Governor Harding announced that more drastic deflation, under direction of the Federal Reserve System, was necessary. Thereafter the screws were on: money flowed into the Federal Reserve's vaults and the life flowed out of Montana. This second phase of the economic destruction of a state entailed the "additional collateral" scheme. It appeared to Montanans then, and appears still, to be nothing more nor less than a racket, a gigantic shakedown which helped to break more than a third of Montana's banks and enabled a good many of their "reorganizers," whose jobs were much sought after, to wax fat on assets which the Federal Reserve had held to be virtually worthless.

This is how it worked:

Bankers who during the war had been urged by the Federal Reserve to lend up to 80 per cent of the current inflated value of agricultural collateral (Harris says the Reserve Banks "displayed unjustifiable eagerness to lend their resources") were suddenly confronted by demands that they post additional collateral as security for loans they had already obtained. Ground for the demand was that declining market values were impairing the validity of the agricultural paper. Federal Reserve officials today will acknowledge that a livestock or wheat note (especially the former) which is impaired in value this year may be perfectly good next year, and some of them deplore the fact that their institutions have little if any agricultural paper. No such humane or farsighted consideration moved the System in the '20's, however. In some instances notes sent to the Minneapolis Bank for rediscount were retained by that institution and the banker who had sent them was curtly notified that they were being held as additional collateral for notes already rediscounted. The point finally was reached when the Reserve Bank declined to rediscount notes individually and insisted instead that the frantic banker negotiate a loan directly on a group of his notes—with the Reserve Bank taking its choice of his paper as security for the loan—*and taking up to three times the face value of the loan.*

Under these circumstances, a banker who sought $1,000 in a hurry lost $3,000 of the best notes in his portfolio, and found himself in a hopeless position if he should be in urgent need of cash—for instance, in event of a run.

The racket even drew the fire of the Comptroller of the Currency. In his 1921 report he struck out sharply at the Board's policy:

With one exception, the Federal Reserve Banks require collateral from banks rediscounting eligible paper. This requirement tends to take a too large proportion of the best paper out of the rediscounting bank . . . [and] has at times left the institution in a difficult position if called upon to face extraordinary demands from depositors, because the bank finds itself without sufficient desirable paper to sell, to rediscount, or to offer as collateral for cash needed. The one Federal Reserve Bank which does not require collateral insists that each rediscount operation shall stand on its own bottom . . . This seems to me to be the plain intent and purpose of the law.

The Comptroller's strictures may have been partially impelled by his resentment over a suggestion that his office be abolished and its functions assumed by the Federal Reserve Board; but since the wind of adversity was beginning to blow down his national banks almost as freely as it did the state banks, undoubtedly his primary motive was concern over the Reserve System's harsh policy toward its own members. (Federal Reserve membership is mandatory for national banks. State banks may join or not join, as they see fit, in principle; actually they are under constant pressure to come into the fold.)

Sound practice or not, the additional collateral racket did the trick: it got the Liberties out of the banks. Governor Harding, says Harris, asked the press to omit from his written version of a speech of January 8, 1920, this sentence: "Henceforth the activities of the Federal Reserve Board will include efforts to bring about a complete distribution of Government bonds to investors and their elimination from the assets of banks." The Board reported in 1921 on the progress of this "elimination":

A noticeable development of the year was the largely increased use of government securities by member banks as collateral for short-term notes . . . The people as a whole in asking accommodation at their banks likewise made free use of their government securities and borrowed upon that collateral.

In the course of this liquidation of Liberties, the value of the government's promise to pay $100 fell to $80 and the confidence of thousands of investors was severely shaken; but such bargains as $100 federally guaranteed bonds at $80 did not go begging: they merely changed hands. The Reserve Board's 1922 report told what happened to them:

In New York and other Reserve cities investment in government securities increased practically without interruption from September, 1921, to the latest report date. At country banks, on the other hand, government security holdings declined from the beginning of 1921 to June 30, 1922. . . . Holdings of corporate securities, which show a decrease in New York City and only a slight increase in other Reserve centers . . . show a practically uninterrupted growth at country banks for the entire two-year period.

Senator Thomas E. Watson of Georgia, denouncing this "crusade of outlawry against its own bonds" undertaken by the government through the Reserve System, said in 1921 that it was then threatening 20,000,000 American investors with the loss of some $300,000,000. Speculators, he complained, were buying up the bonds "at discounts ruinous to the holders." But speculators were not alone in this profitable piracy: the Government of the United States, through Treasury Secretary Andrew Mellon, boasted that government purchase and retirement of its depreciated issues was saving the taxpayers money. The Treasury in its 1920 report, says Harris, "maintaining that the Government was not under any obligation to guarantee the holders of Liberty bonds against fluctuation in the market rate for money, defended the action of the Board [in imposing penalty rates on notes secured by the bonds.] "

When the Liberties were gone from Montana banks and their customers' safety deposit boxes, distress selling of wheat and livestock to meet the overdue notes on which the Reserve Bank was demanding payment began in earnest. The average Montana farm price of wheat in 1919 (when there was no wheat) was $2.43 a bushel. In 1920 it was $1.45, in 1921 it was $1.02, and in 1922 it was 92¢. From $9.92 a hundred pounds in 1919, beef cattle plunged to $5.42 in 1921. Sheep dropped from $10.34 a hundred to $4.49, wool from 58¢ a pound to 19¢. A Montanan's debt which in 1919 had represented 1,000 bushels of wheat (that he didn't have) in 1922 represented 2,500 bushels: in terms of his production, his debt had increased 2½ times. But the products of industry which he had to buy to keep on operating were still, on an average, 1.73 times the prewar price: a binder which cost him $165 in 1916, for instance, cost $335 in 1921.

At the same time that this crushing burden of new debt was being imposed, the Montana producer found it impossible to get new credit or extension of his old obligations. Montana notes rediscounted with the Minneapolis Federal Reserve Bank during 1921 totaled about $65,000,000; in 1922 the total dropped to $28,000,000, in 1923 to $17,000,000, in 1924 to $7,000,000 and in 1925 to less than $2,000,000. Between 1921 and 1922 some $37,000,000 in credit was squeezed out of the state; figures after 1923 are not significant other than to indicate the waning importance of the Federal Reserve, because in 1923 the newly created Agricultural Credit Corporations began to take over the farm finance function for which the Reserve System ostensibly had been created.

The Federal Reserve Board, in one of its annual reports, says that the Reserve System is one "of productive credit." In the three years 1919, 1920, and 1921 the System earned $310,000,000, the greatest profit in its history—because, the Board explained, in those three years "there was a strong demand for credit and the Reserve Banks made a large volume of loans." Yet in 1919, one of the best of those years from the standpoint of Federal Reserve earnings, agricultural paper included among Federal Reserve Bank assets *decreased* $3,000,000 and livestock paper *decreased* $1,000,000, while bankers' acceptances *increased* $16,000,000 and trade acceptances $3,000,000. One may question whether this was "productive credit" in the economic sense in which western producers understood that term when the Reserve System was founded, though from the commercial banking standpoint acceptances are considered "productive" investment. At any rate, it was at this time that the internal wrangling developed within the Reserve System as to the System's proper function. Earlier "indiscretions" which had led the country to believe that the primary function was maintenance of a steady flow of credit were regretted; it had been discovered that reserves were not inexhaustible. The conception of the System as a commercial banking agency clashed with the views of wartime Secretary of the Treasury McAdoo and Comptroller Williams, who had said System credit would enable farmers to hold crops for good prices; and it was even more widely at variance with the position that the primary function of the System was to maintain reserves. Bailey of the Kansas City Bank is quoted by Harris as saying in 1920 at the Reserve Board conference: "You have made the Federal Reserve Bank of Kansas City a broker shop, you have changed it from a reserve bank to a commercial bank, and I want to get it back. . . ."

But by 1921 (the damage had been done in Montana) it was clear, according to Harris, "that Reserve officials were once more impressed with the need of accommodating trade . . . Mellon discussed the close relations of Reserve Banks to industry and proposed that business be stimulated. The Board began to liberalize its eligibility rules and to adopt a liberal acceptance policy."

Thereafter the Reserve System began to deny responsibility for price movements or any desire to control them. By 1926, says Harris, officials of the System "concerning their ability to control or influence prices . . . now expressed a skepticism which undoubtedly was exaggerated because their opinions were for publication."

The Board's 1925 report sought to explain the responsibility of the System for judicious use of the funds entrusted to it and perhaps to apologize for the deflationary process by which it had been accused of wrecking the wheat and stockraising west. Reserve Banks *outside of the financial centers*, the report said, considered not only the eligibility and soundness of the paper offered to them for rediscount but also the general position of the borrowing bank, the volume and character of its outstanding loans and investments, and to some extent the character of the management. Then the Board added: "The Reserve Banks are influenced by the consideration that funds obtained from the Reserve Bank on the best possible security may be utilized by the borrowing member banks in granting loans of a less satisfactory character."

Such considerations, presumably, were held to justify the System's fettering of Montana agricultural credit—on the ground that its commodity base was precariously tied to unjustifiably inflated prices. The same considerations, however, did not impel the Board to restrain its member banks when they financed reckless speculation in domestic and foreign securities. The same year the Board laid down the rules quoted above for banks *outside the financial centers*, it actually objected, according to Harris, to an increase in New York rates which had been ordered because of increased speculation, the board "holding it unjust to penalize business." Harris continues on this point:

In the latter part of 1927 and the early part of 1928, the attitude of officials was that the diversion of funds to speculative uses had not been costly to legitimate users of bank credit; they thus justified the equanimity with which they countenanced the increased use of banking resources for speculation.

Later in 1928, however, the Board—its legal and economic position by this time was "extremely weak," says Harris (and no wonder!) —did attempt to curb the boom by demanding that member banks liquidate speculative loans as long as they were in debt to the Reserve Bank. But the New York Reserve Bank refused to adhere to the program, although, says Harris, "it was prepared to bring pressure on country banks that were lending on the call money market: the assumption being that the brokers were normally the customers of the large New York banks, and that control was difficult because member banks in New York City were generally in debt but a few days."

It has been estimated that on Black Thursday, 1929, member banks of the System had $6,634,000,000 loaned out to brokers, dealers, and speculators in stocks—a sum greater than the average volume of money in circulation throughout the United States during the preceding year. Was this "productive credit"; were these loans of a more "satisfactory character" than loans on Montana-produced foodstuffs or meat on the hoof?

In 1924, the year which the Montana superintendent of banking said "witnessed the culmination of Montana's banking tragedy," the Reserve Board was reporting, without censure, great expansion of its member banks' stake in the stock market:

When repayment to the Reserve Banks had brought the volume of borrowing by member banks to a low level, these banks used further additions to their funds for enlarging the volume of their outstanding credit, chiefly through the purchase of investment securities and the making of loans on stocks and bonds . . . In the financial centers, where the growth of deposits was largest, the increase represented in part a growth of balances held for banks in the interior. This concentration of funds in the money centers, which usually occurs during periods of declining business activity, contributed to the ease in the central money markets and was one of the factors responsible for the low level of rates prevailing during July and August. [The low interest rates, of course, were encouraging the speculative joyride.]

At this time *more than one in three of Montana's banks had closed*—a total of 191—and their depositors had lost about $30,000,000 in four years.

The banks of the financial centers were so full of money that interest rates had to be cut to get it into circulation; gold held by the Federal Reserve to redeem its notes exceeded the value of these notes by $83,000,000, and $1,000,000,000 more of surplus lay idle in Federal Reserve Banks—*but half of the farmers and ranchers of Montana had gone bankrupt for lack of a little credit.*

The Federal Reserve's "unheard of surplus," commented a Montana newspaper editorial writer bitterly, "is due in great measure to forced collections in the northwest." Was *that* productive credit?

Nor did the Reserve System's advertised caution about the way in which the member banks' money was used extend, apparently, to foreign fields. Beginning in 1918, the Board pounded away in every report on the duty of American finance to support foreign trade extension by the purchase of trade acceptances—drafts drawn by the seller on the purchaser of goods and secured by the goods themselves. In 1919 the Board proposed amendment of the Reserve Act to facilitate purchase of trade acceptances by large banks "to an amount not exceeding 200 per cent" of the banks' capital and surplus, of which domestic acceptances were not to represent more than 30 per cent. "By limiting . . . the larger amount to foreign transactions," the Board said, "there would be no possibility of the added acceptance privilege being used for the expansion of domestic credits."

Unquestionably these trade acceptances—again from the commercial banking standpoint—were sound and profitable short-term investments. The Board's policy was dictated by the emergence of this country as a great creditor nation. The Comptroller of the Currency, noting in 1919 that the United States had become the world's banker, pointed out that its banking power was three times as great then as that of the whole world in 1890, and that its excess of exports over imports in 1919 totaled more than $4,000,000,000—"a debt which the rest of the world has to find some way to settle with us."

Nevertheless, this emphasis upon foreign trade was indicative of a trend. A few years later, American investors who had been persuaded to share this enthusiasm for overseas ventures lost more than a billion dollars when their foreign debtors defaulted. The Senate finance committee, investigating this disaster, wanted to know "how had the headlong rush into foreign money lending occurred?" "Clarence Dillon supplied the answer," according to Charles and Mary Beard in *America in Midpassage:*

The capital exported was "surplus" capital—wealth not needed at home—and the bankers had merely channeled this flow. Senators were not convinced. One member of the committee thought the outward flow of capital was largely due to the higher rates of interest offered by agents and bankers for foreign governments . . . Another insisted that by promoting foreign loans at higher rates of interest the bankers had perhaps contracted credit at home and exerted a deleterious influence in slowing down domestic enterprise.

Certainly Montana enterprise was slowed down. Farm bankruptcies, in proportion to total number of farms, were greatest of any state in the union and cost creditors $35,000,000.

A Montana banker whose institution was a member of the Federal Reserve System saw the crash coming in 1920 and hurried to Minneapolis to talk it over with officials of the Ninth District Bank, some of whom were personal friends. He was told flatly that the prices of Montana's products had to come down, and he objected that if the Reserve System chose the method it seemed to be favoring—ruthless credit curtailment—it would break every bank in the northwest. A Reserve Bank official pounded his desk: "Nevertheless, prices have to come down!" The Montanan came home to borrow all he could on personal notes in a fruitless effort to save his bank.

Several years later the same Montanan—no longer a banker—happened to meet again one of the men who had been in the Minneapolis Bank's office that day he had protested the deflation policy. The Reserve official asked him how the "other banks" were doing now that the "weak" ones were gone and the Montana situation had quieted down.

"Their presidents," the Montanan snapped, "are out in front of their banks with razor blades scraping the gilt words 'Member of the Federal Reserve System' off their windows!"

President Woodrow Wilson signed the Federal Reserve Act on December 23, 1913, and announced that he was presenting it "as a Christmas gift to the American people." It took less than ten years to teach Montanans that there was no Santa Claus—for Montanans.

XXI. SIGN ON THE DOOR

The Montana bank disaster began in October, 1920, but it was not until 1924 that it won special attention in the annual report of the Federal Reserve System—and then only as a result of fear that the disease might spread. In the 1924 report the Reserve Board is quoted as having addressed this inquiry to its Advisory Council:

The Board would like to have your opinion as to whether the lack of confidence in these small banks [in the northwest] is likely to spread far enough to do any serious injury to banks in the larger cities or to any banks outside of the territory principally affected by agricultural depression.

To that the advisory board replied, somewhat smugly:

It is the opinion of the Council that it is unlikely that the lack of confidence referred to will spread enough to do serious injury . . . It is also the opinion of the Council that the present unfortunate banking situation arises largely from the fact that the number of banks in the sections involved has been much greater than local needs for banking accommodations required . . . This, coupled with unsound and inexperienced management, resulted in inevitable disaster . . . There are no means that can prevent banks from suffering the consequences of mismanagement or dishonesty.

Montanans, had they not been too disheartened to care, could have chuckled grimly soon after this when they found out just how wrong the Federal Reserve Advisory Council could be. By 1926 the Montana tornado had blown itself out, and Montana that year lost but 8 national banks; but Minnesota lost 92, Missouri 58, North Dakota 59, Kansas 46, Nebraska 18, South Dakota 115, and Iowa 135. All this, to be sure, occurred in "territory affected by agricultural depression"—but it was different territory and a lot of large cities and large banks were caught.

There had been sounder, less complacent counsels in 1924

than those of the Federal Reserve Advisory Council. Even
calm Calvin Coolidge, President of the United States, took
alarm: he suggested some form of refunding for the farmers'
past due indebtedness to bolster up the then-collapsed northwestern banking system. But in Lewistown, Mont., which had
gone bankless for some time after the biggest failure in the
state, the *Democrat-News* editorial writer was skeptical and
bitter:

> The refunding . . . to restore impaired capital of banks, as well
> as to restore confidence in the banks, is somewhat like locking the
> door after the house has been robbed. The pressure of the federal
> reserve upon country bankers has had the effect of placing them
> in such an embarrassing position with their clients that confi-
> dence has melted away like ice in a July sun. The matter of re-
> storing confidence is much easier said than done. . . . The neces-
> sity of having to restore it is one of the most regrettable features
> of the situation.

Sound counsel came also in 1924 (remember that that was
too late, however, to save Montana) from Garet Garrett in a
famous *Saturday Evening Post* article, "That Pain in Our
Northwest." Garrett's study moved Montanans to loud cries
of rage—nobody likes to have a stranger usurp the individual's traditional right to talk about his own operation—but
his facts and conclusions were nevertheless incontrovertible,
especially this warning:

> Farmer and banker bankruptcy on such a scale [as that in Mon-
> tana] creates a state of general anxiety. The elements of sympa-
> thetic danger are fairly obvious. No bank stands alone like a
> solitary cedar tree . . . no bank can fall anywhere without in
> some degree affecting other banks. Nor does any one section of
> the country stand alone and self-contained. When an agricultural
> section is in distress it will buy fewer automobiles and less of all
> the products of industry, and if this continues long there begins to
> be unemployment in the industrial centers, which causes the in-
> dustrial population to buy less food, which reacts in turn upon
> agriculture, and so on in a circle.

But Garrett's Montana critics felt that his emphasis upon
the monotonous old refrain, "a delirious way with credit, too

many banks," was merely re-playing the worn record upon which eastern capital had grooved a theme song to the effect that Montanans had made their bed, etc. Such superficial reading overlooked his weighing of causes:

Do you speak of the causes, thinking perhaps to stalk the effects? There all controversy truly begins. The cause, did you say? It is that the government, having moved the farmer dangerously to increase his production for reasons of patriotism, left him afterward to the mercy of bankers, who outrageously deflated him, the Federal Reserve System assisting; it is that big business is organized against the farmer to exploit him; it is that industry receives the benefits of tariff protection while agriculture does not . . . or it is that the American wheat grower is not an agriculturist, but a soil miner, a land gambler, a reckless borrower of credit, a planter without slaves who pays his I.W.W.'s six or eight dollars a day to reap his one crop, buys his food in the city, and charges his loss to the government. . . . There is no doubt that the radical explanation of agriculture's dilemma has been the excessive supply in the last three years of certain great staples, principally cattle and wheat, the production of which was enormously stimulated during the war.

Nevertheless, Garrett did overlook something: he neglected to explain *why* there were too many banks in Montana. There were rich profits, for a brief time, in the "rainbow banking" which he described in considerable detail, but another struggle, bigger than that of individuals or moneylending corporations for these profits, was going on behind the scenes. This was the fight of the Federal Reserve System for control of the nation's banking structure, and the dog-eat-dog rivalry of national and state banks which grew out of this fight contributed largely to Montana's fatally overbanked condition. Montanans had nothing to do with it, save that some were encouraged (for a price, in money or prestige) to set themselves up as bankers in communities which needed bankers, and could support them, about as much as they needed and could support the Metropolitan Opera Company. A lot of these communities had bankers already, sometimes two or three. Some of the others probably never had heard of a banker.

Consider as possibilities among these last, for instance, the two hamlets so insignificant that they had no post offices, yet which found themselves hosts to national banks, chartered in 1917! The proud bankers had to drive to other towns to get their mail. That was the year the Comptroller of the Currency chartered in all the United States 176 banks—and nearly a quarter of that number, 41, in Montana! That was more banks than any other state got, and quite a feather in Montana's Stetson. The year before, 1916, Montana also was given more banks than any other state, 11 out of a nation-wide total of 122. Fifteen more were chartered in 1918 and the same number in 1919. They were all bright and smiling new members of the Federal Reserve System, for membership was compulsory for national banks; but after 1920 members of the club began dropping out. The Federal Reserve lost 11 Montana members in 1922, 15 in 1923, 34 in 1924, 19 in 1925. (Some of these were state banks which had acquired Federal Reserve membership).

According to the Comptroller of the Currency, certain considerations dictated the decision of his office on the chartering of new national banks. These, according to his 1916 report, were:

First, the general character and experience of the promoters and of the proposed officers of the new bank; second, the adequacy of existing banking facilities and the need of further banking capital; third, the outlook for the growth and development of the town or city in which the bank is to be located; fourth, the methods and banking practices of the existing bank or banks, the interest rates which they charge to customers, and the character of the service which as quasipublic institutions they are rendering to their community; fifth, the reasonable prospects for success of the new bank if faithfully and efficiently managed.

The Montana experience made it apparent that the Comptroller's fourth consideration—"the methods and banking practices of the existing bank or banks"—should have been ranked first. The methods and practices of no bank could be considered satisfactory, it was indicated, if it shunned membership in the Federal Reserve System. As a result of this crusade, the growth of national bank assets in the five years following the Federal Reserve System's creation was greater than the increase in these assets during the preceding twenty-five years. The resources of Montana national banks alone increased more than 500 per cent in twenty years.

National banks were established in communities already adequately, or more than adequately, served by state banks—especially if these, as was their legal privilege, had refused to join the Federal Reserve System. The town of Belt, Mont., had 1,000 citizens and two state banks which had been functioning for several years without the questionable benefit of Reserve affiliation; suddenly a third bank, a national institution, was chartered. All three closed in the '20's; after reorganization, one, a state bank, has survived into the present time. Great Falls, with 20,000 people, had three state and two national banks. Over the protests of managers of these institutions that the city could not support any more, a third national bank was established, apparently on the theory that there was plenty of room as long as state banks remained in the field. The two original national banks and one of the state banks survived.

Stanford, population 300, county seat of fabulous Judith Basin County, had its Basin State Bank, established in 1911 and not a member of the Federal Reserve. A competitive national bank was established. It closed, as did thirty other banks in central Montana's three counties. The Basin State alone survived among this group, and when the biggest bank failure in the state occurred in the neighboring county, only six depositors withdrew their money from the Basin State. It is still not a member of the Federal Reserve System and manages to get along very well as it always has: lending money on wheat and livestock, local real estate, farm land; it has never bought a foreign bond or an American industrial. But propagandists for group and branch banking (who have had considerable encouragement from the Federal Reserve) insist that such small country banks cannot survive local economic crises because their loans are "not sufficiently diversified."

It is true that for a few years almost anyone could set up a bank in Montana and almost anyone could get a loan. As Garet Garrett put it, money went to people the bankers knew nothing about "except that they owned land, wore spurs, and smelled of cattle."

Some of the banks which thus eagerly disposed of their money were little more than loan agencies for eastern and midwestern finance companies or individual capitalists. Others were semi-independent "branches" of eastern correspondent banks, which competed vigorously for Montana wheat and cattle boom business. Their officers, if they were Montanans, were usually successful ranchers or businessmen with little or no banking experience; if they came in from "outside," they occasionally knew banking but almost invariably were wholly ignorant of the economy in which they had to operate, and yet were eager to involve themselves in its hazards by personal ventures in wheat, livestock, or land. Some of their borrowers in turn used the easy money to buy stock in the bank from which they had obtained the loan. A few even became directors that way.

Certainly it was bad banking. It couldn't survive four successive years of drouth followed by one of history's worst winters (1920–21), or mismanagement and ignorance, or ruthless government-enforced deflation. So Montana lost 38 per cent of its state banks and 30 per cent of its national banks, a fifth of its farms, half of its manufacturing establishments, nearly half of its retail businesses, 15 per cent of its population, and some of its towns. The outcry with which it greeted "That Pain in Our Northwest" indicated that it had come darned near losing its sense of humor and its traditional go-to-hell spirit; but it hadn't lost them, quite.

That spirit carried Montanans through drouth, fire, flood, and blizzard, and it sustained them now, when their banks were bust. All America got a brief glimpse, during the 1933 bank holiday, of what it meant to live in a bankless town. Montanans were used to it by that time: they had known what it meant to live in bankless counties, even bankless regions as big as eastern states. They had known the business paralysis which lasted until some industry, perhaps a flour mill or a store, brought in some currency and cashed a few checks. They recalled the bitterly jocular competition among townsmen for the unhappy distinction of having been the last depositor: "I had just handed my money over the counter when Jim walked by me and stuck that sign on the door." Then there was the deadly suspicion that So-and-So had been warned, and got his money out; and the panic among the

down-on-their-luck whom the bank had been carrying because
it was so deeply involved in their fortunes that it had to keep
them solvent or go down with them.

A Montana bank superintendent of that period pointed
out that the closing of a bank is one thing "that can never
be done right." It is no secret that statutory reserve requirements were frequently waived by state bank examiners after
1921, that irregular practices were winked at in a conspiracy
to save the banks, or failing that, to keep them above water
as long as possible. The banking superintendent went so far
one year as to suppress publication of his department's annual report. It would have been easier to let the great mass
of weak banks go in 1920 and 1921, but the state administration chose to spread the impact of the disaster over four
years. The superintendent later told why:

Those who lightly remark that "that bank should have been
closed two or three years ago" speak thoughtlessly. . . . Maybe
it would have been better to have closed it two or three years ago,
maybe it would have been better never to have organized it, but
this is certain: that it would have caught twice as much money in
it then as it did finally catch . . . and would have done twice as
much harm.

Another consideration which induced banking authorities
to ignore the letter of the law in order to maintain the tottering banks as long as possible was the vital one of "confidence."
In their effort to preserve this intangible prop of the financial
system they were not very successful; and perhaps that was
partly due to the fact that national bank examiners were not
so liberal. National banks suffered to a greater degree than
state banks when this confidence was lost, however. When
prices did return to the point at which a Montana producer
could profitably sell and he found himself with a little cash,
if he still had respect and gratitude for his bank he made a
payment on his note. If he had "lost confidence," the money
went into hiding or into postal savings. Because of this, when
the state closed a bank it usually permitted the banker and
his staff, unless proven incompetent, to participate in liquidation and reorganization. But when a national bank was closed,
frequently an outsider came in "to clean up the mess." And
the farmer-borrower's assets, especially those with four legs,

vanished into the hills with singular celerity when one of these despised "carpetbaggers" appeared to check up on the assets behind a bank's notes.

Resentment of the national banking system's coldly impersonal supervision was an important factor in the state banks' resistance to the effort to draw them into the Federal Reserve. It is still a factor—along with the conviction of many bankers and producers in the hinterland that regional financial and economic problems cannot safely be entrusted to a central board in Washington, especially when that board is a quasi-political body subject to the influence of the administration in power. In the '20's the Reserve System met this opposition by propaganda and pressure. It attempted to sell depositors the fiction that only Reserve member banks were "safe," and it adopted punitive measures. One of these latter was the practice of forcing state banks to clear Reserve members' checks at par and then flooding them with paper from distant points and thus putting them to heavy clearing expense.

If a state bank was in trouble, its president could go to the capital city and talk it over with officials of the state banking department. He had known them for years and they helped him all they could. The Federal Reserve member, on the other hand, found in Minneapolis a group of employees bound hand and foot by arbitrary rules dictated in Washington, rules not sufficiently flexible to cover special regional conditions; these men could not help him if they would. And their principles were the traditional textbook principles of conservative banking, taking little account of variants from the norm which might arise in a regional economic situation —the result perhaps of a storm, a hot sun, or just a high wind.

The same resentment of bureaucratic bigotry figured in the country bank's stubborn cleaving to its big city correspondent bank in the face of the Federal Reserve's demand that the rediscounting and other business of its members go to the district Reserve Bank. Correspondent banks were anxious to get the little banker's business and put themselves out for it, in competition with other city institutions. The Federal Reserve, noncompetitive, couldn't be bothered. In the panic of the '20's the correspondent banks at first were generally liberal, but as pressure on them increased (many, of course, were Federal Reserve members) they too called in the Montana paper. Nevertheless some of them acted as buffers for a few months and thus saved scores of Montana institutions. The War Finance Corporation, by emergency loans, also helped to prevent complete collapse. In 1921 and 1922 it loaned about $14,000,000 in Montana and in two years Montana banks had reduced the debt to $700,000. At the beginning of this same period the Federal Reserve System had $13,601,000 loaned out to Montana banks and in two years the debt stood at only $490,000. This remarkable repay-ment record would seem to indicate some reserve strength in the Montana commodity economy of the period and call into question the justification for the merciless liquidation forced upon the state.

It was the fashion—even apparently in the Federal Reserve, if one may judge by the quotation at the start of this chap-ter—to blame Montana's bank disaster partially upon "dis-honesty" of the bankers. Today, however, federal and state banking officials agree that to the best of their knowledge dishonesty did not break one of the 191 banks which closed. Several bankers and employees went to jail, but in nearly every instance the offense was falsification of the books in desperate attempts to keep their banks alive, and with no effort to profit personally.

Actually, a good many of these bankers lost everything they had, including their spirit. "I used to sneak down to the bank early in the morning before my neighbors were up," one of them said. "I had to sit and wait a long time before the ex-aminer finished his breakfast at the hotel and came down. He took his time; it was just another bank to him. We'd work together all day, with the shades drawn. . . . I found ex-cuses to wait until after dark to go home."

Perhaps this man was a poor banker; perhaps he was one of those who made five-year loans with no provision for re-payment by installments—for some did do that. His bitter-ness and that of many others toward the Federal Reserve might be discounted, therefore, on the ground that they seek a scapegoat for their own sins—were it not for the fact that the national banking system gave a charter to this "inefficient" banker and the Federal Reserve Board encouraged him to make the loans which, within a year or two, it denounced as worthless and ineligible for rediscount.

There was a rueful comradeship among these banker victims. One of them, fugitive briefly from his home town because he could not face his friends, met on a street the banker of the town in which he was hiding out. "I want you to know," this banker said, "that your name is still good at my bank for any sum you need." Two years later they met again, and the other bank had gone. The first victim said sheepishly: "I have three salary checks in my pocket—I was afraid to deposit them in your bank. You're welcome to two of them if you need the money." Contrary to some popular misconceptions about bankers, he did need it.

Montanans have long chuckled over an apocryphal story —it is attributed to an ex-banker who retained his sense of humor and his gift for homespun tales (and that's all)— about a farmer who suddenly, to his own astonishment, found himself a director of his home-town bank. For months Ole attended directors' meetings, at considerable expense to himself and without pay, and sat dumbly listening while well-dressed strangers representing the national banking system or Federal Reserve scolded him and his fellow directors for the bank's "frozen assets." Ole finally got up the courage to inquire of one of these visitors, "What are 'frozen assets'?" He was told scornfully that they were the cattle, sheep, and wheat which were collateral for the bank's paper.

The bank went broke, and so did Ole. It was reorganized; but this time it shunned the frozen assets which had ruined it before. Now it loaned money on stocks and bonds. An effort was made to draw Ole back into the directorate, but, once burned, he spurned the offer.

The bank went broke again, and Ole, chuckling, dropped in to see the young men who were reorganizing it a second time—some of the same young men who had lectured him years before. "You fellers," he said, "you got frozen assets, yah? Well, we had frozen assets once before. . . . Now, by God, let's see you *eat* yours!"

When the worst of it was over, when prices had started up

again and Montana had decided it might live, though in a state of semi-invalidism—at that time (1925) the will of William Andrews Clark was admitted to probate.

The estate was valued at $47,000,000.

That sum would have paid every depositor in Montana's 191 closed banks 100¢ on every dollar. And there would have been $17,000,000 left over.

XXII. MAN ON HORSEBACK

Dan McKay was a gaunt and unkempt and unlettered Scot, one of the men whom Jim Hill's railroad attracted to northern Montana. Like Hill, Dan discovered he had a mission. Its objectives were not very clear at first, and even less clear later; but when Dan found that he could talk there was no holding him.

Dan got to talking by the simple process of "horning in" whenever he saw a few farmers together in the road, in town, or chatting over fences. He'd offer an opinion, shrewdly phrased; gradually he earned a reputation as a "pretty smart fellow." The first speeches were made from the improvised platform of a manure spreader, in farmyards. Dan used to say brightly as he began, on this humble rostrum, "I'm a Democrat, but I'm speaking from a Republican platform." He was crude and coarse and his grammar left much to be desired; his language, therefore, was that of his listeners, and any smart aleck who heckled him about his shortcomings was soon put in his place.

The new homestead communities began to hold little meetings, and they asked Dan to come and tell a few jokes. He had a brick plant, and such visiting about was good for business. (He didn't mind when tenants of a building he erected in Glasgow, commenting on the quality of his brick, urged him to put scarecrows on the roof to keep the sparrows off; the birds shook the building when they alighted.)

The early speeches were formless—"booster stuff," jokes, flag-waving. Then Dan discovered that most of the homesteaders' villages had delusions of grandeur and hankered especially for the prestige and profit which resulted from being a county seat. There is a suspicion that Dan's prospects were cannily "salted" so that he would find this bonanza—that smarter men than he saw it first but needed Dan to "front" for them. At any rate, Dan became a "county splitter."

County splitting was new to Montana, although some other states had had unhappy experiences with it. Dan McKay's career in that field began (about 1912) shortly before the great homestead rush, flourished during the boom, and ended when the boom collapsed in the '20's. During that decade he did very well indeed for himself, but what he helped to do to Montana is the point of this chapter.

Montana law provides that a county may be created by petition and election within the county or counties to be divided. (Certain minimum valuations for property in the new county and for property to be left to the old county are established in the law, and it was by raising these minimums that the state legislature finally managed to check the rush to establish new units of government). Dan approached men who could expect to be political officeholders in the new county, and property owners who would benefit by the expected boom. For a flat fee plus expenses he would get the petitions signed, campaign for the new county, do the necessary scheming and bribing and rabble-rousing. Among his first sponsors was usually the owner of lots in the prospective county seat which might be bought for a courthouse.

The money wasn't important to Dan McKay, although he was careful to see that he got it. He wouldn't spend it, however, on dress, on his family, or home; and his own business suffered because he found his mission so much more exciting. The campaigns gave him a sense of power and everybody knew his name—a name cursed and cheered in the newspapers, on street corners, in the wheat fields and in the legislature. Dan was happy because he loved fame, he loved to talk, and he loved to ride his big horse.

Glasgow, like all the prairie towns, was always celebrating something so the cowpokes could ride up the street and back and show off their outfits, and Dan was riding his big horse in a parade one day when the boys gave him the "hokey-pokey." Dan was a professional friend of the farmer by that time, and for this parade he had dressed the part even to the extent of donning a wig. Farmers were not very popular in cowtown Glasgow, and pseudo-farmers were rated even lower. If Dan, on his high horse, chose to personify the contemptible honyocker, that was his funeral.

"Hokey-pokeying" the rider alongside of you was a familiar sport of the period; you might break his neck, but that was a minor hazard. "Hokey-pokey" was a foul-smelling sulphide compound obtained from a druggist and carried in a pocket in a medicine or whisky bottle. In contact with bare flesh it was harmless (thus a thumb over the mouth of the bottle enabled one to flip out a drop or two and aim as desired) but when it struck flesh covered with hair, it burned and stung fiercely. A few drops flung on a horse's rump were certain to cause unscheduled and highly diverting incidents in any parade.

That's what happened to Dan, aboard the biggest horse in the Milk River Valley. His mount, suddenly attacked by what felt like a red-hot poker at the base of the tail, reached for the sky with his hind feet and Dan went headfirst into the gumbo of Glasgow's main street, losing his wig. Dan wasn't hurt much, but it was reported afterward that the mud flung from the horse's hoofs had been found atop Glasgow's tallest building, which was two-and-a-half stories high.

Such little embarrassments didn't bother Dan McKay. He knew people; they'd laugh at him, but they'd turn out to listen to him the next time he made a speech. The Glasgow incident made him talked about, and his audiences grew. One day an attorney who was associated with him in a county-splitting venture watched Dan getting the worst of a street argument, and asked him, when it was over, why he didn't stop his continual disputing and go about his work with more suavity and silence. "George," Dan replied, "I'd rather be kicked hard by a mule than have the mule not notice me at all."

The "Company" (Anaconda), the railroads, and sometimes the big stockmen (not always these last, because under certain circumstances they could control a new county politically) fought the county splitting tooth and toenail. They probably did not recall Powell's sound arguments against overorganization of a sparsely-settled country with a hazardous economy; but they knew the threat of new taxation when they saw it. McKay, who had always been against "big business" on principle, therefore became the little man's angry voice: fallible but loud. Newspaper warnings of the new counties' costs he brushed aside: the editors wore "copper collars." He rode across the high border country on his big horse, in buggies, or on trains, talking persuasively to the eager owners of weedy town lots and the political hopefuls, getting signatures on the ruled lines of his petitions, making deals to end county seat fights or selling his services to the highest bidder in such contests, whispering, shouting, damning "the interests."

The county seat fights were terrific. Some farmers slew each other with pitchforks, businessmen battled in saloon and street. A few times, on hostile ground, Dan actually risked his life; but he always escaped unmarked. He could talk himself out of nearly every such crisis. Occasionally, however, a county he already had established got away from him. Most of the divisions were fought to the state supreme court: there were petitions, and petitions withdrawing names from those petitions, and petitions withdrawing the withdrawals; there were comic intrigues, and considerable corruption of a penny-ante type; lifelong friendships, sometimes even family relationships, were broken up. All that went before the court, and sometimes a county division was annulled.

Dan helped to split up a dozen counties before disaster overtook his clients and the bankruptcy notices of the taxpayers went up in the nearly deserted halls of the little new courthouses. Some counties he mangled twice, and counting such incidents, he probably figured more or less prominently in creation of a fourth of Montana's present 56 subdivisions. A few of the new counties had some slight justification: there were instances where an inert and immovable bureaucracy, loyal to the old livestock industry, neglected the interests of the county's new wheat-growing citizens. Some such grievance appears to have contributed to the success, after a twenty-year fight, of the effort to create Blaine County.

The first attempt to wrest from Chouteau County that section which became Blaine preceded the law providing for popular vote on county divisions and therefore had to be made through the legislature. This was in 1893, and the attempt failed by one vote in the senate. It was renewed in 1903 and it failed again by one vote in the senate, when the member who could have assured a tie vote and victory (the presiding officer was pledged for the bill) unaccountably overslept and missed the roll call. This was the next-to-last day of the session, but because the erring member had assured Blaine's backers that he was very sorry, a desperate attempt was made to get a new bill with slight changes through the legislature before the session ended.

The house quickly approved the bill and ordered it printed. The state printers refused to tackle the job in the time available. A private printer was engaged to get the bill out during the night. At 9 o'clock he was kidnaped and borne off to some obscure bar or hotel room and plied with liquor. The new county's backers, finding the shop deserted and the job unfinished, located another printer and posted guards. At 11 P.M., with the bill in type and ready to go to press, the power was cut off. A hand press was found, and by working all night the committee managed to get sufficient copies printed to supply the house and senate. The house passed the bill on final reading immediately and it went to a vote late in the evening in the senate. Members of the committee had been riding herd on Senator J. M. Kennedy of Deer Lodge County, who had "overslept" the day before, and Kennedy was in his seat, wide awake . . .

He voted *against* the bill.

It was nearly ten years later that Blaine County came into being, by popular vote. Dan McKay helped. But the new county's Republicans got off the reservation and went Bull Moose in defiance of Ben D. Phillips, big sheep and mine operator, who had dictated to them in old Chouteau County. Soon Blaine and its neighbor Valley lost sizable chunks of territory to another new county. Its name was Phillips.

Justified or not, all county division was expensive, and it soon became apparent that Montana could not pay. Tax levies on the stricken dryland farms soared, to support the new courthouses, to build schools and roads, and finally to provide relief for those same taxpayers on their drouth-ruined farms. Thus the empty circle was closed, as a dog, after great expenditure of effort, may finally grasp in his teeth the tip of his own tail.

Montana's per capita tax levy, $26.83, was the highest in the United States when county splitting began in 1912. Nine years later it had grown to $50 and taxes upon property had risen from 11 to 27 million dollars. The population of the state increased 23 per cent in that period—but the cost of county government increased 108 per cent; interest on county indebtedness went up 271 per cent; the counties' expenditure for roads, bridges, and buildings increased 300 per cent and "miscellaneous" county expense rose 592 per cent. From 1914 to 1920 the number of schoolchildren increased 42 per cent; the cost of their education increased 145 per cent.

Support of Golden Valley County cost nothing in 1918, because the county didn't exist; but in its first year of life after it had been torn out of Musselshell County, 1920, its new commissioners spent $120,000 on governmental costs and $75,000 on construction. Yet taxes in Musselshell County rose also: the remaining property had to bear a heavier burden to make up for the revenue lost in the division. McCone County, formed in 1919, managed to get rid of $250,000 in two years, and finally (during the depression of the '30's) reached the point at which more than 40 per cent of its taxes were delinquent.

As the drouth crisis deepened, demands upon the new counties for relief and seed loans grew more insistent and bond issues to support these emergency services contributed to the rapidly growing debt. The law permitted county commissioners to spend over their income up to a constitutional limit of 5 per cent of the valuation of taxable property in the county: refunding bonds could be issued without a vote of the people, and could be exchanged for due bonds or warrants.

In 1913 the state and its 33 counties owed approximately $16,000,000, which was $39.68 per capita. In 1921 there were 54 counties and the debt totaled more than $60,000,000, or $110 for every man, woman, and child. Between 1918 and 1920 the debt of counties alone rose from $9,500,000 to nearly $25,000,000; as their tax *levies* grew, to "service" this enormous burden, their actual *revenues* dwindled because of foreclosures on farm property and declining assessment valuations.

So by 1921 a score or more counties were bankrupt and the state treasury reported a deficit of nearly $3,000,000. Ten million dollars were outstanding in delinquent taxes, nearly all due from farmers and ranchers because virtually the entire burden of increased taxation had fallen upon real estate.

Montana had reached the point at which it was confiscating its citizens' property to maintain the functions of government. Taxes per acre on farm land had risen from 7¢ in 1913 to 16¢ in 1921, or 140 per cent.

The rate of tax foreclosure soared, to become highest in the United States with the exception of that in Mississippi. Delinquent taxes ultimately reached $18,000,000; adding to this the sum of taxes against property which had been acquired by counties on tax deed, the total of uncollected taxes was $30,000,000, which meant that taxes were unpaid on one third of all the agricultural land in the state. In five years—to 1925—the valuation of Montana farm land dropped $320,-000,000. County ownership of land in the next ten years increased 4,731 per cent; today individuals have but 38 per cent of the total land area, corporations have 15 per cent, and public agencies 47 per cent.

Political megalomania could not be blamed upon any outside "exploiters": for this phase of their disaster Montanans could only hold themselves responsible. Dan McKay and his supporters were Montanans: none but citizens could sign his petitions and vote to create new counties. Outsiders had had a hand in the homestead boom, in price deflation, in the banks' collapse, in freight rate boosts, and in other panic factors, but the political picnic was a private party.

Regardless of who was host, however, the party was over in the early '20's, and the guests were sick. These people—the farmers and stockmen—up to that time had contributed 42 per cent of the revenue for their state's support, and they could do so no longer. That was the immediate issue confronting the commonwealth: how to survive.

But this county splitting had also had an intangible, long-range effect. It had made the farmers politically conscious and had given them enlightening experience in democracy. Dan McKay's damning of the "interests" and the object lesson he had taught in political processes were more effective than even Dan had ever dreamed they could be: his hearers discovered that the "interests" could be licked, after all, by the mass weight of disciplined votes. Democracy worked.

Thus Montana by questionable means attained good ends.

Its citizens might be broke, but they were not yet disfranchised; and so after thirty years of indulgent or timid submission to the dominant economic power—the mines—a desperate people launched a political revolution.

XXIII. "A RUSSIAN JEW NAMED LEVINE ..."

A bluntly mercenary legend, "Oro y Plata," gold and silver, is inscribed upon the Great Seal of Montana. It was adopted as a Territorial motto in 1864, and some Montanans ever since have protested it and contrasted it unfavorably to the idealistic rhetoric adopted by other states. Enemies of the slogan have seen in it an acceptance of the exploitative colonial tradition and an implicit acknowledgment of the mining industry's dominance.

Similarly, Montanans objected to the sheathing of the state capitol's dome with copper: better that the weather should work its will on the granite, they said, than that the capitol should thus publicly assume a garment indicative of the subjection of the state.

It has always been the central political conflict in Montana, this effort of the people to cast off the shackles of copper as they groped their way out of a colonial economy. It was the conflict which Burleigh, the cowtown lawyer, forecast in the constitutional convention when he fought fruitlessly to give the people legislative opportunity to tax the mines. It was the conflict the farseeing Colonel Sanders had in mind when he described Montanans as "profligate of our lives, of our labors, and of our sacrifices," when he warned that the mining men, "by the forethought and adroitness of greed," had won and held unfair advantage over the other producers in the state. If Montanans were to be masters of their own future, he said, they must call upon the "ceaseless vigilance, independence, courage" inherited from their commonwealth's founders to correct the founders' mistakes—specifically, their overgenerosity to the mining industry.

Burleigh and Sanders were dead (Burleigh in 1896, Sanders nine years later) when the conflict entered its climactic phase in the '20's.

There were preliminary skirmishes. The legislature had directed the establishment of a tax investigating commission in 1917, and it had presented statistics showing the relative contribution of the various economic elements of the state toward support of government; but it had carefully refrained from suggesting any change in the system of mine taxation— that system, the commission had explained hurriedly, was established by the Montana constitution. Chairman of the commission was a Butte mining counsel.

But in 1918 Chancellor Elliott of the University of Montana, distressed by declining educational revenues, ordered an economics professor on the university faculty, Louis Levine, to make a thorough study of the state's tax system. The chancellor innocently assumed that out of such an expert study there might come valuable suggestions for the legislature; and, though much to his own chagrin, as it developed, Chancellor Elliott was right.

Suddenly in January, 1919, he ordered Levine to abandon the project. "From every standpoint of sound public policy," the chancellor wrote the professor, "it is untimely and inappropriate for the University to intrude itself into discussion of the tax problem; such intrusion is bound to be misunderstood by the public and legislature." Word of the trend Levine's study was taking had got around, and the chancellor's enthusiasm for this brain-child become a monster had died. But Levine had finished his research, had a book virtually ready for publication, and refused to assent to its suppression. The chancellor suspended him from the faculty, but his 141-page essay, *The Taxation of Mines in Montana*, was promptly published by B. W. Huebsch in New York.

This was the first thorough analysis of Montana mine taxation in relation to other revenue sources, and the Anaconda Copper Mining Company's interest in its suppression became instantly apparent. A storm of protest over Levine's dismissal broke in eastern liberal papers and the economist found himself the center of a roaring controversy over academic freedom. Indignant Montanans forced the state board of education to reinstate him and give him his back pay; thus the people, hardly realizing yet that the epic battle had begun, won the first engagement.

The most recent professional history, friendly, like all others, to the Company, retains an echo of Anaconda's resentment at being thus persecuted by an upstart economist. Raymer's *Montana: The Land and the People* has this to say of the incident (italics mine):

... The chancellor called to his aid *a Russian Jew named Louis Levine, later known as Lorwin.* ... Levine, *refusing to be governed by his superior officer,* published "Taxation of Mines in Montana" ... Two months later, *after a furore had been raised over the "autocracy" of the suspension* ... [he was reinstated].

The "Russian Jew named Levine, later known as Lorwin" —writers as well as criminals have been known to use aliases —left Montana to join the institute of economics of Brookings Institution, for which he later did distinguished work. Meanwhile his little book and an earlier, less technical work, *The Comical History of Montana* by Jerre Murphy, Butte newspaper foe of Anaconda, provided the ideological fuel for Montana's political prairie fire.

It was an unhappy Company which confronted the 1920 state election. Democratic candidate for Governor was a young Butte lawyer, former United States district attorney who had resigned that job in 1918 because he refused to be stampeded into a hysterical "witch hunt" for "German spies." In the 1920 campaign he had the backing of the Nonpartisan League. This young lawyer's name was Burton K. Wheeler, and his experiences in this campaign had much to do with shaping his future political course in the United States Senate.

The Republican candidate was Joseph M. Dixon, a progressive former United States Senator from Montana who had managed Theodore Roosevelt's Bull Moose campaign for the presidency in 1912. For the Company the lesser of two grave evils, Dixon had at least its tacit support in the 1920 campaign. Nevertheless he as well as Wheeler promised to seek mine tax revision; for the first time the Company was unable to present to the voters at least one candidate it was certain it could control.

Posters, handbills, and newspaper stories proclaiming Wheeler's alleged approval of bloody revolution and "free love" flooded Montana. His steadfast defense of civil liberties in wartime was twisted into sedition, he was denounced as pro-German, as "Bolshevik Burt." Dixon won the election (the Harding Republican landslide undoubtedly helped) and Wheeler, whose anger over the abuse heaped upon him in this campaign has never subsided, learned some of the

hazards of tying a political career to leftist economic principles. That lesson some Montanans believe to have changed
his direction and his methods slightly, but it did not deter
him from running for the vice-presidency on the LaFollette
third-party Progressive ticket in 1924, two years after Montana elected him to the United States Senate.

Dixon's first message to a Montana legislature (January,
1921) earned rank, in the undistinguished records of that
apathetic assembly, as a great state paper. It went to the roots
of Montana's economic disorder, yet it was temperate and so
scrupulously fair that the Company, in its own subsequent
campaign pamphlets, quoted from this "enemy" document to
support its argument that it already was taxed enough. In
1921 it was paying approximately 3 per cent on each mine's
"net proceeds" plus a new levy voted in 1917, a corporation
license tax of 1 per cent of net income.

As a result of Dixon's first efforts, an additional license tax
of $1 plus 1.5 per cent of the "net proceeds" was imposed
upon each metal mine. But the flaw in this became obvious
at once: a mine which could show that as a result of a poor
market or a bad operating year it had no "net proceeds" could
escape wholly untaxed save for the surface property levy provided in the state constitution. Besides, the definition of "net
proceeds" permitted deduction of all improvement and expansion costs which could be crowded into one year.

Farmers and ranchers had had no "net proceeds" either, for
several years, but, as Governor Dixon pointed out, they had
to pay their taxes, good season or bad. He went before the
1923 legislature with some startling figures and a harder-
hitting message.

The metal mines' production in 1922 had been worth more
than $20,000,000, but the net proceeds tax collected by the
state was only $13,559. In contrast, the oil industry's gross
production had been worth less than $3,000,000, but it had
paid net proceeds taxes of $28,000. Coal production had been
valued at only $9,000,000, but coal had paid $147,000, ten
times as much as copper, in proceeds taxes to the state. Oil
was paying 1 per cent of gross production and coal about 1.5
per cent, whereas on a basis of gross, copper was paying only
.06 of 1 per cent.

The answer, Dixon said, was a license tax of 12¢ a ton on

the gross tonnage of ore produced. This levy, the first striking at gross production of the mines, he asked the legislature to enact. But, under pressure of various kinds from the Company lobbyists, the majority which Dixon had counted upon in the assembly faded away and the proposal was defeated.

The constitution, which had provided for taxation of the "net proceeds" of mines, had also, in another section, specifically authorized imposition of "license" taxes on individuals and corporations doing business in Montana. Taking advantage of this provision, supporters of mine tax revision now drafted Initiative No. 28 and submitted it to the voters of the state at the 1924 election.

This was the showdown. Initiative No. 28, exempting mines with an annual gross production of less than $100,000, established a graduated levy upon production exceeding that sum, ranging from .25 of 1 per cent to a maximum of 1 per cent. It repealed the earlier 1.5 per cent license tax on each mine's net proceeds. Its supporters said it would bring in half a million dollars a year.

Dixon, seeking reëlection, campaigned for the Initiative. The voters were reminded that the state tax commission had found the mines contributing but 8.79 per cent of Montana's revenue while the stricken farms paid 32 per cent, livestock more than 10 per cent, and railroads 17. They were advised to read Levine's conclusions on the unreliability of the old "net proceeds" system: he had found indications that Montana assessors took the Company's word for what its "net proceeds" were. Arizona's mines in 1916, Levine reported, produced a net of $41,845,604 from a gross of $82,036,342, whereas Montana's net totaled but $28,605,355 from a gross half again as large as Arizona's—$146,500,000. Arizona's assessed mine valuation for tax purposes was $209 for each $100 of gross proceeds; Montana's was $29. And some mines in both states were under the same ownership.

The Company, never noted for subtlety in its political dealings, made what appears to have been a serious strategical error in the campaign of 1924. Angrily determined to drive the dangerous Dixon out of Montana political life, it leveled its guns on the candidate rather than upon the issue: Dixon was damned as extravagant and .wasteful; the new tax proposal would never have arisen had there been "conservative" government of the state. Even the cost of a gravy boat, part of a set of dishes purchased for the executive mansion, provided fuel for the flames in the Company press. As a result, the Anaconda's campaigners were even more effective than Dixon himself in convincing the people of the desperate condition of Montana's finances. Party loyalties vanished. Thousands of Republicans deserted the "radical" Dixon. Labor unions were whipped into line under threat of "curtailed operations, less expenditure, less work, loss of market for Montana producers." Sidney M. Logan, Kalispell attorney and son of a frontiersman killed in an Indian fight, deplored the bitterness of the campaign: publicity of this kind "hurt the state." Chambers of commerce snatched up his cue, rang changes on the theme: eastern capital would shun Montana, fearful of confiscatory taxation; the fact that the Company had never been known to encourage another major industry to enter the state and offer competition in the labor market was overlooked.

Dixon lost the governorship to a complaisant small-town lawyer, John E. Erickson; but Initiative No. 28 carried by more than 20,000 votes.

Dixon said:

In years to come the people of Montana will gradually realize the great step forward that has been taken toward equalizing the tax burden. . . . With these things accomplished I have every cause to feel fully content with my four years' service as governor.

The Company promptly forgot the threats of disaster which it had hurled about in the heat of combat. "The mining industry cannot stand any additional tax load," it had complained; but it reported a net profit for 1925, after taxes, of $17,540,532, almost three times its net for 1924. Far from curtailing operations and reducing expenditures, its underground development in Butte in 1925 was 34.19 miles, an increase of 36 per cent over 1924, and new mechanical and electrical equipment was installed there at a cost of $416,297. In addition, Anaconda authorized in 1925 the expenditure of $2,250,000 to equip three mines with high-speed electric hoists, and it spent $1,500,000 for plant expansion in Great Falls.

The gross proceeds license tax didn't reach its sponsors' goal of $500,000, but from 1925 on it did bring in $300,000 to $400,000 annually (in 1942, $382,502), whereas in 1922, a bad year, "net proceeds" and license taxes together had only cost the Company $24,527. It was in 1922 that John D. Ryan, chairman of the board, said in Butte: "No disgrace to this Company could be as great as to have the majority of Montanans feel that we had not fulfilled our duty to them, had not done the fair thing. . . ."

The shades of Burleigh and Sanders, chuckling, probably agreed that while the shame, after 1925, must have been almost more than the Company could bear, that difference between $24,000 and $300,000 was going to mean a lot to Montana. . . .

And, even though the mining industry still had the state's motto, still controlled most of its political machinery and its press, still dictated to most of its businessmen and industrial workers—despite all this, it had begun to look as if Montanans could be masters of their own destiny.

The struggle was just beginning and there would be other formidable adversaries. Well, they'd licked the Company, hadn't they?

...and, at Long Last,
Planning

XXIV. FIRST IN TIME FIRST IN RIGHT

A PIONEER Great Falls cattleman, E. L. Dana, who, though nearly eighty, is still riding his range, told a story at a meeting of the Montana Stockgrowers' Association in 1925, a bad year, which won a chuckle even from ruined colleagues attending their last convention. It was a story about water:

Once when a Missouri River steamboat was stuck on a Montana sandbar and its donkey engines were laboring to pull it off into deep water by means of cables looped around trees on shore, a woodchopper came down to the stream from his cabin and took a bucket of water.

The steamer's captain glared at him, and shouted above the din of the pounding engines:

"Hey! You put that back!"

The steamboat captain's rebuke to the woodchopper was no

more fantastic than the legal challenge which confronted the first northern Montana farmer who decided to use for his crops a little of the water flowing past his door. T. C. Burns brought his family north to Chinook from the Yellowstone country in 1889. He had done some irrigating at his former home, and after acquiring eighteen hundred acres in the Milk River Valley under the old Desert Land Act (which required the settler to irrigate) he dug canals from the river to his fields.

The Great Northern Railway Company, whose line reached Havre in 1887 and was completed to the coast six years later, promptly obtained an injunction to prevent Burns' use of the water, alleging that it owned rights on the entire Milk River, which runs alongside the right-of-way for about one hundred and seventy-five miles, to provide water for the boilers of its locomotives. Litigation dragged on for several years, but finally Burns won. Canals were constructed at Chinook and Harlem—the first irrigation in northern Montana. Jim Hill's railroad may not have wanted word to get around that irrigation was necessary or desirable; but it probably actually was concerned about the possibility of its locomotives running dry; that was a drouth period. In later years it has given irrigation valuable support.

Montana's water problem is the same as the nation's food problem in depression times: the supply is adequate but distribution is no good. The aridity might be said to be of the heavens above and not of the earth beneath: rainfall is insufficient for some types of agriculture, but few states have greater water resources. Two of the largest rivers in the United States, the Missouri and Columbia, rise in Montana, only state which can boast of rivers draining into the Pacific Ocean, Gulf of Mexico, and Hudson Bay. The annual flow of all its rivers would cover the entire state (146,997 square miles) with 6 inches of water; this flow would irrigate 10,-000,000 acres, but actually only 2,000,000 acres are irrigated and less than two thirds of these have adequate water all the time. For various reasons only another 3,000,000 or 4,000,000 could feasibly be put "under the ditch."

Montana has hundreds of lakes, thousands of springs. Biggest body of water, Flathead Lake, has an area of 200 square miles, and 3 miles east of Great Falls, Giant Spring pours 388,000,000 gallons of water into the Missouri River every 24 hours.

But storage and diversion of water are expensive processes. Construction costs, because of Montana's great distances, are high. An antiquated legal system militates against development in conformity with the modern water rights principle of "greatest beneficial use," and forces water users to engage in exhausting and expensive litigation. Interests other than those of Montana—regional and national needs—have to be considered, for few of the major streams run their course within the state's boundaries and those which do are tributaries of the rivers which form the arteries of America. The Missouri, fifth longest river in the world, serves an agricultural basin of 500,000 square miles, an area almost twice that of the original thirteen colonies. The mighty Columbia governs the economy of the whole Pacific Northwest. Montana asks only that it be permitted to so manage this life-giving resource that it will be conserved, and not wasted; and used for the greatest good of the greatest number before it goes on downstream to be used again. Often enough Montana is not permitted to do these things with its own rivers.

The valley of the Upper Missouri originally was a part of Missouri Territory, and the congressional act adopted June 4, 1812, providing for government of that Territory said the Missouri River was to remain a common thoroughfare for all time. Montana stands on that word "common," which means, Montana thinks, that this resource shall be commonly, and not privately, owned.

The rivers of this state make an average descent of 3,000 feet from their source to the points at which they leave Montana. They could supply 3,700,000 horsepower of electrical energy, about one tenth of the estimated hydroelectric capacity of the entire United States. Only four states—California, New York, Oregon, and Arizona—have greater potential power resources. Yet Montana's actual production is less than 500,000 horsepower.

Several factors, then, contribute to the difference between the promise of Montana's rivers and their performance. One of the most important of these factors is water rights, which will be discussed later; another is the instability of the water resource itself—changing channels, silting, extreme variation in flow, or other unpredictable obstacles to planned use. The steamboat probably drove itself onto a sandbar which hadn't been there the season before, or which it had safely passed over a month earlier: the discharge of the Missouri River at Fort Benton has ranged from 107,000 second-feet, on June 7, 1908, flood year, to 1,420 second-feet on August 17, 1919, drouth year. There's no telling about Montana weather: an early spring, accompanied by warm rains and chinook winds, brings flash floods which spill over the reservoir crests and the river's banks to destroy farms, highways, bridges; a late one may retard runoff to the point where a power drouth threatens. Under such circumstances, river management becomes predominantly a question of storage, which, as has been noted, is expensive; so here again water rights and the issue of public versus private resource control enter the picture. It may be that because of the expense and the uncertainty of the market for power, adequate water management will never be possible for Montana under private auspices; or it may be that the uncertain market, the dearth of industrial development, is an effect rather than a cause of the private power interest's timidity and lack of initiative. The power company, say some Montanans, is in a rut.

The Montana Power Company of New Jersey, a subsidiary of the Electric Bond & Share of New York, is the successor in interest to 4 small firms, largely Montana-owned, which merged in 1912, and to 34 other small companies acquired since that date. It is reputed to have one of the largest, if not the largest, single industrial customer of any American utility —the Anaconda Copper Mining Company, which buys power from it to operate its mines, mills, smelters, reduction works, and other plants. At the end of 1940 this one company, according to Montana Power's annual report, was using more electric power than the estimated combined consumption of the entire airplane industry of the United States. In that year Montana Power's industrial load (mostly to the A.C.M. and to the Milwaukee Railroad, which operates electrified trains through the state) represented 76.3 per cent of the total horsepower sold by the company, while the residential load represented only 4.5 per cent.

The utility serves about 90,000 customers with electric

power produced at 14 hydroelectric plants and 1 storage reservoir in a linked system, with 5,358 miles of transmission lines. It both sells and buys power outside the state, depending upon its own supply. It operates water systems for 3 cities in Montana, steam heating plants for 2, serves 15 cities and towns with natural gas, owns an operating subsidiary in the oil and gas fields which produces gasoline, and has large real estate holdings, which included in 1943 Great Falls' leading hotel.

Montanans have been thinking seriously about water management since about 1937. Daily newspapers of Great Falls, power heart of the state, on April 2 of that year recorded precipitation, rain and snow, of .14 of an inch. For more than two months thereafter the citizens scanned the sky for rain clouds, and saw none; but they dodged indoors, locked their windows, and cursed despairingly as other clouds—dust—blotted out the Rockies sixty miles west.

When rain came in June it was too late to save much of the wheat crop, but this could be borne—there had been short crops before, and no crops at all; Great Falls was used to that. Now, however, a new frightening specter hung over the community and the state. Its name was power exhaustion. The same newspaper which reported a meager shower early in June also reported, less conspicuously, the closing of several units of the Anaconda Company's Great Falls zinc plant because of lack of power. The Missouri River, reduced by drouth and burdened with erosion silt, could no longer turn the turbines which operated the plant. It was the fourth such shutdown since 1936, when a shocked and unbelieving community had learned for the first time that its mighty "Big Muddy" could fail it. The zinc plant, copper refineries, and wire mill constitute Great Falls' only large industry: when the smoke is rolling from its 506-foot stack and its 1,400 (more now, for war) members of the CIO International Union of Mine, Mill, and Smelter Workers are busy, Great Falls prospers. But a shutdown may cause a 15 per cent business drop overnight in the downtown stores, and more later.

By July Butte's great mines had begun to go down, and the newspapers were no longer minimizing the story. Montanans who had read Stuart Chase's *Rich Land Poor Land* found something familiar in their situation, and re-read the end of his chapter on Ducktown:

Here is the whole story of the future—"if present trends continue"—highly simplified and very clear. Metaphorically speaking, the smelter is industry, feeding on a declining resource. While . . . that resource lasts, the people of Ducktown have jobs and automobiles. The world congratulates Ducktown on its high standard of living. Meanwhile the land crumbles away and the waters become wild and useless. This does not matter—for men without eyes—if other lands grow food and if copper keeps coming out of the mines to exchange for it. But no mine can be operated without power, and finally the outraged land and water cut off the power. What happens then?

Montana had begun to find out what happens then.

Throughout 1937 the Montana Power Company was unable to fill the demand for power, even though it bought what it could get from outside the state. It resisted, nevertheless, establishment of hydroelectric facilities at the government's great Fort Peck Dam on the Missouri in northeastern Montana. Testifying on March 3, 1937, at a hearing on this project before army engineers in Great Falls, President F. M. Kerr of the company said:

I will admit that for the moment it [adequate power] doesn't exist, but just as soon as the sun shines again and gets the temperature up to 40 degrees, there will be plenty of water in the Missouri River, and we will get plenty of power, and I don't anticipate another shortage; I don't see how there can be one.

Shortages which Mr. Kerr's company did not anticipate subsequently closed Butte and Great Falls plants of the Anaconda Company and threw thousands of men out of work.

The utility opposed the Fort Peck power development on the ground that potential demand did not justify new facilities, and pointed out that Fort Peck itself was contributing to Montana Power's difficulties by reason of the contract the company had signed to supply 60,000 kilowatts for Fort Peck construction. This convinced the army engineers, who in July disapproved the project; but next month the Federal Power Commission told Senator Wheeler flatly that Montana's serious power shortage was due not only to water deficiency but also to failure of private utilities "to provide additional dependable power facilities in anticipation of such a water deficiency." Wheeler initiated new hearings, and with Great Falls labor and farmer groups from eastern Montana represented, the fight was won: installation of equipment to generate 105,000 kilowatts was authorized in May, 1938. The power ultimately will provide cheap rural electrification and pumping for irrigation in a large section of eastern Montana.

Reporting on Wheeler's bill to provide power at Fort Peck (originally a flood control and navigation project) the United States Senate committee on commerce challenged the utility's claim that it would be able to supply future demand. Less than 73 per cent of the current demand was then (1937) being satisfied, the committee said, and added:

Completion of another hydroelectric unit by the Montana Power Company in 1938 [Kerr Dam on the Flathead] will increase the available supply of power by nearly 60,000 kilowatts, but with the natural increase in use of electrical energy the ability of the Montana Power Company, notwithstanding completion of the new unit, to adequately serve and well serve its users may be doubted and challenged.

The new unit mentioned by the Senate committee had been eight years in the making. The delay illustrated the conflict between the Federal Power Commission's concept of the duty of a public utility to provide "additional dependable facilities" and a private corporation's reluctance to sacrifice profits. Kerr Dam on the Flathead River had been started in May, 1930, and work stopped a year later. In June, 1933, Mr. Kerr, pleading a surplus of a billion kilowatt hours of electricity, won postponement of the obligation of the Rocky Mountain Power Company, a Montana Power subsidiary, to finish the dam. The company finally resumed work in July, 1936, after the drouth's effect on water reserves had become unhappily apparent, and after widespread agitation for governmental erection of the dam as a public works project. Kerr Dam is on Indian lands.

An attempt to inject this issue of "additional dependable facilities" outside of the Missouri River watershed into a subsequent lawsuit in which the company, as plaintiff, demanded adjudication of its water rights, brought from the utility's counsel this statement:

There isn't any law that requires the Montana Power Company to operate any plant on any other river or build any plant on any other river. It has its water rights on the Missouri River. If the Montana Power Company does choose to operate a plant on another river, should the defendants be given credit for the amount of water saved from the Missouri operation by that? That contention would be too far-fetched. This lawsuit affects the water rights on the Missouri River. What is done on other streams has nothing to do with it. . . .

The company's seven Missouri River plants have an installed generating capacity of 233,500 kilowatts. In 1933 United States Army engineers presented to Congress a plan for potential power development on the Upper Missouri and its tributaries (all in Montana) which envisaged construction of 15 power dams and a reservoir dam, in addition to the Montana Power's present facilities, providing installed capacity of 910,800 kilowatts—also in addition to the company's production. The engineers' program called for replacing the power company's Canyon Ferry plant, which is forty years old; the new installation would have an installed capacity of 50,000 kilowatts against the present 7,500 and store 455,000 acre feet instead of 37,200. The cost of developing such a tremendous system, the engineers said, would not be justified by any immediate prospect of industrial expansion, though they did call attention to one resource Montanans are still waiting for someone to develop: "Enormous deposits of iron ore have been recorded within short transmission distances of the main stem potential power developments. Notable among these are the Running Wolf and Sheep Creek deposits in Cascade, Judith Basin and Meagher counties."

Perhaps such industrial expansion must wait upon a definition of the rights and duties of the dominant public utility, and upon determination of whether the utility's major dependence upon a single customer tends to discourage new ventures; for new industries might force that valued customer to enter into competition for workers in Montana's already-high-cost labor market, and might challenge its political controls.

Among other things, this definition must encompass water rights.

The water rights system of Montana grew out of placer mining practice, when rivers were turned on gravel beds or diverted into sluices. The unit of measurement was the "miner's inch"—the amount of water which will flow through an opening 1 inch square with a pressure head of 6 inches above the top of the opening. It was many years before this gave way to the cubic-foot-per-second standard which is more efficient in gauging use of water for modern agricultural or industrial purposes.

Powell and scores of others warned the new Territory of the danger in permitting individuals other than actual users of water to acquire water rights, but a loophole in Montana law for a while did allow speculative appropriation of rights and sale of the "surplus." This encouraged absurd excesses; though even those who could prove "beneficial use" went far enough. Many streams were claimed a dozen times over; for instance, the first settler to appropriate the water of Trout Creek in Lewis and Clark County "took" 2,000 miner's inches, which was four times the actual discharge of the stream. Hundreds of others recorded similar claims. Up to 1913 a total of 40,000 water appropriators had filed on 225,-000,000 miner's inches, or 56,250,000 second-feet—a volume of water sufficient to irrigate an area more than twice the size of the state of Montana.

A water rights claimant merely filed with the county clerk and recorder a notice of appropriation stating the amount of water desired, the point of diversion, and the place of use. The amount appropriated was left to him, and he almost invariably claimed more than he needed. In times of ample supply—when the practice started—this did not matter, for he soon learned to take only what he could use; excess water is damaging, or at least inconvenient. But in dry years the first claimant might be able to take the whole stream. Under such circumstances, priority in filing the claim came to be all-important in legal adjudication of water rights. A principle was established in Montana law and maintained by numerous court decisions: *first in time first in right*. No provision was made, or is yet made, for "preferential use": some other states have decreed that domestic users have first right, agricultural users second, and industrial (including power) third. In some instances where such safeguards have been set up, however, they are nullified by practical application in the courts of the same "first in time" principle, which is hard to kill in the frontier west.

In the Gallatin Valley in 1934, water was sufficient only to satisfy those claims which had been filed in 1886—nearly half a century before. Similar shortages have occurred on scores of Montana streams year after year, notably on the Yellowstone and Musselshell. It is not surprising that occasionally in drouth periods men armed with shotguns have sat all night near the gates of irrigation canals while other men angrily watched a trickle of water slip past their fields to those of someone who owned an older water right. Frequently the older rights have been at the lower ends of the valleys, and in order to satisfy them several times the quantity of water they called for had to be reserved at the upper end, to allow for seepage and evaporation en route. This has been wasteful and has fed the bitterness of those who had to stand aside and watch the precious stream go on past their scorched crops.

Today the whole question of water rights rests in the courts of the United States, which are being asked, in the "Broadwater-Missouri case," to decide, in effect, who owns the Missouri River.

The record of this action—as this book goes to press it is before the Ninth Circuit Court of Appeals in San Francisco—comprises some quarter of a million words in five printed volumes. Despite its length and the wearisome repetition inevitably to be encountered in legal transcripts, it is not at all dull reading. One learns, for instance, that Benjamin Harrison, before he became President of the United States, fell into the Missouri from a boat near Helena. And one chuckles over the outburst of Operating Engineer Arthur C. Pratt, loyal old veteran of the Montana Power staff, as he comes fiercely to the defense of some antiquated but beloved machines: "They are damn good old generators; boy, they are good old generators!" Or his succinct account of what happened to the original Hauser Lake Dam, coupled with his sly dig at the lawyers—they had been arguing endlessly over the issue of navigability of the Missouri, a point excluded from the case by the judge. . . . Asked what happened to the dam, Pratt said "It failed."

Q. What did you mean by "failed"?
A. It busted.
Q. Did you see it bust . . . Was water running out of it when you were there?
A. About fourteen feet below the eaves of the power house and it looked nice and smooth, good navigability and everything.

The "Broadwater-Missouri case" is of supreme importance to Montana and the whole west, though few, as yet, are aware of it. Upon its outcome may rest the whole program of water conservation by states, a movement pioneered by Montana, which established its state board by legislative action in 1935. This board, which was empowered to sign contracts with the Public Works Administration, to issue bonds and collect water rentals, was the first such agency in the country to obtain federal allotments of this type for water conservation projects. Eighteen were built with PWA help at a total cost of approximately $8,500,000, of which $3,000,000 was grant. In addition the board sponsored about 130 WPA projects, 3 in coöperation with the Civilian Conservation Corps, and built several with its own funds. Altogether Montana invested more than $12,000,000 in its water conservation program benefitting 500,000 acres of land by water storage or diversion, canals, pumping facilities, or municipal water systems. The board also planned and helped to develop rural electrification projects, in coöperation with local associations, and recently has been planning $8,000,000 worth of water conservation jobs for development after the war.

Each water project is managed by a local water users' association which signs a water purchase agreement with the state board and thereafter operates the undertaking on a "home rule" basis. One of these local agencies, set up in November, 1938, was the Broadwater-Missouri Water Users' Association, to handle irrigation of 21,000 acres near Townsend, Montana, by means of a concrete diversion dam across the Missouri River and a series of canals. The Broadwater-Missouri project cost just under a million dollars and operated for the first time in 1941.

On May 23, 1939, the Montana Power Company filed suit

in United States District Court, district of Montana, against the association, the state water conservation board, and the board's members, who include the Governor of Montana. The utility asked that title be quieted to its asserted prior water rights on the Missouri River and that a permanent injunction be issued to prevent the Broadwater-Missouri Association from diverting the 400 second-feet of water which it had appropriated for use during the irrigation season. The association's dam is above the Montana Power Company's seven hydroelectric installations on the river.

On October 1, 1942, after a series of hearings, arguments, and legal wrangles which take up 2,014 printed pages, Federal Judge Charles N. Pray "forever enjoined" the defendants from using the water they claimed except when the plaintiff's needs "under prior water rights" had been satisfied. The water users and state board, assisted by the state attorney general, the Federal Power Commission and the United States Department of Justice, appealed and announced that if necessary the dispute would go to the United States Supreme Court. The issue, say the appellants, is basically this:

In this case the court wrongfully ignored the fundamental principle that the corpus of running water belongs to the public and is not subject to private ownership or control. Under the constitution and laws of the state of Montana, its public waters are held inviolate as a community resource for the benefit of all of the people of the state and for all time and no person, natural or artificial, may destroy or impair the right to this common resource. The court wrongfully extended and applied the doctrine of priority so that it may permit by a corporation the manipulation, waste, exploitation and unlimited control and an absolute monopoly of the waters of a great river.

Who, in short, owns the upper basin of the world's fifth greatest river? Can the state, which by law prohibits sale of the "corpus"—the water itself—outside of the state, be forced to permit export of the water's product, electric power?

The defendants, said the power company in its original complaint, should be permanently enjoined from "diverting by said dam or otherwise *any or all* of said Missouri River and be permanently enjoined from interference in any manner with the flow of the waters of the Missouri River and the plaintiff's use thereof." In Section VIII of its complaint the utility set forth:

That the plaintiff, and its predecessors, have used, and plaintiff is now using, and will continue to use all of the waters flowing in the Missouri River for the uses and purposes aforesaid, and that the use of *all of said waters* at each and every dam, hereinbefore described, is necessary for the uses and purposes herein set forth; that the *uninterrupted and undiminished* flow of said Missouri River at said dams at all times is necessary and essential to generate the electrical energy with which plaintiff serves, and may continue to serve its customers, and fulfill its obligations to the public as a public utility. [All italics are this author's.]

Counsel for the company explained that the plaintiff actually meant to claim the natural flow of the river to the extent that it is required to operate each of the seven plants to capacity when necessary, and in addition storage water to make up any deficiency when the natural flow is inadequate. Separate water right appropriations had been filed for each dam by the company or its predecessors. Acknowledging that an appropriation "of the whole stream . . . made in that way we would concede would not be a valid appropriation," company counsel John V. Dwyer argued thus:

If we appropriated 100 inches in the stream that at times in the year has only 50 inches and the water right is prior [to the rights of others], we are entitled to the whole stream. If we appropriated 7,000 second-feet in the Missouri River and our water right is prior and there is only 4,000 feet in it, we are entitled to the 4,000 feet.

Subsequent cross-examination of M. E. Buck, operating vice-president and general superintendent of the utility, brought this exchange into the record:

"Q. You claim all the water in the river, don't you?

"A. Certainly."

The court, however, ordered the question and answer stricken from evidence on the ground that this question of "all the water" had been disposed of previously by the company counsel's acknowledgment no such claim would be valid in that form. The water users' counsel, Wellington D. Ran-kin, former United States District Attorney, then pressed Buck for an answer to a question as to whether improvement of one dam to provide additional storage would not "save a lot of . . . water for the farmers at very slight and reasonable expense so that you both have enough water?" Objections of plaintiff's counsel were overruled and Mr. Buck answered.

"A. We don't have to save any water for the farmers. They take it.

"Q. Is that agreeable to you?

"A. I wouldn't say that it's agreeable. I am telling you what the condition is. . . ."

Plaintiff's capacity-operation argument to justify the amount of water claimed was challenged by the defense on the ground that such operation of a dam might occur "for just a few minutes at a time," on a few days in a few months out of the year. This brought from the company's chief engineer, H. H. Cochrane, the reply that capacity operation, in order to show in the records introduced in evidence, had to continue for at least one hour. However—

"Q. It might be sixty-one minutes in a month and that might be the entire period during that month the Morony plant was operated at capacity?

"A. Sure."

Cochrane explained that the lower the flow of the river, the less valuable the company's investment became. In the last twenty years, he said, the utility's records indicated that whereas formerly 40 per cent of average precipitation in the drainage area passed down the Missouri River to Great Falls, during the last two or three years this supply had dropped to about 20 per cent. "The difference is used up by more and more irrigation, which seriously depleted our water supply. That's what we are trying to stop now."

The original judge before whom the Broadwater-Missouri action was filed, James H. Baldwin, before relinquishing the case on being charged by the defense with prejudice, granted "in its entirety" the plaintiff's motion to strike from the issues to be heard numerous portions of the defendants' answer and all of the defendants' four affirmative defenses. Among the contentions thus excluded from the case was the water board's claim that it was the *alter ego* of the state, that the action therefore was against the state and the court was without jurisdiction; that the channel, bed, banks, and water of the Missouri and its tributaries were the property of the state and the state's rights were paramount and superior; that the rights of the plaintiff might depend upon whether the waters claimed were actually needed, whether water passed by the plants unused, whether the plaintiff, by improving storage facilities, could avoid depriving defendants of the water they needed, and whether the plaintiff could not secure adequate energy for its needs elsewhere, or did not already possess it. The fourth affirmative defense asserted that the utility's claims constituted a monopoly contrary to public policy, that other plants in the company's system in Montana disposed of electric power outside the state and could develop "at a reasonable expense, all energy, if any, which the plaintiff might lose by the operation of the Broadwater-Missouri project on any occasion" if such operation caused a shortage of water for the Missouri River plants. Judge Baldwin, by ordering this defense stricken, ruled out of the case the whole issue of system operation and limited it to the seven Missouri River plants.

Defendants moved to amend their answer in line with the famous New River decision of the United States Supreme Court (December 16, 1940), bringing into the case the issue of the navigability of the Missouri River, alleging its consequent ownership by the federal government and asserting that the dams of the Montana Power Company had been maintained unlawfully in the river and without license of the Federal Power Commission. This motion to amend the answer also was denied by Judge Baldwin.

An affidavit of prejudice was filed against the jurist by W. G. Kirscher, secretary of the Broadwater-Missouri Water Users' Association. Kirscher alleged that during presentation by defense counsel of a motion for continuance, the judge "entered upon an extensive discussion as to his views" and counsel "was prevented from further explaining the position of the defendants. . . .

. . . In the discussion above described the most noticeable feature, as observed by this affiant, was that the said judge spent a considerable portion of time condemning and criticizing the Broadwater-Missouri Water Users' Association and the farmers who were seeking to secure water from said project; that in particular the said judge, addressing his remarks to said counsel [C. J. Dousman] stated that you have a handful of farmers over in Broadwater who are trying to put the Montana Power Company out of business; that in said statement the said judge expressed his personal bias and prejudice against the defendant . . . and . . . the judge stated that the claims of the water users . . . were of small importance as compared with the rights of the plaintiff in this case; that it was ridiculous of the government to assist such farmers in the growing of further crops, while at the same time the government was paying other farmers to destroy and plow under crops which could already be grown. . . . The judge then discussed at considerable length the great importance of the functions of the plaintiff. In particular he stated among his reasons for his interest in the welfare of the plaintiff that the services rendered by the plaintiff to the state were of the utmost importance; that in order to protect the industry of the state it was most important that the plaintiff's right to generate electricity should not be destroyed; that two railroads were dependent upon the electricity from the plaintiff . . . that the functions of the plaintiff enabled people to read by electricity and not use candles for such purpose; that any interference with the plaintiff would interfere with the defense program . . . and with rural electrification. . . .

The said judge . . . further stated on said occasion that the defenses of the defendants . . . were based upon wishful thinking rather than any sound foundation of facts; that said statements made by the said judge were not based upon any evidence before him in said case, or upon any affidavits or proof at said hearing, or at any other time. . . . That the remarks of said judge are not exactly quoted herein but this affiant has recited the substance thereof as accurately as he can remember them, and that the remarks of said judge were substantially as stated in this affidavit.

Judge Baldwin then called in Judge Pray, before whom both sides laid a statement of issues. The defense position was virtually as outlined hitherto, with additional contentions, among others, that:

. . . Neither plaintiff nor any other power company should be permitted to retard the ordinary development and use of the water resources of the state of Montana, in accordance with the laws of such state. . . .

. . . The use of water for raising food is a use which is superior in right and equity to the use of such water for power purposes, when power can be developed by other means.

To all this the Montana Power Company complained in answer that the action had been instituted simply "to adjudicate water rights," and "the defendants . . . have endeavored to broaden the issues, to complicate the case, and thus necessitate a lengthy trial and a long delay in determining the rights of the parties to the action during a critical water period." Another defense contention—that it was entitled to "credit" for all return flow into the Missouri of the water used by the Broadwater project before the plaintiff could establish injury—was not an issue, the power company said, because "plaintiff is entitled to have the water at its point of diversion." Most of the defense contentions, the utility pointed out, had previously been ruled upon and stricken out of the case by Judge Baldwin.

Judge Pray, at a pre-trial conference, upheld the plaintiff's position that most of the defense contentions had previously been held immaterial, and ruled that the special master whom he appointed to hear evidence, Howard Toole of Missoula, in general would be limited in his acceptance of testimony to the bounds established by the two judges, Baldwin and himself. In his subsequent decision for the plaintiff, Judge Pray explained that he had "declined to disturb the rulings on the law of the case as settled by Judge Baldwin, thereby conforming to well-known decisions in our own circuit and to the greater weight of authority in general."

As a result of the court's rulings on admissibility of evidence, the hearing itself was primarily concerned with ability of the plaintiff power company to prove that it could and did make beneficial use of all the water it claimed at each of its seven Missouri River plants. This it succeeded in doing to the satisfaction of the special master and the court.

The defendant water users and water board attempted to show that the utility's use of water was wasteful. Definition of the term "waste" was a moot point throughout, the power company insisting that water spilled over the crests of its upriver dams and not carried through those power plants was not "wasted" because some or all of it might be used below, the defense contending that a water right of the size claimed

by the utility at an upriver plant meant excessive spill at the
last downriver plant because of the inflow of tributary streams
between the installations. The special master in his findings
of fact defined "waste" thus: ". . . All water flowing by any
of the water projects of any of the parties and not being used
by such party at a time when such water is needed and could
be used for the efficient or beneficial operation or use of such
project at such time."

The water board and water users objected to this definition, the record shows, on the ground that it was opposed to
that of the Montana Supreme Court, that it was ambiguous
and unintelligible; that, for example, it could not be told
from the definition whether water which leaked through the
dams of the plaintiff was or was not "waste." Leakage was not
waste, the utility's witnesses said, because leakage at Canyon
Ferry, oldest and least efficient plant, would be caught and
used at other plants downstream.

The definition also, by confining waste to water passing by
the plants unused "at a time when such water is needed,"
tended to disqualify the defense contention that the plaintiff's
storage facilities to conserve the water when it was not actually needed to operate the water wheels were inadequate.
This point came out during cross-examination of Mr. Cochrane by Willard Gatchell, an attorney on leave from the Federal Power Commission, appearing for the defense:

Q. Now, could there be any adverse effect on the operation of the
seven Missouri River plants by diversions of the water through
the Broadwater-Missouri irrigation development during those
periods of this year when the flow has been greater than your
water wheel capacity at your seven Missouri River plants?
A. Not if the reservoirs were full, but if the reservoirs were
largely empty and we were in doubt as to our ability to fill them
I say yes, because we think we are entitled to the water to fill the
reservoirs every year if there is water in the river.
Q. Have you filled the reservoirs this year?
A. Yes, sir, we didn't know if we were going to fill them.
Q. But they are all filled?
A. That's right.
Q. And did you offer to permit the Broadwater-Missouri irri-
gation development to take water—to divert water out of the
Missouri River this spring?

A. No, they first gave notice they had already taken it, so there was no object in our offering it.

Q. Did you consent to their continued diversion?

A. No.

Q. Didn't you refuse to consent to their continued diversion?

A. Yes, sir.

Q. If they had not diverted it but that water had remained in there in the river during the entire time they have diverted it this year, wouldn't it have been waste of water as to your Missouri River plants?

A. Not in the sense we have used the word "waste," spill. [It would have been "spill" rather than "waste," in the witness' interpretation.]

Q. There would have been a larger spill?

A. Yes, sir.

Q. So the water would not be used by them or by you?

A. That's right.

Q. So far as you are concerned, these farmers can go without their crops.

A. Not at all.

Mr. [J. E.] Corette [plaintiff's counsel]: We object. . . .

During the hearing on suggestions for the master's tentative findings of fact, the defense, through Mr. Dousman, presented this argument on the issue of adequate storage:

We specifically object to that finding to the effect that the Montana Power Company has made all adequate storage in this river, and that the defendants have not made adequate storage. . . . We were not permitted to offer expert testimony on that question. . . . We might conceive that there were [times] years ago when the storage was adequate and commensurate with the operating plants . . . but we insisted that that is not the case at the present time, and it is our position that there is no proof of adequate storage on the part of the plaintiff, and that the findings and conclusions of law that all further storage must be made by appropriators are proof of monopoly. . . . If we study the records of the power company at times when they claim they were short of water, you will find that in three years they were short of water, as they say, for all their electrical demands. One of those was just before they built the Morony plant in 1929, so that perhaps if their own foresight had been better, there wouldn't have been any shortage that year. The other two years were 1936 and 1937, just before the Kerr plant was constructed. . . .

Efficiency of the plaintiff's plants also figured, Mr. Cochrane testifying that the over-all operating efficiency ranged from 57.5 per cent at Canyon Ferry to 82 per cent at Morony, with an average for the seven Missouri River plants in 1936 of 75.5 per cent. Though the defense attempted to challenge these computations, they were accepted by the master and the efficiency represented by them was held to be adequate. "Over-all efficiency" as defined in the case was the ratio between average kilowatt output of a plant for a year and the average power contained in the water used by the plant or passing through it at the total gross "head" available there.

The special master was called upon constantly to rule on objections to testimony which the defense sought to present and lengthy arguments resulted; "we are coming now again," he said wearily one day, "to the point where counsel are testifying."

Where its testimony was excluded, the defense was permitted to insert in the record an "offer of proof" in which counsel gave the gist of what the defense believed it could elicit from the witness had he been permitted to speak. In this manner Mr. Gatchell made offer of proof that at least 40 per cent of the water diverted by the Broadwater-Missouri project would return by springs or seepage to the river; but the plaintiff retorted that under Montana law such seepage would belong to the water users' association, the original appropriator, anyway, and thus would not be legally the property of the power company.

Similarly the defendants offered to prove:

That there are a number of available reservoir sites in the Missouri River watershed above the power company's plants;

That in the opinion of an excluded witness, Thomas H. Means, a consulting engineer, "the facilities of the Montana Power Company at the seven power plants on the Missouri River which are the subject of this litigation are not reasonable and do not make a reasonable use of the water. . . ."

That stored water purchased by the Broadwater project on an upriver tributary of the Missouri would reach the project;

That the Missouri is a navigable river upon which boats have operated in the region of the project and the company's dams (and that from one of them Benjamin Harrison fell in);

That on installation of a second unit of 56,000 kilowatts at Kerr plant on the Flathead for which space exists in the power house there would be no shortage of electricity in the company system;

That power generated at plants other than those on the Missouri goes into the general power system of the company and that by full use of other plants "there would not be any water shortage on the Missouri River";

That the Montana Power Company sells electricity for transmission outside the state of Montana.

To the last point, which the defense endeavored several times (fruitlessly) to introduce, the plaintiff replied that in the decade in which it had had interconnecting lines with the Washington Water Power Company, Montana Power had bought from the Washington firm more than five times as much electricity as it had sold to it. This was "a political argument," the utility's counsel said, and stated the power company position thus: "There is no more reason why electricity, made by Montana water, should not be shipped out of the state, than why potatoes, alfalfa, or any other irrigated products, made by Montana water, should not be shipped out of the state."

But the defense, arguing principle, put it differently. In its objections to the master's findings, it said of his decision that the plaintiff had a prior water right superior to that of the state board and water users' association:

[This] grants to the plaintiff a complete monopoly of the waters of the Missouri River for its own corporate profits, and violates that part of Section 9 of Article XV of the state constitution which provides that:

"The police powers of the state shall never be abridged, or so construed, as to permit corporations to conduct their business in such a manner as to infringe the equal rights of individuals, or the general well being of the state."

. . . Said finding in effect grants to and confirms in the plaintiff the right to control the waters of the Missouri River as against the defendants and wrongfully and unlawfully deprives the state of Montana, and its agent, state water conservation board, of the right to control the waters of the Missouri River, and places same under the arbitrary control of the plaintiff corporation.

The Broadwater-Missouri case, beginning as a simple action for water right adjudication like hundreds which had been tried in state or federal courts, decided, and forgotten, has grown almost without the conscious volition of anyone to the point where alert planners and watchers of straws-in-the-wind can say of it, "This is the showdown." Unhappy Montana politicians reluctant to offend the Montana Power Company may wish they had never heard of the case, and it is conceivable that the utility's counsel may have occasional misgivings; but no one can stop it now. It is too big to stop; and besides, the "government" is interested. As the case went to the circuit court* the Department of Justice assigned a water rights litigation expert to assist counsel for the Montana defendants. The Federal Power Commission and Reconstruction Finance Corporation already were interested. The Power Commission called upon the corporation to show cause why it should not be forced to obtain a license to operate in the Missouri, and why the Commission should not take other steps to conserve a "navigable stream."

But "government's" interest, Montana planners have discovered, is not always an unmixed blessing. The Broadwater-Missouri case may be more than just a struggle between a state agency and a utility. In the spring of 1943 Montanans had occasion to recall the boy who induced the big fellow across the street to rout a bully attempting to steal his marbles—and then had to fight his rescuer for them.

Army engineers working on behalf of the federal Bonneville and Grand Coulee power projects in Washington state presented to the Bonneville advisory board a set of proposals for additional water storage on the Columbia and its tributaries. Citizens of Montana and Idaho discovered that dams built or raised in accordance with these plans would lift the levels of lakes in the two states to the point where they would destroy thousands of acres of productive land, some industries, and even some communities. Montana's Governor Sam C. Ford, the state water conservation board, and thousands of citizens protested the project at public hearings before the army engineers, who acknowledged that the plan had been for the government to take over the Montana Power Company's Kerr Dam and raise it seventeen feet. This would have caused Flathead Lake to flood much of its valley, one of the most beautiful and fertile sections of the state; several small

* See n., p. 274.

communities would have been wiped out and at least a portion of the city of Kalispell inundated. The engineers said it
was the easiest and cheapest method of providing additional
storage to obtain power needed in Washington for war industries; but as a result of the vigorous Montana protest the
state was assured that the project would be abandoned. Bonneville turned its attention to Idaho, where a dam at Albeni
Falls would back up Lake Pend Oreille, flooding part of Bon-
ner County. Citizens' opinion in Idaho was divided, but the
Governor and others protested.

Montana has proposed in place of the Bonneville program,
which would make the state simply a reservoir, a feeder of
water to distant power plants, that the government proceed
with construction of power projects long since reconnoitered
and proven feasible within Montana. After abandonment of
the Flathead proposal, support of the Bonneville administration was pledged to these.

Coördination of the vast resources of the Columbia and
Missouri River watersheds so that power facilities are equitably distributed among states and beneficial use, power and
other, assured to the limit of the water, undoubtedly cannot
be left to private enterprise. It is, likewise, too big a job for
any one state; and it is certainly too big and too fraught with
dangerous possibilities to be entrusted to planners of a single
power project in the Pacific northwest.

The Bonneville scheme gave Montana a very bad scare. It
was an ideal issue for the Company press because the fact that
Montana Power control of the Flathead River was threatened
was only incidental to the disaster which loomed for the common people of the valley. The power company itself remained in the background and let the citizens, including
some of its enemies, do the fighting.

Nor has alarm been relieved by recent discovery of the ease
with which the federal government can "confiscate" vast
chunks of western territory. President Roosevelt's executive
order in the spring of 1943 seizing without warning Wyoming's 221,000-acre Jackson Hole as a "national monument"
was instantly protested by all western governors. And Interior
Secretary Ickes' sneer at the ranchers who defiantly drove
their herds across the area (he called them "mail-order cow-

boys") will live to cause much subsequent grief to Mr. Ickes and whatever federal planners are unfortunate enough to be assigned to the cow country.

Westerners are quick to resent and challenge the domineering note which they recognized in the Jackson Hole and Bonneville incidents. Grass and water are the west's most precious possessions. Federal appropriation, or threatened appropriation, of these treasures has now inspired among western governors a new "state's rights" movement, born in hurried regional conferences, and this may have considerable political significance in the future. The west's own planners have found themselves unhappily but determinedly aligned with the utilities, which have used the "state's rights" argument for less justifiable ends.

Federal and regional planners should take warning from the fact that a rash proposal to flood Montana's rich valleys for the benefit of Washington industries drove the people of the state overnight into a temporary but effective alliance with the powerful utility interest which they had dared, at long last, to challenge to a finish fight.

* On Jan. 4, 1944, the circuit court reversed the lower court's judgment (p. 262) and specifically dismissed the action in so far as it concerned the water conservation board and its members. The majority decision was based solely upon jurisdiction: it held the water board to be in fact "a mere arm" of the sovereign state which thus could not be sued in federal court. Because the entire action was reversed, however, the Montana Power Company was not entitled to judgment against the water users' association, though the way apparently was left open for future proceedings against this defendant if the utility chose to initiate them. The basic issue—validity of the company's water right—did not figure at all in the decision, though in notes accompanying it the majority said: "That appellee's [company's] rights were not per se invaded by the enterprise in question is shown by the fact that the Board's project was completed during the course of the trial and water was diverted from the river during the 1941 irrigation season, concededly without interfering with appellee's prior rights. Indeed it was found that with the exception of the months of July and August the flow of the Missouri has normally been more than sufficient to supply appellee's requirements."

XXV. SOIL BLOWING IS A DISEASE

Canada is the land of agricultural miracles.

In recent years the farm scientists have recognized the identity of interest, for planning purposes, of Assiniboia's prairie and the plains of Montana, the Dakotas, Wyoming, and Nebraska. But long before they got around to it, the people of this region had learned that frontiers of weather are not fixed by international agreement.

Southern Saskatchewan and Alberta have always been an economic unit with the northern states. A map prepared in 1942 by the Northern Great Plains Agricultural Advisory Council for an experimental report on present-day planning needs outlines the identical section over which the buffalo ranged and were pursued by Indian and métis hunters sixty years ago. These people acknowledged no nationality save their own, no government save those of God and of the hunt. Their flag was the flame of a sunset, the stinging smoke of a prairie fire, the great plume of white and shining ice which swept their world when a blizzard struck. Many still living do not know on which side of the boundary they were born.

It has taken the white man a long time to learn what these predecessors of his took for granted: you can fit your economy to nature but you can't fit nature to your economy. Buffalo, wind, sun, and snow pay no attention to boundary lines.

Planning—grass-roots planning, the only kind that can ever succeed—was born in the agony of northwestern drouth. The victims of drouth themselves originated it, though accidentally, and not the scientists; there is always a gulf between them, a morass of pedagogical jargon. Planning had to come more simply, as a practical device to implement purely mechanical processes—new ways to grow wheat. The new farm practices (and some were not actually new—just rediscovered) wouldn't work for just one farmer in a district or a county. There had to be coöperation, agreed upon in advance. It was coöperate or perish; and with coöperation, there was planning.

The most important of the new farming practices—born, like large-scale mechanization, during the drouth decade— was strip farming. It had an interesting history.

Four thousand years ago the Incas of Peru and the Chinese and Japanese terraced their crops—planted contour strips on hillsides, alternating a strip of crop and a strip of some soil-binding plant, usually grass. This slowed down and guided the water runoff, and checked erosion. Centuries later the Germans adopted the practice for the steep banks of the Rhine. Perhaps it was their descendants who introduced the practice to America, in Pennsylvania.

But there are few cultivated hillsides in the northern plains. There would seem to be no need for terracing in this flat land. The practice originated in countries which had too much water, where floods rushing down hillsides uprooted the plants. How could it serve a country which had hardly any water on the crops?

The story of its adaptation to dryland agriculture proves again the role of accident in history, the strange interrelation of seemingly distinct and irrelative events. For instance: the Northwest Rebellion.

In 1870 and again in 1885, a handful of people set themselves up as a nation and fought two futile wars against the Dominion of Canada to preserve their way of life against the advance of mechanical civilization. They were the métis, the "breeds," led in both struggles by Louis Riel. He was briefly a Montanan, as were many of his people. For a few months after the first uprising they held Manitoba. The scene of the second conflict was moved westward to Saskatchewan, which was Assiniboia then. The causes of both wars were the same: resentment of the invasion of their north country by English and Scotch farmers, driving off the buffalo by which the métis lived; and, linked with that invasion, the English system of surveys which pushed the original settlers away from the water. The métis were beaten, the nation dispersed, by machines: the Canadian Pacific Railway transported thousands of troops to crush them, and an American machine gun, the Gatling, cut down the skilled hunters—its first use on this continent in actual warfare.

At Indian Head, Assiniboia, there lived a Scotch farmer named Angus McKay. In the spring of 1885, as Paul de Kruif tells the story in his *Hunger Fighters,* his farm help went off to fight the foolish métis who resisted the blessings of Anglo-Saxon civilization. One of McKay's fields was plowed, but not planted; alone on the farm, he did not have time to sow the wheat. McKay was a careful farmer, however, and he found time somehow to keep the plowed field clean, cultivating it to kill the weeds. It lay fallow all that year, and next spring he planted it. This was a time of severe drouth (the beaten métis, disarmed and cropless, drifted by hundreds across the border to beg from the more prosperous Americans, and soon became known as a worthless bunch); McKay marveled when the field produced thirty-five bushels of wheat to the acre. A continuously cropped field beside it yielded but two bushels to the acre.

McKay had "discovered" the principle of summer tillage or "summer fallow." It was not new, but he was probably the first to use it on the northern plains.

News of the miracle spread. A quarter century later, when the Montana homestead rush began, some of the shrewder and less impatient newcomers adopted summer tillage. The fallow field, storing up at least part of an extra season's moisture, invariably produced a better crop than a field sown to wheat year after year.

The railroads urged the practice upon the honyocker; it seemed to be the answer to the dilemma of drouth. Scientific agencies such as the government experiment stations were, however, more cautious; and in this instance wisely cautious, as it turned out. There were serious drawbacks to summer tillage and they became more and more apparent as the "soil mining" of the homestead era continued. One, of course, was expense: permitting half of one's acreage to remain out of production year after year meant that a larger operating unit was necessary to support life, for summer fallow could not offset continued drouth; there had to be rain sometime, if the field were to store up any moisture. And the crop ripened later on summer-fallow fields. It was only a few days later, but a few days are important where harvest races with winter, always lying in wait just the other side of Height of Land. Still another and ultimately the fatal flaw in the practice was the incessant cultivation it required to keep down the weeds. An elaborate theory of the beneficial "dust mulch" thus created was dreamed up; it was nonsense. The soil was loosened, the clods broken up, the surface pulverized—and the fields began to blow.

The first to adopt summer fallow succeeded, for several years. Alvin C. Hull of north central Montana produced excellent crops in two years of disastrous drouth; a St. Paul bank had a pamphlet printed describing his methods and distributed thousands of copies. Other farmers, desperate, seized upon the practice as a last hope. Better some crop on half of their acres than no crop at all on any of them.

But the dust clouds became bigger and blacker. Summer fallow wasn't working, even on the farms where it had worked before.

The wheat rancher was stumbling upon a great truth:
Soil blowing is a *disease* of the land.

Summer fallow worked fairly well when only a few farmers practiced it; the soil on their neighbors' fields, even in fields parched by drouth, was held in place by their miserable crop. But once blowing started, it was almost impossible, it seemed, to check it. A twister drilled into a patch of light, powdery soil, the blow spread fanwise across the field, the wind rose— and an adjoining field also in fallow was infected, just as it could have been infected by insects, or as humans could be by a germ. Contact was fatal, and once infected a field would blow forever if it lay fallow, for each cultivation reduced more cloddy soil to dust, ready for the wind.

This disease was deadlier even than the drouth which was its preliminary stage. Every inch of topsoil lost by blowing contained plant food equal to the amount removed from the soil by twenty crops of wheat yielding fifty bushels to the acre. That meant a loss equal to ten years' wheatgrowing on the summer fallow system; with wheat worth as little as $1 a bushel, it was a loss of $1,000 an acre.

Thus summer fallow, like everything else ever tried on the northern plains, appeared to be defeating itself. A practice designed to conserve moisture was hastening loss of the soil. For a little while there had been hope; now again there was none; and the experiment itself had left the plains farmer worse off than he had been before.

It was time for another miracle. Again it came from Canada, which had given the high prairies their quick-ripening, drouth-resistant hard wheat strain, the Marquis, and had applied to the dryland wheat farm the principle of summer fallow, which should have worked, but didn't.

This second miracle was also one of adaptation.

Leonard and Arie Koole of the Nobleford-Monarch section of Alberta ("sunny southern Alberta," said the railroad and the little boards of trade, but a man on a desert learns to hate the sun) were brothers and Dutch. They also were intelligent and determined men. In 1917, first of the four great drouth years which burned out Montana's homesteaders, they watched as the wind snatched the topsoil from their fallow fields. They talked it over with their neighbors, other Dutchmen in the little colony. Someone (the Kooles did not claim the credit) remarked that the westernmost edges of the fields broadside to the wind had not drifted; the blow did not start until the wind had swept some distance into the fields. It would be a fine thing if one could only have more western edges on one's fields. . . . They had the answer. Why not narrow the fallow field? Why not alternate strips of crop and strips of fallow? Why not place the strips at right angles to the wind so that the furrow would always be broadside to it, with a shelter belt of crop or stubble to protect the fallow strip?

The Kooles tried it in 1918, on 240 acres. It worked; and so came strip farming, salvation of the northern plains. It was the ancient terrace, laid out flat and combined with summer fallow; it was the water-erosion principle applied to wind. At first the strips were very wide, 80 and 40 rods; later they were cut to 20 or 10, and today in many sections a 5-rod strip is standard. But variations in width are only modifications of the principle, to fit different wind, soil, and mechanical conditions. Strip farming couldn't cure the disease of soil blowing but it arrested it. The Kooles' discovery, said an Alberta College of Agriculture bulletin simply, "saved a region apparently doomed to destruction." There were no medals for Leonard and Arie Koole and few even among the plains farmers whom they rescued from starvation ever heard of them.

But Montanans heard of this second miracle, and drove north to see it. Within a couple of years the Smail brothers were trying it in Fergus County, then H. D. Myrick of the Square Butte country and A. P. Anderson of Cascade County. W. H. Reed of Turner, Blaine County, just south of the

border, came back from Alberta determined to sell the plan
to his neighbors. A pioneer of summer fallow, Reed knew this
new method would fail as that had failed, unless it were applied coöperatively. Reed was a crusader: he carried boxes of
soil around with him, built little demonstration models, explained the principle simply. He and Myrick and others
formed strip farming clubs, organized their districts so efficiently that alternate crop and fallow strips ran through from
one farm to the next, preventing drifting which would occur
if two fallow strips lay side by side with only a fence between.

Most of these men had been homesteaders, of whom the
state agricultural commissioner had said: "They had had no
previous experience, such as clerks, barbers, etc." As a matter
of fact, Reed had been a barber. He had been hailed out,
dried out, blown out, for year after year.

Today strip farming is the accepted method of wheat raising wherever there is wind on the northern plains. The Agricultural Adjustment Administration's Montana committee
virtually forced general adoption of the practice in the state
during the '30's, but even without this compulsion it would
have spread, because farmers saw it proven in the field.

Mechanization, summer fallow, strip farming—all these
were forcing those who had survived the panic period toward
the larger operating unit. The transition was not easy. "The
tractors," wrote John Steinbeck in *The Grapes of Wrath*,
"came over the fields and into the fields, great crawlers moving like insects, having the incredible strength of insects."
Then . . .

The driver . . . could not see the land as it was, he could not
smell the land as it smelled; his feet did not stamp the clods or
feel the warmth and power of the earth. He sat in an iron seat
and stepped on iron pedals. . . . He did not know or own or trust
or beseech the land. If a seed dropped did not germinate, it was
nothing. If the young thrusting plant withered in drought or
drowned in a flood of rain, it was no more to the driver than to
the tractor.

He loved the land no more than the bank loved the land. . . .
Behind the tractor rolled the shining disks, cutting the earth with
blades—not plowing but surgery, pushing the cut earth to the
right where the second row of disks cut it and pushed it to the

left; slicing blades shining, polished by the cut earth. . . . And when that crop grew, and was harvested, no man had crumbled a hot clod in his fingers and let the earth sift past his fingertips. No man had touched the seed, or lusted for the growth. Men ate what they had not raised, had no connection with the bread. The land bore under iron, and under iron gradually died; for it was not loved or hated, it had no prayers or curses.

Metaphysical fantasy? Perhaps, and undoubtedly, as some of the critics pointed out, far beyond the mental scope of the Joads who were the ostensible protagonists of the piece. But was it beyond them, except in its poetic form of expression? This is what a Montana wheat grower had to say of the difficulties of that transition period:

I have always figured that one of the chief troubles was the failure of the people to recognize the fact that the tractor deprived them of the opportunity to convert hours of work into production. With the advent of the tractor, the Montana farmers were paying eastern manufacturers for labor they formerly had provided themselves—and they had to do this with an even lower income than they had had before.

Put it another way: most of the Montana farm work was now being done back east, in Detroit or wherever the tractor came from. The money that had gone before to pay labor at home, to buy horses and take care of them—money that had gone to the towns and to other farms and ranches—was going back east to pay for the tractor. And not enough of it was returning to Montana. Whereas before we had fed our own hay to our own horses, now we bought gasoline and repair parts from outside the state.

Then there was the factor of all that new power. There was a tremendous increase in power without, in most cases, a corresponding increase in land area. Few of the farmers had places big enough to justify use of this new and expensive power; a lot of it was wasted. And that meant a lot of farmers didn't have enough to do.

There, stated more practically, more in economic than social terms, is Steinbeck's thesis or an extension of it. The Montanan quoted was far better educated than the Joads; a highly successful operator, he was one who had increased his land area to attain a skillful balance of mass production and declining mechanical costs. But other farmers, ex-homesteaders, seized quickly upon his statement when it was repeated to them; maybe, they said, it explained what had gone wrong with their farms and towns in that period, something they had not been able to figure out.

So in Montana the machine, adopted eagerly to save an unplanned agricultural system, only hastened that system's passing. Acquisition of the machine and its employment on the wrong soil in the wrong way entailed added economic and social strains which the homestead economy could not survive.

It is significant that while crop acreage in Montana increased 205 per cent from 1910 to 1920, machinery investment in the same period jumped 450 per cent. True, the "value" of farm lands in that period rose correspondingly to the machinery investment; but this land figure was largely speculative and much of this "value" was paper; the machinery investment was mostly cash, even if borrowed and secured by liens on the crop. The tractor—initial cost and maintenance—represented an actual drain of wealth out of the state which was not compensated for by improved production because the fictitious increase in land values tended to prevent enlargement of units to accommodate the increased power provided by machines.

Then there were damaging lags within the process of mechanization itself. The tractor speeded up greatly the planting operation and increased the area which could be seeded; but until the appearance of the combined harvester-thresher several years after the tractor, the farmer could not harvest the additional acreage. The "combine," when it did appear, was expensive to buy and to operate, and its use entailed some risk of storm losses since the grain had to stand longer in the field than under the old methods.

The whole post-panic readjustment of Montana agriculture —mechanization, new farming methods, new land policies— tremendously increased the risks of farm operation. On the other hand, it tended to eliminate the unfit. Equipment expense is now estimated at 40 per cent of the crop cost. Lack of mechanical efficiency, or arbitrary price increases beyond the farmer's control (such as gasoline, distillate or oil), can quickly ruin the wheat operator. Also there have been important social consequences. Added efficiency of the tractor and truck for hauling grain, for instance, permits longer trips to railroad points and eliminates some communities whose chief excuse for existence was the grain elevator.

Mechanization forced a shift to cash operations: the farmer had to pay for his production needs whereas before the advent of the machine he had grown most of the supplies needed to put in his crop. Beset by uncertain markets and (especially in Montana) capricious weather, he had to increase the efficiency of his operation greatly or go down. In short, he had to be immeasurably more alert and intelligent than his predecessor of a generation or even a couple of decades ago.

What the full social effect of this expanding caliber of the farm operator will be is yet to be seen; certainly it already has given rise to new cultural demands upon Montana communities which are unable to meet them. And, while one cannot "scientifically" attribute one social attitude to diverse individuals merely because they are included within a single economic group, it is permissible to speculate upon a trend. Thus it may be guessed that much of the state's reversion to political conservatism after eras of stormy agrarian movements may be due to the rise of this new, more "businesslike" farming.

The violence of the human exploitation during the homestead era brought about, as it has so frequently as waves of "cultures" have washed over the state, equally violent reaction. The Nonpartisan League, revolutionary in base, sought producer-coöperative control of agricultural finance and marketing. Born out of agrarian anguish, it figured in a few political campaigns, though it never gained the power it did in neighboring North Dakota. Later farm troubles brought the Farm Holiday Association, neither as radical nor as determined as the League: it fell apart as soon as its value as a protest organization was gone. Today's Farmers' Educational and Coöperative Union, strongest agrarian body in the northwest, is more powerful than any of its forebears, but probably would be regarded by them as somewhat pedantic: its members solemnly study economics, cooking, and finance; its leaders, respecters of property, preach a gentle refashioning of the capitalist system by means of coöperatives. The Union trains planners, but it fights the larger operating unit; it stands alone as spokesman for the small-scale operator against an apparently inexorable trend, currently assisted by government policies which are slowly squeezing the little fellow out.

The Union's alarm over this trend is well-founded. No one doubts the ability of the big, mechanized operator to plan— now that he has learned (and learned more thoroughly, perhaps, than the small farmer) that agriculture cannot survive in semi-arid country without coöperation among those who live by it. But there will be no room in his plan for Montana's nine thousand "stranded" farm families, no room for the Joads.

Thirty years ago, Jim Hill's fear of the "bonanza farm" hastened his unwise promotion of the homestead rush. Now it is coming, unless the grass-roots planners can stop it—and there are two sets of planners, little and big. The signs and portents are to be read in the statistics: bigger and bigger operating units, more tenants, fewer owners; less than 18 per cent of the land owned by individuals who actually are farming it. Linked with this trend is "sidewalk farming," a development which probably has taken firmer root in Montana than in any other state. The term designates the practice, growing for many years, of operating a farm from a home in town, or moving into town for the winter; it is a direct result of mechanization on the farm, and of the automobile and good roads.

"Sidewalk farming," once started, grows like a snowball. Families which choose at first to remain on their farms find themselves isolated as their neighbors move; next year they move too. Social and cultural community are lost. The farm becomes merely an economic apparatus like a factory; its owner, in town, joins a luncheon club and the Chamber of Commerce and is persuaded that his interests coincide with those of other substantial businessmen.

Discoveries like that of strip farming do not come from such men as these; and Montana is apt to need more discoveries. Montanans must be opportunists because of the precarious conditions under which they live; they must be more enterprising and more courageous than the residents of states in which the land-use pattern has been well established and is protected by stable natural forces. Montana always has been, and will be until the sun cools and the ice creeps back from Keewatin, a "next-year" country. Therefore even in planning there must be provision for some recklessness, for an intrepid spirit.

Nothing is certain. Montana could become a desert in fifty years, though there is no evidence at hand to indicate that it will. Climatic studies based on tree rings and other indicators by M. A. Bell, former superintendent of the northern Montana branch experiment station at Havre, disclose that there have been drouth periods lasting half a century. Bell's studies carry the state's weather history back to the late 1600's. Planners have been forced to acknowledge this possibility of fifty-year drouth, too; in fact in the early '30's it looked as if that were happening.

A cycle of low rainfall began in 1929, and it was the worst in the memory of the oldest settlers. It lasted for nearly ten years, though with some interruption—there was good moisture in 1932 and 1933. During this drouth period the annual average precipitation for the state fell to as little one year as 9.7 inches, and the wheat yield to 6.6 bushels. The price collapse incident to nationwide depression intensified Montana's disaster: wheat worth $100 in 1920 was worth $19.23 in 1932, and that was the first year in four in which there had been a good crop! Montanans sold their grain for 25¢ a bushel, and even at that figure sometimes found it hard to locate buyers.

In 1931, twenty-eight of the fifty-six counties of the state had applied for emergency Red Cross relief, and this time it was forthcoming. Four fifths of the total population of Garfield County requested help to get them through that winter. At harvest time that year wheat was worth 45¢ a bushel. There were very few Garfield County farmers who had any wheat at all, but granting for the sake of argument that one may have had a 10-bushel-to-the-acre yield, this is the situation he confronted:

It cost him $2.50 an acre, 25¢ a bushel, to "combine" his crop. It cost him 35¢ a bushel to haul it to market, 50 to 100 miles. Total, 60¢. Market value of the wheat, 45¢.

By 1935 a fourth of the population of Montana was on relief. Livestock operators as well as grain farmers were destitute. It took an investment of $150,000 to $200,000 in cattle to enable a rancher to make $10,000 to $15,000 a year, and one bad season required the sale of substantial portions of his herd at the bottom of the market. Cattle worth $9.10 a hundredweight in 1929 brought $3.34 in 1934; sheep were $8.14 in 1929, $3.12 in 1934. The government instituted its drouth-purchase program in 1934 to save the west's herds from starvation on the dusty ranges and 350,000 of Montana's cattle, 492,-000 of its sheep were sold under this plan.

This catastrophe cost the people of the United States $1 apiece. Total federal expenditures for relief and public works in Montana approximated $125,000,000; the state and counties provided $8,500,000 more. It was the first large-scale federal help; at last America knew what Garet Garrett meant: "The elements of sympathetic danger are fairly obvious. . . . Nor does any one section of the country stand alone and self-contained."

Also the catastrophe, coming just as Montana had begun to recover from the previous one, just as it was taking its first hesitant steps toward planning its future, provided the final chastening experience needed to clear the way for that planning. Not even the blindest booster in the stupidest Chamber of Commerce could now insist that the behavior of nature in the '20's had been "unusual"; finally it was acknowledged that two or three years in every ten would be years of serious and perhaps disastrous drouth. For once Montana was thoroughly scared, scared enough to listen respectfully to the men who had been working quietly throughout the '20's trying to sell their fellow citizens the idea of planning.

XXVI. THERE'S FOOD ON THE TABLE

But the planners had to be Montanans, with dust on their pants, able to sit down at the same table with the farmers, the stockmen, the merchants, and bankers; nor could they talk too fast and too glibly. Better to get others to do the talking, and gently guide the discussion, as did Robert Clarkson, Teton county agent.

Besides Clarkson, to mention only a few of the outstanding ones, there were Evan Hall, a Milwaukee Railroad agricultural development agent, down in Miles City, who had been a county agent too; Otto Wagnild of Choteau and A. W. Ziebarth of Chinook, assessor and clerk, respectively, of their counties; Nic Monte, a stockman, Hall's friend; and Henry Lantz, another county agent, in Malta.

Because such men as these finally won a hearing, Montana was able to establish this remarkable record of leadership in planned agriculture:

It was the scene of the first experiment in unified county planning;

It originated the coöperative grazing district, set up the first such district in the United States, and provided the practical basis for the nationwide Taylor Grazing Act program;

It originated farm resettlement and has America's first (and still the largest) project.

All of these were born in the troubled '20's. First, growing out of little things, out of farmers' picnics and talks over the line fence, was the "guinea pig county," laboratory for a social and economic experiment on the great plains.

Teton County, Mont., is a vast wind-swept plateau. Rising sheerly in the west is the flat gray-blue silhouette of the Rockies; there are hardly any foothills, and the mountains are like gigantic paper cutouts against the sky. To the east there is a gradual slope to the hazy brown monotony of the prairie.

This was the buffalo range of the Pikuni, the Piegan-Blackfeet. Valorous fighters, they defended it for hundreds of years against raiders from the camps of the Assinniboines, the Gros

Ventres, Crees, Flatheads. But the white man pushed the Blackfeet north to a bleak reservation, bleaker even than this high cold plain which the newcomers called "Freeze-out Bench." Their herds took over the plateau and fattened on its rich grama grass. The town of Choteau, originally Old Agency, had been reservation headquarters, then a trading post named for a famous St. Louis fur operator, Pierre Chouteau, Jr. (The misspelling was permitted to stand, to distinguish it from older Chouteau County, of which Fort Benton was county seat). Finally Choteau became a prosperous little livestock community, capital of Teton County.

Today Teton County—so recently a primitive hunting ground that it still yields rich returns to collectors of Indian artifacts—is the scene of one of America's most important social experiments. Planners in Washington, private financial agencies, and farmers and farm theorists everywhere have been watching the progress of something new in democratic, coöperative management.

It is one of the forty-eight counties selected throughout the country (one for each state) by the Department of Agriculture, the agricultural colleges and experiment stations, for experiments in creation of "unified county programs"; but it is unique in that its planning began, at home, long before Washington got around to this scheme in 1938. Indeed, there is reason to believe that Washington got some of its ideas from Teton County, relayed through the alert Montana extension service to Montanans who held strategic agricultural positions in the capital, including M. L. Wilson.

The "unified county program" is based upon planned land use, but it is not "rural zoning." That is a land conservation measure tried in some other states with considerable success; and it may, with some modification, fit into the Teton County plan. But the Teton project is of vastly greater scope. It embraces not only soil conservation but also tax revision (it began with this), water utilization, erosion control, curtailment of weed and pest damage; range management, financing, tenancy, standards of living—even health and recreation.

The experimental value of Teton County, a tilted prairie shelf ranging in altitude from 3,500 to 9,000 feet, is enhanced by the fact that it is one of the "best" counties of the northern plains. It is almost equally divided between stock-raising and farming; it has both irrigated and dry land; and, above all, it never was as destitute as were so many other counties and thus affords a fair test of new methods. Some of the others were so badly off that any change was improvement. Not so Teton County. But it was because the county agricultural extension agent, Robert Clarkson, saw the collapse of counties all about him and was determined to forestall it in Teton if possible that planning began.

In 1922 Clarkson undertook to prepare an agricultural outlook report for the county and found himself embarrassed by the scarcity of statistical material. To bolster up the report and make it worth mimeographing, he hit upon the idea of including a study of the distribution of the county tax dollar. The little report which he had hesitated about issuing was an immediate "best-seller," and the farmers and ranchers clamored for more. Clarkson prepared some large charts based on his taxation studies and carried them around to farmers' picnics in 1923. Out of the picnics grew his planning round tables.

A study group consisting of about twenty farmers was organized by Clarkson and met twice a month. Soon the center of interest had shifted from where the tax dollar went to where it came from; delinquency had begun to appear in some sections of the county. The twenty homespun economists could see that there were inequities and injustices in the outdated system of land valuation. They called in Otto Wagnild, county assessor, resident of Choteau since the '90's, to see what could be done about it.

Wagnild had been worrying, too. Teton land was assessed like that of most other counties—upon inflated market value, or upon its contiguity to shipping points. A farm near Choteau might be assessed at $18 an acre and a better farm twenty miles away at $8. Income and taxation were out of joint. Wagnild sat down with Clarkson's study club to work out a solution. They found it in reclassification of the land for taxation; Clarkson and Wagnild and the study club sold the idea to the county commissioners in 1928. Reclassification on the basis of the land's potential productivity represented merely a restatement, in agricultural terms, of the classical theory of taxation based upon ability to pay; but in a county the size of Montana's Teton, larger than the state of Delaware,

it meant that the planners faced a tremendous task. They decided that there should be analysis of the agricultural capabil-
ities of at least every 40 acres in the county—and Teton
county has 1,500,000 acres.

The job took ten years. Now in Wagnild's office in the little
sandstone courthouse (Wagnild is usually out working for
the state tax board and teaching other counties how to do it)
the deputies will proudly display their colored maps showing
every square foot of land in the county and their trim card
indexes listing names of taxpayers, description of property,
and classification of soil.

The actual determination of classifications was done by the
county surveyor and his assistant, who for the first year had to
depend a good deal on their laymen's judgment and on the
experience of farmers who knew the soil in which they
worked; but then came Leonard F. Gieseker of the Montana
experiment station to make a "reconnaissance survey" of the
county, one of a series ultimately covering the whole state.
Gieseker took actual soil samples every two miles, made chemical analyses of them, and prepared a map. Thereafter this
served as a guide for the more specialized Teton County
study. A 40-acre unit on the county's maps now may show 20
acres of second grade plow land, 10 acres of fourth grade plow
land, and 10 acres of second grade grazing land.

The county planners adopted the experiment station classifications but found it necessary to add a few. To begin with
there were four classes of plow land (wheat) and five of grazing land; but something had to be devised to describe those
soils which were being plowed to crop but should not have
been; thus fifth, sixth, seventh, and eighth grade plow land
were added—so far had land abuse gone in some sections. For
taxation purposes, first grade plow land was that capable of
producing 22 bushels or more of wheat to the acre, and so on
down to fourth grade, 8 to 11 bushels. Grazing land was
graded on the number of acres necessary to maintain a 1,000-
pound steer for 10 months; first grade was that of which 18
acres or less were required, fifth grade was so poor it took 56
acres to support one steer.

Today there is hardly an acre of farm or grazing land in
Teton County which is not "paying its way." In other words,
virtually all acreage owned by the county (and compared

with other counties, it is very small) , is under lease at a rental sufficient at least to cover normal taxes. Despite soaring poor fund expenditures in the '30's (from $400 monthly in 1928 to more than $5,000 monthly in 1939) the county paid off its entire bonded indebtedness and its resources now total approximately $1,000,000. Taxes rose with added relief costs, but the higher bills were collected with little or no protest: every owner of agricultural land soon realized that there was no favoritism. Some taxes were raised, some lowered; many farmers had both things happen on their relatively small holdings. And not even absentee owners were victimized; there were no costly tax appeal fights for the assessor.

The Montana extension service began preaching planning in 1927. Clarkson's study club had already been working on improvement of production methods, conservation, and recreation. Under the last heading came Clarkson's "fun feed," annual event attended by hundreds of farmers and their wives and townspeople, too; and his Chautauqua, supposed to have been the only three-day home talent show in the United States. Scores prepared for it for months. A typical Teton Chautauqua (it has been suspended for duration of the war) included a historical pageant, a three-act play, musical numbers including a concert by an all-county chorus, and competitive orations by earnest high school students on such topics as "Man and the Machine" and "A Planned Economy for Future Generations."

"That Chautauqua," wrote the editor of the state's biggest daily in an adjoining county, "is the way to build community unity and spirit and to make a western locality more mature and more satisfying."

Clarkson moved on to become regional planning representative of the Bureau of Agricultural Economics at Lincoln, Nebraska; he died on special assignment in Washington, D. C., in 1941, at the age of forty-nine. In 1934 his job in Teton County fell to Fred Willson, who later moved up to become superintendent of the experiment station near Havre, a research depot noted for its work on grass, cereals, and tillage methods. Willson's task in Teton County was to integrate the county's homegrown planning program with that of the Montana extension service and to fit into it the complicated activities of the new federal agencies. A countywide economic con-

ference was held in 1936, and next year the organization
which still is functioning was established: community committees were elected, and their chairmen, with representatives
of farm organizations, county, state, and federal agencies became the county planning committee. The governmental
members had advisory privileges but no vote. The communities which formed the base of the pyramid were those established by AAA boundaries, usually surrounding a village, a
school, or meeting hall of some sort—groups of neighbors.

The planning procedure was, and remains, voluntary and
democratic: nothing can be imposed upon the farmers without the approval of at least a majority. This "town meeting of
the farm" has developed into a good deal more than a device
to implement federal agricultural programs such as the AAA;
it has been in fact a local "defense" against hastily imposed
planning from above. Teton County farmers have been saved
some of the confusion, some of the squabbles which have
arisen elsewhere as a result of hurriedly instituted federal
programs administered arbitrarily and at long range.

By means of their organized strength and determination
they also have forced or maneuvered federal and other governmental programs into general conformity with their grass-
roots plan. Thus the federal land bank, whose aim in the past
had been only to sell its holdings as quickly as possible, was
persuaded to dispose of land only to farmers who coöperated
in the land-use program, and to adopt a flexible system for re-
payment of loans, based on price and production. So successful has this been that the land bank, a part-federal, part-
private institution, has now disposed of all its Teton County
acreage, most of it to purchasers or lessees who needed it to
maintain an adequate economic unit in conformity with the
county plan.

The Agricultural Adjustment Administration fell in with
the county's policy of discouraging cultivation of low-grade
land, and as a result of this, plus the land bank policy, conver-
sion of individual farmers to the planners' program and other
factors, there is today virtually no sixth, seventh, or eighth
grade plow land in cultivation; it is returning to grass. Some
fifth grade land, because of several fortunately wet seasons, is
still producing crops. There is no Teton County operator,

however, who is still attempting to make a living on wholly submarginal land; the fifth grade which remains in production is in small parcels interspersed with good soils.

The AAA did not go so far as to adopt the Teton planners' most radical proposal—that unbroken sod land capable of producing good crops be brought into production, offset by retirement from cultivation of enough poor land anywhere in the state to equal the new production. Thus 50,000 acres in one county might go back to grass and be balanced by the production of 10,000 good acres in another county. AAA did, however, permit application of this principle on an individual unit basis: some Teton County farmers retired poor land within their own fences and plowed good leased land elsewhere; the county was fortunate in that it had some 30,000 acres of good land, unbroken, which could be used in the shift from some 20,000 acres which were hopelessly submarginal for crops. And, as a result of the war and the change in the national objective from artificial scarcity to maximum production, Teton's planners believe they may yet see their broad goal attained. Although AAA regulations penalized them for breaking new land (even good land, in exchange for poor) they have gone ahead with their own land-use program. It is sounder, they believe, than the AAA's "scarcity" ideology, masked though that may be by phony "conservation" measures; and "farm relief," they are convinced, is not necessary if the land is properly used.

The county's planners have also made notable advances in the problem of adequate-sized farms. Their first report listed 160 farms in the "hopeless" class because of lack of sufficient acreage. Today half of these have ceased to exist and the land has been absorbed by others; the remaining half are operated largely by old people reluctant to move and ultimately these farms, too, will be fitted into the county's broad agricultural pattern. Of the 275 farms of "below desirable" size in operation three or four years ago, adjustment has been accomplished for half and the others are operating successfully because of good weather or the adoption of more intensive farming practice, especially the greater concentration on dairy stock, poultry, and hogs.

Farm size, however, remains as a major problem for the

planners. Two recent developments, in the county but not of it, have complicated their task. Both were the result of federal intervention, hurried and heedless.

Although dryland homesteading ceased as a result of executive orders by the President in 1934 and 1935 withdrawing and reserving public lands for soil classification, Reclamation Project homesteads still may be obtained. In the last three years about 200 of these have come into production in Teton County, and because the United States reclamation law persists in an ancient mistake, prohibiting individual holdings of more than 160 acres, these 200 new farms average less than 100 acres; the first 55 to be opened averaged only 80. Desirable acreage for an economically feasible unit is at least 160 plus pasture land. Nevertheless the operators have been reasonably successful, because weather has been excellent, their market abnormally high, and they have been assisted step by step by the county planning committee. Most of them were conservative and well trained; 80 per cent were Montanans and 50 per cent Teton County residents, the latter chiefly the sons of farmers already operating in the county.

The same unfortunate reclamation law governed establishment of a Farm Security (Resettlement) Project in the county —on 80-acre units. The government placed 100 families on these units and burdened each client (or permitted him to burden himself) with debt ranging from $4,000 to $12,000. Few of these farmers can pay this off and make a living on their meager acreage, but the county planners' objective of larger units is gradually being attained. In 1943 the anticipated 13 vacated units were to be subdivided and distributed among farmers already on the project. In addition, land for rental has become available to the FSA clients. But integration of this project in the Teton program will not be easy; it is off to a bad start and it is outside the planners' jurisdiction.

The "unified county" continues its experiment in the face of war handicaps. The Bureau of Agricultural Economics, which took over federal phases of the program, has been virtually destroyed by loss of its appropriation, so the extension service is trying to carry on in its place. The farmers, their production practice, ownership pattern, debt, and taxation adjusted to best land use, today stand ready on the one hand to increase output for war but on the other to resist any move to obtain such increase by exploiting unfit soil.

South of Miles City, two storied rivers meander through rough terrain to empty into the Yellowstone near that old cowtown. They are the Tongue and the Powder, both meager little streams.

The Tongue River's historical prestige rests upon the fact that it gives its name to an Indian reservation which is the home of the Northern Cheyennes, one of the bravest people who ever lived. In the late '70's, sick and starving and surrounded by thousands of United States troops, this heroic tribe fought its way home to the Wyoming-Montana border country from Indian Territory in the southwest, where the government had stupidly insisted it must remain. Readers of the moving account of this bloody pilgrimage in Howard Fast's *The Last Frontier* have found reason to reëxamine the habitual American moral complacency.

Powder River has been famous since the first Texan lost the first trail-driven longhorn in its treacherous quicksands. "A mile wide and an inch deep," jeered the cowboys; actually it isn't wide at all, little more than a creek. And it's more than an inch deep, though sometimes not much more. Events of great significance in western history have occurred in the Powder River country, and even in our time the river's name has come to be a slogan recognizable almost anywhere in the world: a high and challenging, sometimes admiring and sometimes derisive phrase. "Powder River; let 'er buck!" It was the battle cry of Montana and Wyoming troops in World War I. It has long been the yell which greets a bronc rider as he comes out of the rodeo chute on a sunfishing outlaw. Often it is just an expression of exuberance, a toast in a bar, a shout of greeting to a friend across the street. Montanans who never saw Powder River and know less about it than easterners who read Struthers Burt's excellent book in the "Rivers of America" series nevertheless are proud to claim for their state this crooked, muddy, altogether undistinguished stream.

Between the two rivers are two creeks. One is Mizpah, tributary of the Powder, the other Pumpkin, tributary of the Tongue. The country through which they wind raggedly northward is broken by scores of coulees and given a sort of savage beauty by startling red buttes, formed of powdered iron and volcanic lava.

Between the two creeks (narrowing it down at last for a close-up) there is a cattle range consisting of 108,000 acres. In the '20's this range was in a bad way. Originally the grass had been as good as any in Montana, but homesteaders plowed up some of it and after they were gone "tramp" cattle outfits pushed their herds onto the abandoned farms and the near-by public domain. The ranchers who had homes and hay lands along the two creeks confronted ruin because of the over-grazed condition of the range. There were 4,000 cattle, 2,000 horses, and millions of prairie dogs on the 108,000 acres.

The ranchers, some of whom were old-timers in the Miles City country, could see no way out except to get out. The ownership pattern of the range was so complicated, their financial resources so small, that they could not buy or lease the necessary acreage; besides, public domain was interspersed with private lands and the government land could not be fenced, which made it impossible to block off a comprehensive area.

Evan W. Hall, who had just been appointed an agricultural agent for the Chicago, Milwaukee & St. Paul Railway, arrived in Miles City in May, 1926, and heard promptly about the range troubles. He suggested a meeting of stockmen to talk it over, and it was arranged by Paul Lewis, Custer County extension agent. Besides Hall and Lewis, four ranchers participated in this conference, held June 16. All agreed that there had to be more grass, and some method of permanent range control. Finally Hall was left with Nic W. Monte, one of the leading stockmen of the region, and they talked on for hours.

Suddenly Hall said that he didn't see why they could not have the public domain blocked off and organize the stockmen in an association to obtain long-term leases on it and the adjacent private lands. Monte pointed out that the public domain couldn't be fenced and was still open to homestead entry although all of the homesteaders had failed; and what chance would a handful of ranchers whose post office was Beebe, Montana (not even on most maps), have of getting Congress to approve the special legislation which Hall's plan would require?

Nevertheless the railroad man, western-born and a wor-shiper of grass, was afire with the idea, and Monte was eager to try it. Lewis quickly approved and set out to determine ownership of the acreage involved. This data went to Alva A. Simpson, Custer National Forest supervisor, who joined en-thusiastically in the project and prepared a map of the owner-ship status. Another meeting of the stockmen was arranged for July in Beebe's tiny post office. Out of it came the decision to create the first coöperative grazing district in America and fifteen ranchers signed up.

Lewis and Simpson went to work to figure out what a co-operative grazing district should be, and Hall went off to Great Falls to lay their proposition before Montana Congress-man Scott Leavitt.

The congressman, a Republican definitely without any leftist leanings, saw the merit of the plan at once—though he also saw, as the others apparently had not, that it meant a revolutionary change in public land policy and that it might have far-reaching effects upon the range livestock industry. Within a few weeks he was at the site of the project for a two-day horseback trip to see for himself the conditions in the district.

Leavitt determined that he would ask Congress to with-draw from homestead entry the public domain within the area—about 25 per cent of the total acreage—and permit it to be fenced, *for private use*. This would be hard enough to accomplish, but in addition he would have to persuade the Department of the Interior, which controlled the public do-main, to accept general supervision of the project's operation; the ranchers had agreed that the association's executive board would handle details of administration but that general pol-icy would have to come under the jurisdiction of a govern-ment agency. Thus the venerable Department of the Interior would have a new baby on its hands; and that was an experi-ence which long-established government bureaus at that time were notably reluctant to undergo.

Forty-one per cent of the land was owned by the Northern Pacific Railroad Company—part of its original land grant. Private owners held 28 per cent and the state of Montana about 6 per cent. The association asked the state to trade its land to the federal government in exchange for acreage elsewhere, but legal difficulties arose and this deal never was consummated. Instead the state land board gave control of its property to the association. Private owners and the railroad were persuaded to agree to lease their holdings for ten years for rental just covering their taxes—which was more than most of them were getting. Public domain was to be leased for $20 a section, all it was worth, and the Interior Department agreed to rebate the first three years' lease payments to be put into improvement of the range.

Meanwhile Simpson had completed a "capability" survey of the range, to determine the number of head it could safely support. The association, studying this, decided that not fewer than 3,000 nor more than 5,000 cattle were to be placed in the area, which would give the grass a chance to come back.

At first the grazing district pioneers found the Department of Interior's representatives unsympathetic and with little conception of what the association was trying to do. Hall went to Washington and won the support of E. C. Finney, Assistant Secretary of the Interior, for Leavitt's bill; it passed the House in March, 1927. The brief measure merely authorized the Secretary of the Interior to enter into a coöperative agreement with the state of Montana and private owners of land in the defined area for joint leasing of such lands for not to exceed ten years, to stockmen *living in and adjacent to the area;* it provided also that public domain included in the project was to be withdrawn from homestead entry. All this was not as radical as it looked, Leavitt assured some nervous colleagues. He pointed to his last clause, which authorized the Department of the Interior to coöperate with other government agencies in "any studies . . . of operation and results of said coöperative agreements and leases." Just an experiment, he explained, in remote Montana; what did it matter?

But the opposition had become alarmed. Protests came from cattlemen whose home places, if any, were a long way from Mizpah and Pumpkin creeks; some World War veterans were persuaded that withdrawal of homestead land infringed upon their right of prior entry. So Montana's Senator Thomas J. Walsh held the Leavitt bill up and called a public hearing in Miles City in September, 1927.

Hall wrote Monte:

Bring out at that hearing that the future of your section depends upon the establishment of units large enough to maintain a decent standard of living for the operators. Ranches which have hay lands along the creeks can't get by without grass lands back on the bench; grass and hay, summer and winter feed, can't be divorced. Unless balanced units are provided, the people are going to become peasants; and unless there is some central control of the range, it will always be a "football" for the "tramp" stockmen who have no interest in establishing permanent homes in the neighborhood.

Senator Walsh was convinced, and March 29, 1928, Leavitt's bill passed the Senate.

The first coöperative range grazing district was a success from the start. The association quickly finished fencing the area, began range restoration work, hired a rider to watch its members' herds, tend the fences, and keep interlopers from "pushing" their cattle "over the wire" into the district. Scores of stock-water reservoirs were established to prevent overgrazing of those sections which had natural water sources. Nearly $1,000 was spent to rid the area of prairie dogs, and $1,000 buys a lot of poison. Without quarrels or complaints, each member placed in the area that number of cattle allotted to him by a committee made up of members like himself; if his winter feed supported more than he was permitted to put on this range in the summer, he had to find grass elsewhere for the remainder. At first he paid $1.50 a head as fee for the eight-month grazing season; although reasonable enough, this charge was later lowered to $1.25 and stands at that today.

Gradually the range came back, though the association still grazes conservatively. The original ten-year leases expired in 1942 and were renewed without difficulty. Some county land was purchased by a holding company made up of members of the association; this company then leased to the district. In 1942 the association grazed 1,550 cattle and 2,250 sheep. A committee of members passes upon the quality of bulls (purebred Hereford), and the number, put on the range with the cows; the committee purchases bulls coöperatively, pro-rating expense to members on the basis of the number of cows they have in the area. Salt, cottonseed cake, and other supplies are also bought in this manner. The roundup is a coöperative venture, recalling that of the open range.

Mizpah proved itself in 1931, driest year southeastern Montana had ever known. Although stockmen throughout that section were selling off their cattle or moving them out by midsummer, no stock other than that normally shipped in the fall was removed from the grazing district until December, when the cattle as usual went to their winter range. This ability of the controlled range to maintain carrying capacity even in dry years tends to stabilize the hazardous livestock industry: the Mizpah operator knows the number of stock for which he can obtain summer grass over a period of years, and can plan accordingly. Hitherto this was only possible for the rancher who owned all of his range. Without large investment of capital to obtain such security, the grazing district operator can put more money into building or improving his herd.

No one could ignore such an object lesson. In 1933 Montana adopted a "grazing districts" law to encourage and expedite formation of such associations as that of Mizpah-Pumpkin Creek; one year later the United States Congress passed the Taylor Grazing Act authorizing the Secretary of the Interior to make agreements with these associations anywhere in the United States and to withdraw from homestead entry the lands they needed for their districts. The little "experiment" in Montana which Congressman Leavitt, since retired from politics, had persuaded Congress to authorize, changed the nation's livestock practice.

During preparations for establishment of the Mizpah-Pumpkin Creek district, in June, 1927, the Montana extension service sponsored a range management conference at the site. Those who attended, mostly county agents and stockmen, toured the area and heard its promoters describe their hopes for balanced economic units—controlled coöperative use of the grass in summer, feeding on the home place in winter.

Among the visitors was the county agent of Phillips County, Henry L. Lantz of Malta. He went home thoughtful and stimulated, later wrote his hosts "it made a fellow feel good" to find others studying the problem of integrating the dry ranges and the ranch home on a river. Lantz, too, had a dream; the scientists now call it "area diversification."

A recent "study outline" by a planning organization, *The Northern Plains in a World of Change,* says "area diversification" is a "radical and imaginative innovation." Perhaps; but nearly forty years ago President Theodore Roosevelt, who frequently proved that he understood the west's needs better than native westerners did themselves, had something very like it in mind when Montana's Milk River irrigation district was formed. He withdrew from homestead entry not only the irrigable acreage in the river valley which he had been asked to set aside, but also a strip of dry land one township wide on each side of the irrigable section. Asked by puzzled sponsors of the project why he had done this, since they could not hope to get water on this extra acreage in the rough "breaks," the ex-cattleman President replied that the valley's farmers would need that dry land as summer range for their herds. But his foresight was fruitless; a few years later the homestead "locators" brought pressure on President Taft and he reopened the dryland sections.

It was not long before the valley farmers did need those grasslands, but in the meantime the ownership pattern had become so complicated, the burden of debt so heavy, that the farmers could not afford them: they had been homesteaded, lost, sold, mortgaged, and lost again. The irrigated tracts had become a bonanza for land speculators; prices rose so high that many of the original settlers sold out and left. Cattlemen, squeezed by homesteaders on the dry benches, had come down and bought irrigated lands which were suited to intensive agriculture, and held them for hay. The valley's whole agricultural way of life was out of joint.

The Blaine County portion of the district, because it was irrigated first and many of the original tracts had been subdivided and rented, fared better than Phillips and Valley and utilized the land more efficiently. Blaine County Clerk A. W. Ziebarth, comparing the productive fields in his section with the acres of wild roses and useless brush in neighboring Phillips County, carried a suggestion to a meeting of the Malta Commercial Club: why not help some of the destitute drylanders on the benches above the valley to get rid of their wheat ranches and take up these vacant irrigated farms as renters or long-term buyers?

It was a good idea, but nobody could see where the money to finance it was to be obtained.

Meanwhile Lantz had been working with State College soil experts and the Forest Service in analysis of the county's soil types and grass "carrying capacity." In June, 1925, he announced completion in Phillips County, first in the state, of a reconnaissance soil survey by the United States Bureau of Soils with the Montana experiment station coöperating. "We have heard a great deal," he told Malta businessmen, "about getting rid of the scrub cow, the 'star boarder' hen, and so on; but since our soil map has revealed the county as it is, we ought to let our scrub acres alone." He pounded at the stockmen to adopt deferred or rotated grazing, to divide their range into seasonal pastures and rotate these to allow re-seeding and stronger root growth of the grass. In some cases this meant that the ranchers would need more range, and here, as in the Powder River country, their herds ran into the honyocker's fence. It all came back to the need for general readjustment of land use.

By 1930 Lantz was ready with his big scheme and in July of that year he presented it to the Commercial Club. Known as "the Malta plan," it was the first practical farm resettlement program in the country. Lantz, with H. H. Johnson, superintendent of the irrigation project, and three businessmen, Josef Sklower, George Chambers, and Fred L. Robinson, had won from landowners in Milk River Valley an agreement to sell 80-acre tracts to dryland farmers. Buyers of these irrigated properties were to be urged to lease their dryland holdings to ranch operators in their vicinity, for use as dictated by the county's soil map—unless they could afford to maintain both places. Such leases would be on a share-crop basis, with the drylander's share going to pay taxes and interest on his new irrigated tract. If the scheme worked out, he could buy the new farm on the water on easy terms.

Significantly, the announcement of the "Malta plan" said:

The hope is that these farms may be settled by dryland farmers of this community. The local men understand conditions better than strangers; they have faced drouth and discouragement trying to make a living on units unsuited to them. This type of man, it is felt, will be a more desirable settler than would be imported strangers.

While Malta, stricken by depression, was still hunting around for the money necessary to put the plan into operation, Washington got wind of it. The New Deal had moved into the Department of Agriculture, setting up a "Subsistence Homestead Division." And Henry Lantz, obscure county agent with a big idea, was suddenly summoned to the throne to explain his "Malta plan."

The Montanan had little sympathy with "subsistence" as an end in itself, and none whatever, as the announcement indicated, with idealistic schemes for moving starved Arkansans and Okies into Montana; the state had enough hungry farmers of its own. But he had an indorsement for his plan from the late Dr. Elwood Mead, once reclamation chief and pioneer land use economist, under whom Lantz had studied at the University of California and under whom Johnson, the irrigation project superintendent, had worked. He could count, too, on the support of Montana's M. L. Wilson, who headed the new Subsistence Homestead unit. Above all, the "Malta plan" was ready to function and sounded feasible— and Lantz was a salesman. He returned to Montana as manager of the first Farm Resettlement program in America. Cooperating with the Homestead Division was the Federal Surplus Relief Corporation; soon the program was handed over to the Resettlement Administration and finally to the Farm Security Administration, with the Soil Conservation Service coöperating. (So many federal agencies have had their ambitious fingers in the Malta pie that few even among project officials can be quite sure of all of them.)

The first federal step in the program was to buy and retire submarginal crop land in Blaine, Phillips, and Valley Counties, on a scale undreamed of by the "Malta planners." By October, 1934, Lantz' plea for sale of such land had resulted in an offer of 600,000 acres. The biggest land transfer on record in Valley County took place next spring when the county sold to the project for $120,855 approximately 94,000 acres which it had acquired on tax deed.

There was considerable opposition, much of it stemming

from the old suspicion of "government." Thus one farmer wrote to the *Phillips County News:* "We, as a county, own this land and I think we, as a county, can manage it all right. . . . It is easy to talk to our county commissioners, but if you have to go to the department of the interior you will have to take a lawyer."

Politics, said the *News,* also threatened to wreck the project. The weekly's editorial writer commented tartly under the heading "We Are Sick of It":

Ever since the project started there has been a local undercurrent of opposition . . . because chippy local politics reared its ugly head. Henry Lantz was crucified by letter and telegram. . . . We would suggest that before local democrats scuttle this program over a patronage fight they stop and consider what the community result might be.

But some people still think Henry Lantz is crazy. They have read his credo. It might even be socialism:

Every soil type, every water resource adjusted to its best use; every farm family and every community assisted to provide for themselves the best security the resources of the area can furnish for their social and economic betterment.

Nothing about making money, as an end in itself. Lantz, boss of a project of 7,000,000 acres, says resources are there to provide a secure and happy life for everyone in the three project counties; less than 30 per cent of the available irrigable land has been developed. These people wouldn't get rich; but on the other hand they wouldn't just "subsist," and they wouldn't starve. Lantz believes in agriculture as a way of life; others believe in it as a commercial undertaking. Right now the commercial folks have the upper hand. There's a war on, and reform is forgotten. Too, there have been several good wet seasons. But Lantz goes on planning for the dry years.

Raised a Mennonite and conscientious objector, Lantz nevertheless entered the army in the first World War and was in several major engagements. He came out with a lifelong hatred for the regimentation of men's minds and for the occasional arrogance of bureaucracy. This has conditioned his attitude toward his job. His bearing in early dealings with his "clients" is apt to be cynical and challenging, rather than paternalistic: no head-patting, as in some government ventures. "This unit's no good," he is likely to tell a newcomer; "you may starve to death. . . ." The best of the clients, with pride and faith in themselves left after years of defeat on dry land, promptly get mad and set out to prove him a liar. If there is no reaction, or only a weary acceptance of his prediction, Lantz figures the prospect has two strikes on him already and may start him at the bottom, on one of the work units (subsistence tracts). As relations with the clients progress—a lot of them are "on to him" now—the project manager tries to substitute persuasion for dictation wherever possible. He insists always that there shall be no segregation, that units shall not be so closely grouped and isolated from non-project farms that the clients will be inclined to get together and "damn the government." He schedules as few meetings of project farmers as possible, but as many as possible in which they will join their non-project neighbors in agricultural or social activities.

The Milk River Northern Montana Land Utilization Project—its official name—is less than ten years old. Acknowledging that Montana is a "long-time," a "next-year" country, it is too early to reach an honest verdict on the measure of its success; nor is it possible to pass fair judgment upon it when, along with most planning ventures, it is fighting to survive a war.

Of the 7,000,000 acres in the "project area," the Federal Government owns more than 2,000,000. One and a quarter million are in public domain, now included within a dozen coöperative grazing districts which are grouped in Taylor Grazing District No. 1, first in America. About a million more acres, nearly all submarginal for crop agriculture, have been bought by the Land Utilization Division of the Resettlement Administration, later transferred to the Soil Conservation Service, and this latter agency is now responsible for operating the land utilization phase of the project. The Farm Security Administration bought 16,720 acres of irrigable land in the Milk River Valley upon which to resettle some of the farmers displaced by purchase of submarginal tracts. Nine hundred families were affected by the sale of dry land; ninety-seven of them have been resettled on the irrigable tracts in three counties and sixty-seven others whose land was taken over by mortgage holders and by counties for taxes also got resettlement farms. Forty more bought irrigated farms for themselves, outside the project but in the valley. Four hundred families moved out of the area, and the remainder abandoned farming and went to work in valley towns or for other ranchers.

The 150-odd project clients are in three classes—lease clients, operating on a share-crop basis with the government; purchase clients, buying their land and homes on a 40-year payment plan, and a few "labor clients," established on subsistence plots of 3 to 5 acres on which they pay rent earned by labor for private employers. These last have been surprisingly successful; the initial investment in land and buildings was small and the "operating loan," if any, only $150.

Most lease and purchase tracts are 80 or 100 acres, though some consolidation has been effected in the last few years to provide better economic units. When FSA began to buy these irrigable tracts in 1934, only 800 acres, 5 per cent of the total bought, were fully developed. Today 12,500 acres are fully developed out of the 16,720 acres bought. This irrigable acreage cost the government $250,000.

The majority of the clients settled on these farms were deeply in debt even after sale of their submarginal land and application of the proceeds to their old obligations. Many of them arrived owing $3,000 to $5,000. These debts were adjusted, scaled down, and FSA made an average loan of $1,200 to permit their liquidation. Including this sum, the agency made an average operating loan of $3,500 to the client.

Today the *average* client has a "minus equity" of $218 in his place—that is, he owes that sum in addition to his original operating loan. But 12 have paid up in full and 47 others have a net worth of $3,000 more than their original indebtedness. Sixty-one show a deficit—the least successful is $3,000 deeper in the hole than he was when he started; but he at least has, as do all of them, free of encumbrance, his "family living" assets—furniture, clothing, canned goods, and poultry. These items, upon which the government took no mortgage, are worth on an average $800 per family; most of them were acquired on the project because the average client was broke and without credit when he arrived and had few personal possessions.

The majority, then—bearing in mind their debt burden and destitution on dry land—are better off than when they started, and they have been paying $85,000 to $100,000 annually to the government on its investment, in lease fees, loan reduction, purchase contracts, or rent. A study of the "before and after" incomes of 60 families showed that this group, which was earning an average of $450 annually on dryland farms plus $512 from AAA payments, relief, and outside labor, earned an average of $2,300 annually on the project. On dry land, 41 per cent of the average income came from the farm, 40 per cent from relief, 10 per cent from AAA payments, and 9 per cent from outside labor. On the project, 83 per cent of the income came from the farm, 16 per cent from AAA and sugar beet bonus payments, only 1 per cent from outside labor. From $512 annually, the government's contribution to the income and that from outside work dropped to $225.

It is obvious, then, that these clients have a better and more stable life, though not all of them have as yet been able to support it. Instead of homestead shacks, they have modern five or six-room homes; they have planted thousands of trees, and gardens, hedges, flowers, lawns. In just one year, 1940, they bought more than $1,000 worth of nursery stock. They are getting more dairy cattle, poultry, sheep. Their children are better fed and attend better schools, and all enjoy a richer social and cultural life.

Because emphasis is always on livestock, alfalfa hay is the basic crop; but the major cash crop is sugar beets. The fact that cultivation and harvesting of beets require much outside labor, however, is a serious wartime handicap.

Many of the settlers have developed notable initiative and have worked out new farming practices, which they have shared with others on the project. All are Montanans (Lantz successfully resisted importations) and nearly all were dryland farmers in the northeastern section of the state now included in the project area. These drylanders, despite their lack of experience with irrigation, have shown themselves more willing to learn than the irrigation farmer whose practices have been conditioned by residence in some other state.

Near Malta is the project farm of Henry Green, one of the settlers who took up Lantz's challenge and went onto one of the poorer units. "I seen worser places than this," he said. "At least the wind hasn't blowed here yet. If I can get the water I can try." That was in the fall of 1936, and Green had had his fill of wind. The son of a north Russian immigrant, at seventeen he had established himself on a farm near Culbertson, in northeastern Montana. In 1932 he was farming 600 to 1,000 acres, had 75 head of stock, and $20,000 in the bank. He had married at twenty-two and at this time had eight or nine children. Wheat was 18¢ a bushel that year; Green figured it would take 65 bushels to buy one barrel of gasoline and 10 pounds of grease, sufficient to operate a combine harvesting about 30 acres. He had 480 acres in wheat averaging 10 bushels to the acre; the return from it would not have paid for the threshing.

But Green stuck it out through succeeding drouth years until 1935, when the big wind hit. It blew 65 miles per hour most of the time for four days and four nights, buried his house and left great holes in his fields. That finished the Greens. The bank took their land, cattle, and cash, and Henry arrived in Harlem, Montana, with Mrs. Green, nine children, and $2.50.

Miscellaneous farm labor kept them alive for a while: Green got a job at $75 a month tending to the irrigation of 80 acres of beets. The children were too small to help and it was a lot of work for one man: he had to cultivate, clean ditches, handle the water—"very hard work," he said. The family lived in a house made of three combined homestead shacks, lined with felt paper and with a leaky roof. They used apple boxes for furniture and had one bed.

A Froid, Montana, physician, F. L. Darland, who was interested in Lantz's "Malta plan," told Henry about it and in 1936 he applied for a place on the project. By that time, through sacrifice and saving out of his $75 a month, he had acquired a few hogs, a milk cow, and a team of work horses. He still had no money, no chickens, and no furniture.

Four years later Green was prospering on 106 acres of leased project land plus 160 rented outside the project for extra pasture. He owned 15 purebred Holstein cows, 9 horses, 31 pigs, 180 chickens, and 9 geese. He grew wheat, barley, oats, sugar beets, hay; he had increased his oat production on one field from 30 bushels per acre to 65 bushels by a system of his own devising—a sweet clover nurse crop which he plowed under. He said the clover killed the pestilential greasewood which had "burned out" his soil. In his first three years on his new farm he doubled its production. Alkali was a menace, so Henry figured out a way to plow it to the surface on the hottest midsummer day, then turn water on his fields from small ditches and "boil" the caustic salt out of the soil.

Henry's neat and comfortable home by that time sheltered Mrs. Green and ten children, three boys and seven girls. Green, by extra work, obtained the money to buy 162 shade trees, a hedge, 50 apple, plum, and cherry trees, grapevines, raspberries, gooseberries, and strawberries. The three sons helped on the farm and the two eldest had taken several prizes in 4-H dairy competition.

"Good kids," said Henry, "but I like to kid 'em. Came in one night and said, 'I'm getting tired of this place. All the time gumbo, mud; never get away from the mud!' And my little three-year-old said, 'Didn't you get tired of the dust, Daddy?' You know—those kids never forget that dust. . . .

"I ask those kids how they like it now, eh? They say, 'There's food on the table; we don't go hungry; now we have plenty to eat.' Makes a difference, you don't have to worry about your kids having enough to eat. I was just a home-steader but I had $20,000 in the bank, my own place. Then the wind, and I got nothing; the bank, everybody double-cross me, especially the bank.

"But I figure the government won't let us down as long as we keep on trying."

The story of the Henry Greens—the resettlement—is only part of the whole story of land utilization, and a compara-tively small part, at that. This is the function of the Farm Security Administration. The other story is that of the restora-tion of the land, largely the job of the Soil Conservation Service.

The million acres of retired submarginal land cost about $2,000,000. Seventy-five thousand acres of abandoned crop land in this area have been reseeded to grass and the carrying capacity increased from 5,000 "animal unit months"—estimated on the basis of a natural grass comeback—to 18,000 animal unit months. Value of the land, based upon productivity, has therefore increased from $10,000 to $80,000 or $100,000. Reseeding is costly, and most of this new value has been absorbed by the expense of the process; but hereafter the grass will do its own reseeding. Base of all such projects is the invaluable crested wheat grass, which was "discovered" in 1898 in Russia by N. E. Hansen of South Dakota Agricultural College and painstakingly studied and developed for many years at experiment stations, especially by Harold E. Tower and others at Moccasin, Mont., and by Bell at Havre.

The Soil Conservation Service, the National Forest Administration, grazing districts and individuals have reseeded 320,000 acres of Montana soil in the last five years; but that acreage is only 10 per cent of the area urgently in need of this treatment.

Reseeding, however, represents only a portion of the range improvement program on the Milk River Northern Montana Project. The carrying capacity of the other, natural grass, range, which was 13 acres per animal unit when the project was inaugurated is now 6 acres per animal unit, or more than doubled. Better range management and weather have combined in a happy partnership to bring this about. Hundreds of reservoirs, springs, water holes, wells have been developed. More than six hundred farmsteads have been obliterated, old fences taken down, and hundreds of miles of new fences built to encompass the new, enlarged ranges. Corrals, dipping vats, and cattle guards have been installed.

All this meant more adequate operating units for the stockmen and stockmen-farmers left in the dryland country. Submarginal land bought by the Soil Conservation Service became available to them by lease or through grazing associations; as a result the old settlers were able to pay up their back taxes and consolidate their economic position, and some new operators were able to obtain adequate livestock units. The three project counties, therefore, have benefited not only from the payment of back taxes by those who left the land (13 per cent of the purchase money went to delinquent taxes) but by the improved condition of those who remain. Current tax collections increased 20 per cent in the area when the submarginal land deal was consummated. In addition, school costs in the three counties dropped 54 per cent when the closing of ninety-one rural schools, no longer needed, saved $109,200 a year. And, although the government pays no "taxes" as such on the valley land it owns in the resettlement area, it is required by federal law to pay an equivalent sum "for services rendered." In 1934 the taxes on the land included in the sixty FSA units in Phillips County were $2,854. Five years later the project paid, as an "equivalent" to taxes, $4,909 on these same lands; the difference represented the increased assessed valuation of the buildings on the property, since the land itself had not been reclassified. The present farm building cost per unit is about $3,200, though the first buildings, those on the original Malta homesteads, cost $6,000. They were far too elaborate: the project's Washington sponsors were obsessed with housing and succeeded only in embittering non-project farmers who were still living in log cabins or homestead shacks, besides burdening the settlers with excessive debt. Cost of the irrigable land was about $60 an acre, after development.

From 1929 through the panic period of the early '30's about $7,500,000 was spent for relief and made-work projects in the three counties. Since the Milk River Northern Montana experiment began approximately the same sum has been expended—Lantz calls it "invested"—in the readjustment of 7,000,000 acres of land and more than 5,000 families.

In January, 1937, the Resettlement Whist Club challenged the Malta Whist Club to compete in a tournament in the Great Northern Hotel, losers to pay rent of the cardroom and cost of the lunch. The Resettlement Club unfortunately lost the tournament; but it is pleasant to be able to report it could pay the costs with a flourish.

This chapter has told the story of three planning ventures, all of them of Montana origin. It has not touched upon scores of others of equal or greater importance—the never-ending research of the State College, the experiment stations, the extension service; the statewide program of the Soil Conservation Service, with its eleven Montana districts covering

4,000,000 acres in which it helps the farmer to fight erosion;
the Forest Service; the National Resources Planning Board—
even the Rockefeller Foundation, sponsor of an important
recent study outline of northern plains problems.

Planning is new and conflicts are inevitable. There have
not only been conflicts between the planners and non-plan-
ners but very serious rivalries, jealousies, and divergent points
of view among the planners themselves.

Many of the conflicts have arisen as a result of inadequate
coördination of federal programs: most of them have, in fact.
Planning costs money and Montana hasn't any; otherwise,
most Montanans involved in it believe, they could have
worked things out better alone, once they got started.

The government has insisted that agencies which started
from widely separated stations on tracks heading in different
directions shall, willy-nilly, be brought to a junction; and the
sound of rending and tearing has reached to Washington,
where it has been seized upon with delight by the non-
planners. The government has insisted that agencies with
diametrically opposed objectives shall work in the same field
at the same time. Thus the AAA, pitiful makeshift, and to
some extent the venerable extension service, which function
for the benefit of the large operator, are supposed to work
in harmony with the FSA, which plans for the little fellow.
Pressure groups choose sides: Farm Bureau Federation with
the AAA and extension service, Farmers' Union with the
FSA. Everybody gets in everyone else's way; toes are stepped
on. More agencies come in: emergency seed loan committees, production credit associations (which have done well),
and recently, for some mysterious reason, still another financial agency—the revived regional Agricultural Credit Corporation which started badly by basing its loans on inflated
market values, a practice which helped to break Montana
once before.

Some of these agencies think of planning as a relief measure, which it is not. Sometimes even factions within one
agency take sides on this issue of subsistence (a sorry goal!)
versus genuine rehabilitation. The latter, incidentally, starts
not so much with the individual as with the resources upon
which he lives: restore the soil and the water and *distribute
them equitably,* and you needn't worry much about relief

. . . except for some men who, like some soils, are too far gone to be rehabilitated at all. Let them rest. One does a planning agency a disservice by handing these unfortunates over to it with the charge, "You have until the next Congress convenes to make them produce."

Above this battle, studying their wisps of grass, their boxes of seeds, their grains of dust and their books, are the scientists—the earnest research men of the experiment stations and the professors in the colleges. But now, to their amazement, they—and their translators, the extension service—find themselves embroiled in battle, too. They were first, and their field has been invaded by hordes of disrespectful newcomers. Who shall do the planning, and above all, who shall be paid for doing it?

Thus arises the conflict between the old-line agencies and the "action" agencies—most of the latter products of the New Deal. The old-timers awoke one day to find to their horror that interlopers of whom they never had heard were appropriating, sometimes without credit, the fruits of their decades of study, publicizing them vigorously and basing upon them grandiose and costly programs of reform, some of which were not very well reasoned out. These outlaws, the scientists complained, were proving themselves reckless, too eager for publicity, impractically idealistic; and besides they were becoming serious competitors for appropriations.

The action agencies retorted in kind: the scientists had been too conservative, wedded to their bureaucratic process, fearful of innovation. Like careful physicians, they were prone to hold back, to disparage new developments until their efficacy had been proven to their scientific satisfaction—a very different thing from proof for temporary practical use. While the experts tested, tested, tested, thousands of plains farmers were starving to death. . . .

Back in 1911 E. C. Chilcott, in charge of dryland agricultural investigations in the Department of Agriculture, listed among "most serious misconceptions" this one: "That the farmer can be taught by given rules how to operate a dryland farm." That may have been rare discernment, or it may have been a betrayal of weary cynicism of a scientist. If he meant that arbitrary rules unmodified by individual and regional experience could not succeed, he was right; but if he meant the dryland farmer could not learn new ways, he was wrong. And the scientists have been a little slow in their teaching. To this charge they will reply that the American people have been more than a little slow in providing them with the funds to pay for dissemination of the knowledge they have acquired, which is true; Montana is a special offender, with its starved college and university.

The conflict has not been resolved and may never be resolved. Meanwhile a Montana planner for an action agency says in a contemptuous aside, as a breathless representative of science arrives on the scene of his hopeful experiment: "Moving in in a hurry to save his bureaucracy!"

Nevertheless, Montana can thank God for the scientists and their humble voice, the county agent.

XXVII. THE OLD NORTH TRAIL

But now all bets are off.

The rivalry of federal agencies is no longer of any moment, when the agencies themselves are threatened with extinction. The conflict of big and little planners will be resolved in favor of which can better serve a nation at war. So far, the big fellow has all the advantage.

The money with which America had begun to indemnify the western frontier for decades of careless looting has been diverted to help support a more expensive project of killing Germans and Japanese. The brains which enlisted eagerly to plan the rehabilitation of the west have been drafted and taught to plot instead the courses of bullets and bombs.

The Works Projects Administration occasionally dug holes and filled them up. But it also made the first social and economic surveys Montana ever had, providing a statistical base for planning. The Works Projects Administration is dead.

The Civilian Conservation Corps was condemned by a few for boon-doggling. But its well-trained enrollees fought the fires in Montana's forests and helped to put water on the state's dry ranges. The Civilian Conservation Corps is dead, too.

The Farm Security Administration spent some money foolishly on projects dictated by starry-eyed idealism. But it spent money wisely in the first large-scale resettlement of destitute drylanders; its vigor and its vision held the greatest promise of all: area diversification, community integration, education. As this book was concluded, the Farm Security Administration was fighting for survival in a hostile Congress where a few of its friends held out for its continuance, even on a basis of drastic curtailment of its program.

"I figure the government won't let us down as long as we keep on trying," said Henry Green, FSA farmer.

Too bad, Henry; there's a war on. You're in the way.

The first World War left Montana bankrupt, in land, money, and men. Effects of the second may be worse, though there have been some assurances (there are always some assurances). A spokesman for the Department of Agriculture said: "There will be no such criminal waste of the soil in this war crisis as there was before." Perhaps not; but there is more than one way to waste soil. Good land unused is wasted, and hundreds of Montana farmers and stockmen have had to abandon their operations because their workers have been drafted or have deserted them to take jobs in war plants. Hundreds of Montana farmers and stockmen have been drafted themselves, forced to sell off their herds or their land or both.

And some Montanans have begun to worry about the effect of this mechanized war on the state's—and the nation's—store of minerals, especially zinc.

Again Montana's man-power contribution to the armed forces has been proportionately greater than that of many other states. Army Selective Service officials, admitting this, insisted nevertheless that "there has been no discrimination." The excuse was different this time: it took so long for credit for enlistments to get back to Montana draft boards that the draft quotas weren't reduced in proportion; when the war is over it probably will again be found, to the astonishment of everybody except Montanans, that the state put more men in uniform than it should. Its young men were quick to enlist, as they were in 1917, and they were healthy: the proportion rejected because of physical defects was smaller than the national average.

This time Montana complained about the drain on its man-power, something it didn't do before. It had good reason for complaint: it was being urged to produce more food and metals, but when harvest season came in 1942 the supply of farm labor in the state was 58 per cent below normal, the demand for it 5 per cent above normal, and the wages highest in twenty-two years; grave labor shortages impaired production in the vital mines and smelters.

Montana economists predicted, early in 1942, that by the beginning of 1943 the state's population would be down some 40,000 from the 559,456 census of 1940. But before the end of 1942 the state unemployment compensation commission estimated the loss up to that time at 75,000. Of these, about 40,000 were already in the armed services—the same number called throughout the first World War—and the calls were growing heavier. The other 35,000 had streamed out to centers of war industry, leaving scores of Montana towns and a few cities again on the verge of collapse.

Those who are left at home realize that if there is to be any salvation for Montana after this war, planning must go on in the hope of establishing a social and economic system which will induce the young men, this time, to come home.

But can such plans be made, with the young and enterprising group of the population gone?

Probably they can, although there are grave handicaps. For one thing, the morale of the plainsman can hardly be the best considering his experience in the '20's and '30's. He has been robbed, and he knows it. Again he is asked to fight, and to produce, to save democracy. What kind of a job did democracy do for him on farm credit, prices, freight rates, machinery costs, throughout twenty years of anguish? Democracy asked him once before to increase production; he did, and democracy broke him as soon as it had had its fill. Now again he must raise more calves, more lambs—and until the gravity of the national food shortage was tardily realized, the government took his cowboys, his herders, and his sons.

But change does not terrify a westerner. His life is hazardous enough at best; at worst it can only call forth more of his hard-won fortitude and daring. And at least some Montanans realize that the impatient cry, "Let the planning wait until the war is won," means ruin for their state and for all the northern plains. That's what Montana did last time. What is done now will determine the shape of Montana's future after the war is won—determine, indeed, whether the war shall be won, for Montanans.

The state has progressed a long way in technical adaptation of its economy to natural processes on the plains. But there is a task at hand for those who remain at home in the adaptation of the social machinery, especially government. The counties, the schools, taxation—all these have been functioning on patterns established for humid regions. They could be reformed during the war. Such reform would not cost money, it would save it.

There are great changes still to be made in land ownership practices; experience has indicated that private ownership must be still further subordinated to public coöperative control. The older cattlemen know, better even than the young ones just out of school, that grazing is costlier on their own land than on public range; some even rent their privately owned grass to others and hold their stock on leased range in the national forest. But they learned a hard lesson when the homesteaders came, and their generation clings to the fetish of private ownership; it will be hard for them to yield.

Perhaps something could be done, on the ground of war emergency, about eastern domination, through marketing and transportation, of the Montana price structure. Three monopolies squeeze the state's producer: the buyers, who quote him a price based on Minneapolis or Chicago, minus the freight rate from his farm to that market; the railroads, who tell him what that freight rate shall be; and the manufacturers, who sell him at their own price what he needs in order to produce. Because of his distance from markets and manufacturing centers he gets less for everything he sells, pays more for everything he buys. In hard times the manufacturer maintains his price by curtailing production. This the Montanan cannot do with much success: his production must be planned far in advance, and a change to other crops may be difficult or even impossible.

To combat this price squeeze, coöperatives such as those of the Farmers' Union have been established and by annual rebates to members have succeeded in lowering the farm operating cost.

War, with its attendant meat shortage, might provide a good opportunity for Montanans and others in the cow country to woo the American people away from the "baby beef" fad, born of apartment living, smaller families, and the luxury demand for smaller and tenderer steaks. The current practice of marketing calves and long yearlings leaves the stockman with only his basic cow herd and in event of drouth or price disaster he has to sell off the cows, which are expensive and difficult to replace. Before World War I the Montana herds included cows, calves, and one to three-year-old, sometimes five-year-old, steers; the operator could liquidate his herd starting with the heavier, older stock. Steaks from the older critters were tastier, too, according to the old-timers. To the trend to smaller and younger herds to satisfy the "baby beef"

demand could be attributed some of the responsibility for meat shortage; and the government's policy during the present war of permitting and even encouraging slaughter of 300-pound calves which would be 600-pound steers in a few months was sharply criticized by some stockmen.

Finally, those left at home must—if their sons are to be persuaded to return—encourage development of a social culture (by which is meant governmental and nongovernmental organization, mode of thought, and way of life) adapted to the peculiar natural conditions of Montana. This will be the most difficult task of all. Such a culture must be regional, but not isolated; to some extent it must be international, to maintain the centuries-old identity of the Canadian and American prairies. It must make allowances, within limits, for the traditional mobility of the frontier; for Montanans have always moved. Carl F. Kraenzel of the State College, sociologist, found that in a group of typical communities only a third of the families had lived there for a dozen years. This he attributed in part to "frontier characteristics":

The "westward urge" brought many frontier settlers who moved from one frontier to another. These people were brought up on the idea of mobility; their way of life was conducive to migration. . . . Eastern Montana was a peculiar frontier in that it represented the merging of several currents of population movement. One current flowed from the east, another came from the west. . . . And Canadians also entered Montana in large numbers.

It is a truism, of course, that the degree of man's culture may be measured by the efficiency of his integration with his environment. Lewis Mumford puts it this way in *The Culture of Cities:* "The natural conditions of a region, so far from being nullified by the increase of culture and technical skill, are actually magnified."

The establishment of a true and adequate culture for Montana, therefore, must effect a synthesis of all those which have gone before—those "waves washing over Montana." First the proud tribes of plain, mountain, the far north, the people whose names sing: the fierce Pikuni, the Kootenai, the Isahpo; Athapaskans, and the Crees of Calling Valley, and the Salish and the Sioux. They left their travois tracks on the Old North

Trail; they left Montanans a tradition of outdoor living, a regard for stamina and for courage.

Then the ill-starred métis, whose nation was a vision or a mirage, a brief flame against the sky, projected from the brain of a mystic genius, Louis Riel. They were the voyageurs, the trappers, the great hunters; they were the ardent, fearless men. One hundred and twenty-five of them, in their nation's dying agony, stood off 1,400 Canadian troops for four days at Batoche, Saskatchewan, 350 miles north of the Montana line. They left Montana its French place-names, the name of its most pestilential rodent, the gopher (from *gaufre,* honeycomb, because of its intricately tunneled burrow); they helped to introduce Catholicism.

Then the miners: southerners and Californians at first; later they came from everywhere, and trailing them, the outlaws. . . . Theirs the recklessness, the extravagance (personal and governmental), the carelessness with human life which survive to trouble the state today.

The cattlemen: Texans, many of these, and other southern gentlemen, some of them fugitives from Union prison camps; there were enough of them, along with their southern predecessors, to leave the state an upstart rebellious spirit, to leave at least one chapter of the Daughters of the Confederacy (in Bozeman), and at least two Methodist Churches South.

The cowboy: no gentleman, but best-loved Montanan, he was southern too, at the start, but Kansans and Nebraskans and others soon joined him. Their reign was brief, their happy, heedless spirit a throwback to that of the miner.

The sheepman: he brought a leavening of eastern seaboard, British or Scotch culture to Montana; he was a quiet man, and shrewd. . . . And very lonely in this obstreperous state.

The honyocker: miserable Joad, he was lured to the state by promise of quick riches, and he brought what could have been expected: greed and ignorance, but sometimes ambition and courage, too. Most of his kind are gone now, damned as stupid fools because they believed what they were told. They left Montana the beginnings of a healthy skepticism. And a legacy of bitterness, of broken lives, of starved towns, eroded soil, debt, and disintegration.

So much for interim planning. All of this has been diagnosis of Montana's ills, and probable ills; and the value of diagnosis is in direct ratio to the availability and efficacy of curative measures. There is not much use determining the nature of a malady unless the process suggests some course of treatment. Treatment has been suggested; now for the unpopular and hazardous task of prognosis. What could happen as a result of this war; what are the favorable factors?

Well, in the first place, this is a global war. The other was not. Montana has no new major war industries, but it does have large installations for the United States Army Air Forces and other military units.

Thousands of young men and young women are seeing Montana for the first time. Among them are many who say with Thoreau (who always, when he walked, found his steps turning westward), "I love a broad margin to my life." Montana is a land of broad margins. So some of these young people will remain in Montana, or return to it, if there is opportunity. And what are the chances of such opportunity?

One chance is implicit in the promise of this global war to break the stranglehold of the railroads upon the American hinterland. Air transport needs space and conquers space. Postwar industry may follow air lanes, as prewar industry hugged the rigid rails. At least one Montana city, Great Falls, has become a great air transport terminal. Its bewildered but hospitable citizens have entertained Russian and Chinese visitors on military missions; renowned scientists and explorers have taken off there for the north and beyond.

Montana, fortunately, probably never can become a center of heavy industry, or even predominantly industrial in the sense of light manufacture. However, wartime trends toward decentralization (and they are just trends to read about, in Montana; it has seen none of this new industry), if continued after the war, sooner or later will bring acknowledgment of the region's great natural resources, its spaciousness, its ability to provide a better life for workers. Integration of some small-scale industry with its agriculture would help to solve the riddle of its precarious drouth-ridden economy.

The newcomers whom war has brought to Montana have shown themselves eager to learn its exciting story; they have found it an interesting place in which to live. And Montanans finally are becoming aware of their romantic tradition. The popularity which has greeted such ventures as that of Charles Bovey, young Great Falls rancher, is significant. Bovey has rebuilt, with the original structures, an entire pioneer town and housed it in a fairgrounds pavilion. Called simply "Old Town," it is one of America's most unusual historical exhibits: its general store, drug store, saddlery, blacksmith shop, saloon, and barber shop contain their original equipment or merchandise, and its fire department boasts carts and pumpers which raced to Montana's most famous conflagrations. Bovey, as a member of the state legislature, also sponsored legislation empowering counties to establish historical museums.

Before the war curtailed vacation travel, Montana's scores of dude ranches drew increasing numbers of guests annually, as did the rodeos and Indian ceremonials. Glacier and Yellowstone National Parks established new records for summer visitors shortly before the entry of the United States into the conflict.

Finally, this global war has brought home to Americans the realization that Montana was not, after all, the last frontier. There is another, to which Montana may well be the gateway. It is the new frontier of the north.

The white man of Europe and the brown man of Asia again have marched to battle along the Old North Trail. As Japan seized a foothold in the Aleutians, the white man—American and Canadian, but of European blood—hastened to build a military highway over a route upon which the Asiatics may have come into the New World in hunting and warrior bands thousands of years ago. It is the long-sought Alaskan International Highway, now completed to Fairbanks on an inland route extending from the end of an old motor road at Fort St. John, British Columbia. East of Fort St. John this route leads six hundred miles to Edmonton, capital of Alberta Province, where it connects with a major Canadian highway south to the United States boundary at Sweet Grass, Montana.

Probably not more than 10,000 to 15,000 years ago the first of the Asiatics crossed Bering Strait and pushed on into the interior of Alaska, rejoicing in their discovery of a land more hospitable than the bleak Siberian coast from which they had come. Said Aleš Hrdlička, curator of the National Museum: "The chief deduction of American anthropology, in the substance of which all serious students concur, is that this continent was peopled essentially from northeastern Asia."

The newcomers may have tried navigating the Yukon River. Some struck south along the Pacific coast. Diamond Jenness of the National Museum of Canada sees indications that some marched east over the low divide through the Rockies at the head of the Liard River, out onto the windy barrens and south to where the grass shone yellow in the sun.

They were not invaders, these first Asiatics, for they came to an unpeopled continent; they were frontiersmen, curious and courageous. Hrdlička and other scientists are convinced that they formed the nucleus of the Indian race we know as Algonkian, root of the aborigines of the eastern United States and Canada as well as most of those of the west. And the inland course which they may have traveled—which certainly some prehistoric peoples traveled—came to be known to tribes descended from the "pioneers" as the Old North, or Great North, Trail. It is so known today, and in some places it is still visible.

This migration from Asia was not a single mass movement of a people. It may have continued for hundreds of years; and though there is no evidence of any considerable influx since the early centuries of the Christian Era, investigators in 1936 found that "visiting" between Siberia and the Alaskan island of St. Lawrence continued and that some of the island's settlers had come there in recent years. But while the migration was on there were divisions and fusions and quarrels and alliances. Always there was movement, for these were a nomadic people.

America was already "settled" when there came another advance from Asia, and this, because it undertook to wrest from the firstcomers some of their empire, was an invasion. It did not altogether succeed, though Indians of Algonkian stock still hate and fear the people who came in this new wave, the people we know as Eskimos.

And then, probably not more than two thousand years ago, came still another thrust from Asia. It brought the fierce Athapaskans, most terrible of all the races whose skin boots or moccasins or snowshoes (the last of which they invented) had scuffed the sod and snow for centuries along the Old North Trail. Some believe their ancestral home was on the Himalayan slopes bordering Tibet. Whatever their origin, they were born to the sword: for hundreds of years they scourged the Trail, destroying or dispersing weaker tribes, terrorizing whole Indian nations so that they fled clear across the continent, jumbling the Indian and Eskimo cultures . . . until, reduced by incessant bloodshed, they were themselves dispersed and absorbed by their victims. Indians of Athapaskan stock are today the most widely distributed of American aborigines. Dog-Ribs, Chipewyans, Slaves of the North country, Sarcees of the plains and Montagnais of the snowy peaks, the mysterious Haidas of the north Pacific coast, the Navajos and bloody Apaches of the southwest—all these are Athapaskans, and most of them were terrible foes to enemy Indian or to white.

They had spilled too much of their blood and their seed along the Old North Trail. The tribes which had been strewn like tumbleweeds in the wind came back to this road which led to the vast buffalo hunting grounds of the prairie plateau, and fought long and futile wars. Brings-Down-the-Sun, an aged Blackfoot chief, told Walter McClintock about it:

There is a well-known trail we call the Old North Trail. It runs north and south along the Rocky Mountains. No one knows how long it has been used by the Indians. My father told me it originated in the migration of a great tribe of Indians from the distant north to the south, and all the tribes, ever since, have continued to follow in their tracks. The Old North Trail is now becoming overgrown with moss and grass, but it was worn so deeply, by many generations of travelers, that the travois tracks and horse trail are still plainly visible. . . . In many places the white man's roads and towns have obliterated the old trail. It forked where the city of Calgary now stands. The right fork ran north into the Barren Lands as far as people live. The main trail ran south along the eastern side of the Rockies. . . . It ran close to where the city of Helena now stands, and extended south into the country inhabited by a people with dark skins and long hair falling over their faces (Mexico). In former times, when the Indian tribes were at war, there was constant fighting along the North Trail.

And finally came the European, ruthless as the Athapaskan and shrewder by far, master of many deadly devices besides his guns.

The Trail became the Indians' last stand. Chief Joseph lost the last major battle against the whites a few miles east of it in 1877. Directly on the Trail, at Lethbridge, Alberta, in 1896, Crees and Blackfeet met in the continent's last Indian fight. In the latter half of the nineteenth century greedy and careless white men loosed on the Trail three of the biblical horsemen, pestilence and famine and death; they rode it from end to end, taking a greater toll than had the Athapaskans. The last of the great smallpox epidemics traveled north on this route, probably from Fort Benton, Mont., in 1870. Enraged Indians who heard that the blankets of two traders who had died of the disease had been sold to tribesmen retaliated by tearing the scabs from their flesh and rubbing their sores against the door handles and gates of the trading posts; and they dragged the festering, flyblown corpses from their lodges to the windward side of the forts and heaped them there, in order that the polluted air might blow into the white men's houses. Callous as some of the traders were, it is improbable that they were guilty of the outrage attributed to them by the Indians, for plagues were bad for business. But they did send another white man's plague, liquor, trickling north along the ancient road to debauch and beggar the proud warriors of the plains.

In the early '80's the last few hundreds of the doomed millions of buffalo fled north on this road, and their descendants live now in the Northwest Territories. On their heels came the cattle, and in our own time, as the United States tried prohibition, liquor again traveled this and other obscure old trails, to quench the traditionally lusty thirst of the west.

A wandering horseman may still come across some portion of the Old North Trail. West of Choteau, Mont., in a ceded strip which was Indian territory until thirty years ago, a section of the prehistoric road is known as the "Pondera" (Pend Oreille) Trail. A few years ago a boy whose family's cabin is on this route kicked up a gravel-encrusted bronze coin in the yard. It has been identified by the Smithsonian Institution as having been minted during the reign of Emperor Hadrian,

A.D. 138; one theory of its origin is that it was traded by a
Spaniard in Mexico centuries ago and dropped by some traveling tribesman within the stone tepee ring in which the boy
found it. Such tepee rings are not the work of present plains
tribes, and the wanderer who lost his bronze trinket perhaps
was able to read the mysterious hieroglyphics still to be seen
near the trail at "Writing on Stone," a Canadian historical
park twelve miles east of the twin border towns of Sweet Grass
and Coutts. Blackfeet, Cree, and other plains tribes say they
cannot read this record, struck into the face of a sandstone
cliff before their people came.

Construction of the new North Trail to transport supplies
for mechanized warfare required about fifteen hundred miles
of new road building, along the aerial route to Alaska through
North America's last wilderness. Three of the continent's
great rivers, the Liard, the Peace, and the Yukon, rise along
the road's course. Lumberjacks had never entered the vast
forests through which it passes; few white men had ever seen,
much less explored, this empire. A handful of prospectors
risked its loneliness in the days of British Columbia's gold
rush, and about fifty of them starved or died of exposure.
Prior to establishment of road camps, the only "settlements"
in the seven hundred airline miles between Fort St. John and
Whitehorse, Yukon Territory, were three or four fur trading
posts of the Hudson's Bay Company.

Completion of the Alaskan and Pan-American highways
will link Buenos Aires and Fairbanks, joining the most distant capitals of two continents on the greatest road man has
ever built; but of greater immediate importance is the role
of the Alaska highway in opening the north. A winter road
which ultimately will become an all-weather highway now
links the new Alaska route with Fort Simpson in the Mackenzie district of the Northwest Territories, and a 425-mile pipe-
line is being laid from Norman Wells, in the same district 150
miles south of the Arctic circle, to Whitehorse, Y. T. Completion of the Alaska highway also has spurred work on several
shorter roads to link settlements within the Mackenzie district.

Because the 49th parallel is a political and not a cultural

boundary, the north calls strongly to Americans of frontier tradition who live just south of that line. But the covered wagon and the cavalry charge are gone: neither pioneer nor soldier can succeed unless his mechanized transport and his industrial practice can match his competitor's.

The new roads will open to development vast new treasure hoards of resources, in addition to those of Alaska and northern British Columbia—the 47,000,000-acre Peace River section of Alberta, and the Mackenzie district. The latter, with an area of 500,000 square miles, heretofore has had neither highway nor railroad. Once called "Barren Grounds," its name has been changed as a result of scientific investigation and experiment: now it is "Northern Plains of Canada," and there has been some revision of earlier conceptions of the severity of the district's climate. This has been found to be no worse than that of most of the Scandinavian peninsula and little more rigorous than that of the American northern plains. Grazing is feasible, and minerals and other resources abundant—coal, oil, and gas, water power, lead, zinc, gypsum, gold and silver, copper, tungsten, and perhaps beryllium, rare metallic element which hardens copper.

The new North Trail, some of it traversing the same route as that of a centuries-old through highway of mankind, strikes north into the wilderness at Fort St. John. A few miles west on Peace River is Rocky Mountain Portage over which Sir George Simpson of the Hudson's Bay Company climbed a century ago. The way, said Sir George, "is very ruggid, it will occupy upwards of a week in transporting canoes and property. . . . MKenzies tract has not been followed for years, the one now pursued, which is less dangerous, is marked with an arrow."

The new North Trail, a road of war, unfortunately is no less dangerous. But it is marked with an arrow, too—directing the unfailingly enterprising people of the west to the last frontier, the new—and accessible—north.

Montana will enjoy its role in all this, for next to being actually a frontier, there's nothing better than being the jumping-off place for one. Ask St. Louis or Seattle, Omaha or St. Joe! Certainly frontiersmen will always be welcome, always feel at home when they hear the traditional greeting, "Git down an' come in!" (It is not quite polite to dismount until one is asked to do so, but the convention may be modified for aerial travelers.)

There will be room for adventurers here. In Montana everyone has a quarter of a square mile (ten times as much space as the average American can claim for himself) in which to stomp about and shout, or just to lie and look up at the vibrant blue-green sky. It always reaches just beyond the horizon, and the horizon seems always to be still within Montana.

Between the sky and the horizon's edge is rainbow's end. It is there the sun rests in intermission while the spirit dancers of the aurora thread their way, silent and a-tiptoe, through the grave measures of their minuet; there too are the Sand Hills, where wander shades of dead warriors in perpetual pursuit of phantom buffalo. There is the goal of all the mysterious old trails—the green well-watered pasture, the brimming reservoir, the never-failing field of wheat. Even peace is there.

The sky is so big that the newcomers' mighty air transports roaring into the sunset will loom no larger than did the covered wagons creaking over a mountain pass. For an instant they will be noisy and important, and there will be a flick of flame on their wings, celestial tribute to gallantry; then the sky will be still again . . . save for the high chorus of color, which one learns to hear after a while.

The sunset holds infinite promise. Fire sweeps up from behind the Rockies to consume the universe, kindles the whole horizon, and all the great sky is flame; then suddenly it falters and fades atop the distant peaks and the lonely buttes, ebbs and is lost in secret coulees. The Montanan is both humbled and exalted by this blazing glory filling his world, yet so quickly dead; he cannot but marvel that such a puny creature as he should be privileged to stand here unharmed, and watch.

It is as if every day were the last of days. So Edwin Arlington Robinson saw the mountain country:

Dark hills at evening in the west,
Where sunset hovers like a sound
Of golden horns that sang to rest
Old bones of warriors under ground,
Far now from all the bannered ways
Where flash the legions of the sun,
You fade—as if the last of days
Were fading, and all wars were done.

But the sun's fierce ecstasy will return tomorrow night.
And next year . . .

ACKNOWLEDGMENTS AND BIBLIOGRAPHY

AUTHOR'S NOTE

I HAVE not attempted in this book to write a "definitive history" of Montana, whatever that would be. I am a newspaper man, not a historian. Some incidents which seemed to me to be significant, or perhaps just fun to tell about, have been selected for discussion; others, perhaps equally important in a full history, have been merely touched upon or even ignored.

Several important economic fields have been neglected—the fur trade of the frontier, oil, lumbering, sheep-raising—there are limits to the reasonable length of a regional book. At least one major "exploitation" development is not covered. This, the story of the land grants, would require a book in itself. The Federal Government gave the Northern Pacific Railway 20,000,000 Montana acres, every alternate section in a strip 80 miles wide along its line. The gift has had much to do with Montana's troubles because it complicated the land ownership pattern.

Nevertheless, even with these acknowledged shortcomings, a great deal of "research" in the Wilson Mizner definition has gone into preparation of this work. Mizner's definition was this: "If you steal from one author, it's plagiarism; if you steal from many, it's research."

I am particularly grateful to the unhonored, unsung, and poorly paid professors and their associates from whose painstaking studies published by college, experiment station, or extension service I have taken much of the statistical basis and some of the ideas for this book. I have been fortunate in having had access also to several manuscript sources. These included, through the gracious permission of Mrs. Clara Whiteside of Helena, the unpublished memoirs of the late Fred Whiteside which he titled "One Hundred Grand," and the Hauser letters, David Hilger and John B. Ritch manuscripts and other documents in the Montana State Historical Society library.

Hundreds of individuals, in interviews or by correspondence, have helped; for various reasons I cannot acknowledge my debt to all. The point of view from which this book is written, incidentally, is my own and may even shock some good friends who have helped me to obtain material. No one who may be mentioned, therefore, can be held responsible for my opinions.

I owe much to one Montanan who is dead. Ed Cooney, news-paper man, was one of 29 Representatives whose vote W. A. Clark couldn't buy, though the price went to $30,000 and Cooney, like any newspaper man, needed the money. Riding with him along obscure old trails in his top-heavy Franklin, I shared with Ed Cooney the knowledge of Montana and the love of it usually possible only for those who entered the state, as he did, in a covered wagon.

Harry B. Brooks, a veteran Minnesota and Montana news-paper man, has borne with me and counseled me throughout interminable discussions of my project without attempting to direct or divert my course; the book would have been vastly more difficult had I not had the stimulus of his alert, wide-ranging mind. Two others whom I met early in my study also contributed a great deal by virtue of their scientific knowledge and a trait which is not always its accompaniment—vision. They were Carl F. Kraenzel, State College sociologist, and M. A. Bell, formerly superintendent of the Havre Experiment Station, now superin-tendent of the southern Great Plains field station at Woodward, Oklahoma.

And no one who writes, or even reads, Montana history can adequately tell what he owes to Mrs. Anne McDonnell, assistant librarian of the State Historical Society Library in the Capitol. I can only add my thanks to those of other students who regard her with affection as friend as well as ultimate authority.

To these others, and some I may not have named, my apprecia-tion of special courtesies:

Henry Sheffels, wheat rancher; John Survant of the Circle Dia-mond; E. A. Phillips, secretary of the Stockgrowers' Association; Bert Monroe, ranch foreman; Dudley Jones, stockman; Sam Rem-ington, former rancher; the late Walter Shay, Butte newspaper man and police chief; Sid Willis, ex-sheriff, proprietor of the Mint and friend of Charley Russell, who permitted me to use one of his Russell letters and helped me in other ways; Charles Kissack, once a homesteader; Dr. F. B. Linfield, director emeritus of the Montana Experiment Station; W. N. (Bill) Smith, miller; Zachary M. Hamilton, secretary of the Saskatchewan Historical Society, Regina; J. L. Humphrey, land sales and rental agent; Attorneys George Hurd, John L. Slattery, and Harry L. Burns; W. A. Brown, present state banking superintendent; Mrs. Gladys R. Costello, newspaper woman and FSA historian; N. B. Matthews, banker; H. E. Robinson, formerly a machinery dealer; Fred C. Buck, chief water board engineer; County Agents Ted Fosse, N. A. Jacobsen, O. A. Lammers, and S. N. Halvorson; Dr. R. R. Renne, economist and acting president of Montana State College; H. D.

Hurd, assistant state conservationist; M. P. Hansmeier, extension conservationist; H. G. Bolster, extension land economist; A. E. Palmer, assistant superintendent of the Lethbridge, Alberta, Experiment Station; John Clark, Smeltermen's union secretary, Harry Cosner, former sheriff, and R. H. Willcomb, engineer.

The quotation which gives the book its title, by Donald Culross Peattie, is from *The Road of a Naturalist,* and is used by permission of the publishers, Houghton Mifflin Company, Boston. The poem which closes the book is "The Dark Hills," from *Collected Poems of Edwin Arlington Robinson,* reprinted by permission of the Macmillan Company, New York.

Other books quoted in the text are as follows in the approximate order of their mention:

BROWNELL, BAKER, and WRIGHT, FRANK LLOYD. *Architecture and Modern Life.* Harper & Brothers, New York, 1937.

CONNOLLY, CHRISTOPHER P. *The Devil Learns To Vote: The Story of Montana.* Crown Publishers, New York, 1938.

LAWSON, THOMAS W. *Frenzied Finance.* Ridgway-Thayer Company, New York, 1905.

QUIETT, GLENN CHESNEY. *Pay Dirt.* Appleton-Century Company, New York, 1936.

PENNELL, JOSEPH. *The Wonders of Work.* J. B. Lippincott Company, Philadelphia, 1916. Quoted by permission of the publishers and the Library of Congress Trust Fund Board.

STUART, GRANVILLE. *Forty Years on the Frontier.* Arthur H. Clark Company, Glendale, Calif., 1925. Paul C. Phillips, ed.

BRISBIN, GEN. JAMES S. *The Beef Bonanza.* Lippincott Company, 1881.

BARROWS, JOHN R. *Ubet.* Caxton Printers Ltd., Caldwell, Idaho, 1936. Quoted by permission of the copyright owners.

PYLE, JOSEPH GILPIN. *The Life of James J. Hill.* Doubleday-Page, New York, 1917. Quoted by permission of Doubleday, Doran.

STEINBECK, JOHN. *The Grapes of Wrath.* Viking Press, Inc., New York, 1939.

PRESIDENT HOOVER'S RESEARCH COMMITTEE, REPORT OF. *Recent Social Trends in the United States.* Whittlesey House, McGraw-Hill Book Company, New York, 1934.

HARRIS, S. E. *Twenty Years of Federal Reserve Policy.* Harvard University Press, Cambridge, 1933. Quoted by permission of the President and Fellows of Harvard College.

BEARD, CHARLES A., and MARY R. *America in Midpassage.* Macmillan Company, New York, 1939.

CHASE, STUART. *Rich Land Poor Land.* Whittlesey House 1936.

RAYMER, ROBERT G. *Montana: The Land and the People.* Lewis Publishing Company, Chicago and New York, 1930.

MUMFORD, LEWIS. *The Culture of Cities.* Harcourt, Brace & Company, New York, 1938.

McCLINTOCK, WALTER. *The Old North Trail.* Macmillan, London, 1910. Quoted by permission of Macmillan Company, New York.

The author also acknowledges permission by *Survey Graphic* to use portions of two articles of his which first appeared in that magazine; by Garet Garrett for quotations from his article, "That Pain in Our Northwest," printed in *The Saturday Evening Post,* April 12, 1924; and by Harper and Brothers for the quotation from an article by Julian Ralph in *Harper's New Monthly* for June, 1891. A quotation from Robert S. Fletcher's article, "The End of the Open Range," came from the *Mississippi Valley Historical Review,* September, 1929; and the description of a homestead wife's experiences was taken from "Homestead Days in Montana" by Pearl Price Robertson in *The Frontier,* Missoula, Mont., March, 1933.

The following published sources have been used in addition to those heretofore cited from which quotations were taken:

BOOKS

ABBOTT, N. C. *Rocky Mountain Politics.* University of New Mexico Press, Albuquerque, 1940. Thomas C. Donnelly, ed.

ABBOTT, TEDDY BLUE, and SMITH, HELENA HUNTINGTON. *We Pointed Them North.* Farrar & Rinehart, New York, 1939.

BANCROFT, HUBERT HOWE. *History of Montana, Idaho and Washington.* History Company, San Francisco, 1890.

BRIGGS, HAROLD E. *Frontiers of the Northwest.* Appleton-Century, New York, 1940.

BURT, STRUTHERS. *Powder River, Let 'Er Buck!* Farrar & Rinehart, 1938.

BUTLER, CAPT. W. F. *Great Lone Land.* Sampson Low-Marston, London, 1873.

CHITTENDEN, HIRAM M. *American Fur Trade of the Far West.* Barnes & Noble, New York, 1935.

DALE, EDWARD EVERETT. *The Range Cattle Industry.* University of Oklahoma Press, Norman, 1930.

DE KRUIF, PAUL. *Hunger Fighters.* Harcourt, Brace & Company, New York, 1928.

DIMSDALE, THOMAS J. *Vigilantes of Montana.* McKee, Butte, 1929; 1st ed. Virginia City, 1866.

FEDERAL RESERVE SYSTEM, BOARD OF GOVERNORS OF. *The Federal Reserve System, Its Purposes and Functions.* Washington, 1939.

FEDERAL WRITERS' PROJECT, WPA. *Montana: A State Guide Book.* Viking Press, New York, 1939.

FINNIE, RICHARD. *Canada Moves North.* Macmillan Company, 1942.

GEPHART, W. F., and AMBERG, HAROLD V. Papers in *Present Day Banking.* Minutes of regional banking conferences held by the American Bankers Association. American Bankers Association, New York, 1936.

GLASSCOCK, C. B. *The War of the Copper Kings.* Bobbs-Merrill, New York, 1935.

HAYWOOD, WILLIAM D. *Bill Haywood's Book.* International Publishers, New York, 1929.

JORALEMON, IRA B. *Romantic Copper, Its Lure and Lore.* Appleton-Century, New York, 1934.

KRAENZEL, CARL F., THOMSON, WATSON, and CRAIG, GLENN H. with the collaboration of CORBETT, E. A., PARSONS, O. A. and RANDS, STANLEY. *The Northern Plains in a World of Change.* Toronto, 1942. Sponsored by the Rockefeller Foundation, Northern Great Plains Agricultural Advisory Council, and Canadian Association for Adult Education.

LEVINE, LOUIS. *Taxation of Mines in Montana.* B. W. Huebsch, New York, 1919.

McDOUGALL, JOHN. *On Western Trails in the Early Seventies.* Toronto, 1911.

MACKENZIE, ALEXANDER. *Voyages from Montreal,* etc. London, 1801.

MURPHY, JERRE C. *Comical History of Montana.* Scofield, San Diego, 1912.

NOYES, A. J. *In the Land of Chinook: The Story of Blaine County.* State Publishing Company, Helena, Mont., 1917.

OSGOOD, E. S. *Day of the Cattleman.* University of Minnesota Press, Minneapolis, 1929.

OWEN, ROBERT L. *The Federal Reserve Act.* Published for the author, 1919.

PALLADINO, LAWRENCE B. (S.J.). *Indian and White in the Northwest.* Wickerham Company, Lancaster, Pa., 1922.

RUSSELL, CHARLES M. *Good Medicine.* Doubleday, Doran, New York, 1936.

———— *Trails Plowed Under.* Doubleday, Doran, New York, 1937.

STOUT, TOM, ed. *Montana, Its Story and Biography.* American Historical Society, Chicago and New York, 1921.

TREMAUDAN, A.-H. DE. *Histoire de la Nation Métisse*. Levesque, Montreal, 1936.
VAUGHN, ROBERT W. *Then and Now: Thirty-Six Years in the Rockies*. Tribune Publishing Company, Minneapolis, 1900.
WEBB, WALTER PRESCOTT. *The Great Plains*. Ginn & Company, Boston, 1931.
WELLMAN, PAUL I. *The Trampling Herd*. Carrick & Evans, New York, 1939.
WISSLER, CLARK. *Indians of the United States*. Doubleday, Doran, New York, 1940.

MAGAZINES

Agricultural History, October, 1930. Fletcher, Robert S. "That Hard Winter in Montana."
Colorado Magazine, September, 1939. Boyd, Louie Croft. "Katrina Wolf Murat, the Pioneer."
Pacific Monthly, January, 1908. Wilber, C. W. "The Way of the Land Transgressor: How Montana Was 'Done.'"
Rocky Mountain Magazine, Montana Banker, Montana Farmer.

THESES

ALBRIGHT, ROBERT E. *The Relations of Montana with the Federal Government*. Stanford University. Montana Historical Society Library.
FALL, VICTOR HILTON. *An Historical Analysis of the Montana Planning Program*. Montana State College Library.
TRIMBLE, WILLIAM J. *The Mining Advance into the Inland Empire*. University of Wisconsin. Montana Historical Society Library.

NEWSPAPERS

Anaconda Standard, later *Montana Standard* (Butte); *Billings Gazette; The Butte Bulletin; Butte Miner; Cheyenne* (Wyo.) *Sun; The Chicago Times; Chinook Opinion; Choteau Acantha; The Christian Science Monitor* (Boston); *Daily Drovers' Journal* (Chicago); *Denver News; The Eye-Opener* (Butte); *Glasgow Courier; The Great Falls Leader; The Great Falls Tribune; Havre Daily News; The Helena Herald; Lewistown Democrat-News; The Madisonian* (Virginia City); *Meagher County News* (White Sulphur Springs); *The Miles City Star; Malta Enterprise; Mineral Argus* (Maiden, later in Lewistown); *Mon-*

tana Newspaper Association (Great Falls)—inserts for country weeklies; *Phillips County News* (Malta); *The River Press* (Fort Benton); *The Pioneer Press* (St. Paul); *The Montana Post* (Virginia City); *The Reveille* (Butte); *Rocky Mountain Husbandman* (White Sulphur Springs, later in Great Falls); *The Wall Street Journal* (New York); *Yellowstone Journal* (Miles City).

PRIVATE PUBLICATIONS

Annual Report to Stockholders. Montana Power Company, 1940.
Bulletins. Montana Taxpayers' Association, 1921, 1922, 1937, 1939.
Control Soil Blowing by Strip Farming. Circular. Great Northern Railway, about 1936.
Copper Target, The. Pamphlet. Anaconda Copper Mining Company, 1924.
Her Majesty Montana. Series of 52 broadcasts by C. W. Towne for the Montana Power Company, 1939, Pamphlets.
If and When It Rains: The Stockman's View of the Range Question. Pamphlet. American National Livestock Association. Denver, 1938.
Montana: Homesteads in Three Years. Pamphlet. Great Northern Railway, 1913.
Montana Land Bargains. Pamphlet. Montana Ranches Company, Helena, about 1915.
More Free Homesteads, Another Big Land Opening. Circular. Great Northern Railway, 1910.
Summer Tilling in Montana. Alvin C. Hull and Prof. John Bracken. Pamphlet. Capital Trust & Savings Bank, St. Paul, about 1919.

PUBLICATIONS OF THE STATE OF MONTANA

Annual Reports of the Department of Agriculture, Labor, and Industry; State Superintendent of Banks; Board of Equalization; Adjutant General; Water Conservation Board.
Constitution of the State of Montana.
Contributions. Montana State Historical Society, Vol. IV.
Messages of Governors S. V. Stewart, Joseph M. Dixon, John E. Erickson, Frank H. Cooney, and Roy E. Ayers.
Preliminary Report on Development of Economic Opportunities in Montana for Migratory and Stranded Families. State Planning Board, 1939.
Proceedings and Debates. Montana Constitutional Convention, Helena, 1889.

Report. State Tax and License Commission, 1917–18.
Report. State Tax Investigation Commission of the Senate, 15th Assembly, 1916–17.
Revised Codes of the State of Montana.
Staff Report. Montana State Planning Board, 1936.

JUDICIAL DOCUMENTS

Transcript of Record, in the United States Court of Appeals for the Ninth Circuit, Broadwater-Missouri Water Users' Association, Montana State Water Conservation Board and Others *vs.* the Montana Power Company, on Appeal from District Court of the United States for District of Montana; No. 10350 (printed in San Francisco).

PUBLICATIONS OF STATE AGRICULTURAL INSTITUTIONS

Bulletins of Montana State College, Experiment Station, and Extension Service, by Blankenship, Renne, Kraenzel, Saunderson, McIntosh, Eckert, Maughan, Brownlee, Wilson, Murdock, Slagsvold, Starch, Reitz, Hansmeier, Green, Burke, Pinckney, Parsons, Plambeck.

PUBLICATIONS OF THE UNITED STATES GOVERNMENT

Annual Reports of the Comptroller of the Currency, 1917–25.
Annual Reports of the Federal Reserve Board of Governors, 1918–26.
Annual Reports of the Ninth District Federal Reserve Bank, Minneapolis, 1920–26, and its *Monthly Report of Crop and Business Conditions,* May, 1920.
Anthropological Survey in Alaska. Dr. Aleš Hrdlička, Curator of the National Museum. 46th Annual Report, Bureau of American Ethnology, Smithsonian Institution, 1928–29.
Bulletins and *Miscellaneous Publications* of the United States Department of Agriculture by Mead; Kell and Brown; Short; Gieseker, Strahorn and Manifold; Westover, Sarvis, Moomaw, Morgan, Thysell, and Bell.
Bulletins of the United States Bureau of Mines. Harrington, Rice and Sayers.
The Coming of Man from Asia in the Light of Recent Discoveries. Dr. Aleš Hrdlička. Annual Report of the Smithsonian Institution, 1935.

Geology and Water Resources of the Great Falls Region, Montana. Cassius A. Fisher. United States Geological Survey Water Supply Paper No. 221, 1909.

Land Use Planning under Way. U.S.D.A., 1940.

Maladjustments in Land Use in the United States. Part 6 of the supplemental report of the land planning committee to the National Resources Board, 1935.

Message from the President of the United States transmitting report of the Alaskan International Highway Commission. 76th Congress, 3d Session, House Doc. No. 711, April, 1940.

Missouri River: Letter of the Secretary of War dated September 30, 1933, submitting report of army engineers for improvement of the river. 73d Congress, 2d Session, House Doc. No. 238.

The Origin and Antiquity of the American Indian. Dr. Aleš Hrdlička. Annual Report of the Smithsonian Institution, 1923.

Planning for a Permanent Agriculture. U.S.D.A., 1939.

Prehistoric Culture Waves from Asia to America. Diamond Jenness (National Museum of Canada). Annual Report of the Smithsonian Institution, 1940.

Regional Planning: Part I, Pacific Northwest. National Resources Committee, May, 1936.

Report of J. W. Powell, Geologist in Charge of United States Geographical and Geological Survey of the Rocky Mountain Region, upon the Lands of the Arid Region of the United States, April 3, 1878.

Reports of the Bureau of the Census.

Soil Erosion: Critical Problem in American Agriculture. Part 5 of the supplemental report of land planning committee to the National Resources Board, 1935.

Speeches of United States Senator Carter (Montana), 1890–96.

Three-Quarters of a Century's Philosophy, Opinion, and Research on Agricultural Problems in the Great Plains, briefly outlined in chronological sequence; Montana land use planning section, Division of Land Utilization, Farm Security Administration.

Water Rights on the Missouri River and Its Tributaries. Elwood Mead. U.S.D.A. Bulletin No. 58, 1899.

The Western Range: A Report on a Great But Neglected Natural Resource. Letter from Secretary of Agriculture. 74th Congress, 2d Session, Doc. No. 199 (1936).

PUBLICATIONS OF THE DOMINION OF CANADA

BURWASH, MAJ. L. T., F.R.G.S. *Canada's Western Arctic.* Ottawa, 1931.

KITTO, F. H. F.R.G.S. *The Northwest Territories.* Ottawa, 1930.

SMITH, HARLAN I. *Album of Prehistoric Canadian Art* (illustrations of "Writing on Stone"). Ottawa, 1923.

MISCELLANEOUS PUBLICATIONS

RENNE, R. R. *A Preliminary Report of the Butte Economic Survey.* Published by the city of Butte, 1939.

WILLCOMB, R. H., and HOWARD, J. K. *Real Property Inventory and Economic Survey of Great Falls.* Published by Great Falls Housing Authority, 1940.

INDEX